"Erwan Rambourg points amazingly well to the new ideals that luxury will embody: inclusivity; a level of care for people and the planet that is both aspirational and essential; and a commitment to quality through sustainability and circularity."

GUILLAUME LE CUNFF, CEO, Nestlé Nespresso S.A.

"Erwan Rambourg's long awaited new book comes at a time when the worlds of retail and luxury are going through unprecedented changes. His insights about the effects of COVID-19, his predictions about the luxury sector in China, and his knowledge of the retail and luxury industries are second to none. A must read!"

ASHLEY GALINA DUDARENOK, China marketing expert, LinkedIn Top Voice, three-time bestselling author, founder of ChoZan and Alarice

"An inspiring read. Rambourg captures the essence of trends we're seeing across the fascinating world of luxury, and provides practical, strategic advice alongside important insights into the future."

SANDRINE CRENER, Program Director, Harvard Business School

"Tapping into his deep knowledge, extensive experience and vast network of industry leaders, Rambourg provides an insightful roadmap to navigating the global world of retail and luxury beyond the immediate aftermath of the COVID-19 pandemic, into the end of our decade. His analysis of the fundamental shifts in this field is a must-read for anyone who wants to succeed in this sector."

KETTY PUCCI-SISTI MAISONROUGE, Adjunct Professor, Columbia Business School; President, Luxury Education Foundation; luxury entrepreneur

"As an independent company, we always look for ways to benchmark our strategies and results, to check our convictions against others, and simply to broaden our horizons. The insight provided by Erwan's analyses is invaluable!"

JEAN CASSEGRAIN, CEO, Longchamp

ERWAN RAMBOURG

FOREWORD BY FRANÇOIS-HENRI PINAULT

FUTURE LUXE

WHAT'S AHEAD FOR THE BUSINESS OF LUXURY

Figure.1
Vancouver / Berkeley

Cataloguing data are available from Library and Archives Canada
ISBN 978-1-77327-126-2 (hbk.)
ISBN 978-1-77327-127-9 (ebook)
ISBN 978-1-77327-128-6 (pdf)

Design by Naomi MacDougall
Editing by Michael Leyne
Copy editing by Marnie Lamb
Proofreading by Alison Strobel
Indexing by Stephen Ullstrom
Front jacket illustration by Shutterstock/karnoff

Printed and bound in Canada by Friesens
Distributed internationally by Publishers Group West

Figure 1 Publishing Inc.
Vancouver BC Canada
www.figure1publishing.com

To my children, Manon, Benjamin, and Baptiste.
May their future be big and bright.

———————————————

When I was a boy of fourteen, my father was so ignorant
I could hardly stand to have the old man around.
But when I got to twenty-one, I was astonished at how much
the old man had learned in seven years.

ATTRIBUTED TO MARK TWAIN

Contents

PART THREE
THE FUTURE

FOREWORD

CHINA HAS BEEN widely acknowledged to be one of the leading drivers of the sustained growth in the luxury sector. Six years ago, in his previous book, *The Bling Dynasty*, Erwan Rambourg had the foresight to announce that this was more than just a trend but was a structural and therefore lasting phenomenon. Even today, and in spite of the COVID-19 crisis, the Chinese market represents a substantial long-term reservoir of growth. If we look back, while this has not altered the ties between the major houses and their home countries, it has led to a shift in the center of gravity for our sector.

Taking his argument further, the author rightly underlines that this move towards Asia is not the only structural force to be changing the key balances within the luxury industry.

To varying degrees, the sector as a whole has benefited considerably from changes in consumer behavior among the new generations, irrespective of geography. Initially viewed as something ephemeral, the appetite of Millennials around the world for luxury products has proved more sustainable than expected by some industry observers.

This is evidence, if it were needed, that this inclination is the result of a fundamental shift in society, driven by changes in the way of life of young adults, the growth in their discretionary spending, and the new social identities embraced by consumers. These trends will continue beyond the economic slowdown triggered by COVID-19.

Among the factors contributing to this new generation of clientele for luxury brands is the rise of social networks, within the broader context of the digital revolution. The author's comments on the "selfie generation" reflect what is for me a deeply held belief: that modern luxury, enriched by genuine, interactive creativity, will continue to enable individuals to assert themselves and to express their unique personalities. Successful houses are able to provide a response to this fundamental need.

Acquiring a luxury product will always be about far more than mere consumption; it's also about choosing a style, an aesthetic, an attitude. It means becoming part of a tradition that is being reinterpreted and renewed by a creative vision. It means sharing the values that are associated with a particular brand. This is why luxury brands need to live up to the expectations, along with the sense of attachment, that they create. More than ever, modern luxury is a luxury that accepts its responsibilities to the environment and its community, that does not hesitate to take part in debates within society, and that promotes diversity and inclusion. All these characteristics reflect the expectations of the new generation of customers, and together, they represent the major challenge facing our sector but also an opportunity to claim its sense of purpose.

FRANÇOIS-HENRI PINAULT
Chairman and CEO of Kering
Paris, May 2020

PREFACE
THE LIFE OF LUXURY
AFTER COVID-19

I WROTE THE BULK of this book in 2019, before the novel coronavirus (COVID-19) emerged to engulf the world in a pandemic. As you can imagine, I made many revisions through July 2020 as cities around the world shut down and air travel ground to a halt.

Why think about the next decade in luxury when half of the world is living in confinement and fear? Who can imagine consumers will even think about buying high-end, seemingly useless products when they are busy panic-buying staples like pasta, toilet paper, and milk? Who would even think about a Rolex watch or a Chanel handbag as equity markets collapse, unemployment soars, and fatalities escalate? In the U.S., following the shocking death of George Floyd from police brutality and the mass protests that ensued, in a country facing its own pandemic of blatant race inequality, who in their right minds wouldn't feel guilty about purchasing high ticket items?

These are all fair questions of course. As we have learned to become familiar with new expressions such as "super-spreader" or "flattening the curve" and new concepts and habits such as WFH (working from home) and using Zoom or WhatsApp for videoed happy hour with friends, so will the luxury sector learn to evolve and adapt. Luxury brands will have to learn a new vocabulary, observe new rules, and remain open-minded as to what the circumstances might bring about. As Henry Kissinger once said, a diamond is just a chunk of coal that did well under pressure. If luxury brands do away with complacency, COVID-19 may well prove, in hindsight, to have been a catalyst for positive change, made possible by creativity, optimism, and resolve.

I have ventured throughout the book to imagine what the virus aftermath may be in luxury. In essence, I believe that the outbreak and its impacts on consumer behavior will accelerate existing trends.

Some consequences of the pandemic are quite straightforward. Chinese consumers are, and will remain, the key constituent for the luxury sector. The rapid stabilization of COVID-19 cases in China in March 2020, only two months after the onset, implies that Chinese nationals have been the first to come back to premium consumption. The virus episode has proved to be short lived for them, and confidence has rebounded quickly. The trend to consolidation in the luxury industry and the advantages that scale confers will be amplified. The smaller independent brands will suffer more from demand coming to a halt in the spring of 2020. And mergers and acquisitions in the luxury sector should be well supported as the bigger groups continue to aggregate market share.

Some other implications of the virus will come across as counter-intuitive. For example, as quarantine conditions reduce the barriers to online shopping, it may seem reasonable to expect luxury consumers will make the bulk of their purchases online. I argue that luxury will be an exception to that rule because its attributes are incompatible with the principle of social distancing. Luxury will be sold predominantly in stores, not online, even in a post-COVID-19 world.

The most important long-term implication of the virus is on consumer conscience and values. The world likely faces way worse threats than COVID-19—even though it may not have felt this way in 2020—with climate change being the most obvious one. I do not subscribe to the idea that luxury will be a victim of a sort of "quarantine of consumption." COVID-19 has a silver lining of sorts, one that will build on a movement that has already gained strength in recent years: consumers, mostly driven by youth and women, will be more thoughtful about their choices and increasingly buy less but buy better. Luxury clients are likely to ask more questions. Environmental, social, and governance concerns will be under heavier scrutiny, supply chain substitutes will emerge, a circular economy of luxury could develop, and brands will thrive to become more trustworthy.

See, it's not all bad.

ERWAN RAMBOURG
New York, NY
July 2020

INTRODUCTION
A BIG AND BRIGHT
FUTURE FOR LUXURY

I can resist anything except temptation.
OSCAR WILDE

C AN YOU IMAGINE saving up for months to buy something most people would deem completely unnecessary? To many, perhaps most, the demand for luxury items seems completely irrational. Products like mechanical watches or high-end jewelry are seen as discretionary, as superfluous, and whose perceived value is completely disconnected from their utility. Sales of personal luxury goods are forecast to reach between EUR320bn and EUR365bn (USD349bn and USD398bn) per annum by 2025, while total sales of luxury, including cars, dining, cruises, and hospitality, are already in excess of EUR 1.3 trillion (USD 1.4 trillion).[1] How to explain the vast size and continued growth of a "superfluous" sector?

I have been involved in the luxury industry for twenty-five years, first in marketing in Paris (for Guerlain and Christian Dior within the LVMH* group, and then for Cartier, the world's largest high-end jewelry brand) and for the past fifteen years with a bank, focused on

---

* Throughout the book, when a group's name is underlined, you may find further information about that group in A Guide to Luxury Goods Companies, which begins on page 236.

corporate strategy and equity markets. (To this day, when I tell former marketing colleagues that I was relieved to leave marketing for a bank, they look at me funny…) Though my career has shifted away from day-to-day marketing challenges towards a helicopter view of the industry, I have not lost sight of the fundamental appeal that fuels the demand for luxury products. For many wealthy consumers, "luxury" is no mere indulgence but a core priority that serves profound needs and desires. Luxury is about belonging, culture, and meaning.

The main goal of this book is to explain how the luxury industry has great growth potential ahead despite the recent hiccups and offer some predictions on the changes that will accompany that growth. Below, I will discuss the specific demographic, structural, and cultural factors that will influence the industry in the coming decade. Demand for luxury is bound to continue to be rock solid over the long term and is entrenched in deep roots. While COVID-19 may have grounded travelers and caused consumers to (rightly) prioritize immediate needs over luxury purchases in the short term, I believe that after a dreadful 2020, the following decade could be akin to another "Roaring Twenties" for luxury sales. The mass-luxe pyramid (see page 3) should welcome many more consumers.

In my view, the consumption of luxury is not as much correlated to financial means as it is to a desire to prove to society that you belong. In other words, your propensity to purchase a luxury product is more correlated to psychological elements than to your paycheck. When you understand that, it is less surprising to hear that wealth creation has not been the main driver for luxury consumption over the past twenty years. It is true that the development of global capitalism has created tremendous wealth: the gap between the haves and have-nots is widening in many nations, as measured by the Gini coefficient (a measure of wealth inequality), and on paper, at least, wealth disparities support luxury demand. It is important to remember, however, that luxury sales thrived in Japan in the late 1990s, in an

The mass-luxe pyramid

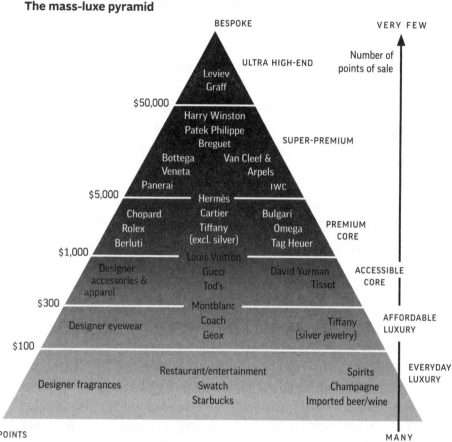

At the base of the pyramid of luxury goods are many brands selling accessible goods through a wide distribution network; at the top are a few brands selling exclusive goods to the wealthier consumers through a more limited distribution network. SOURCE: Erwan Rambourg.

era of economic stagnation so severe it is now called the Lost Decade but ironically could have been called the Luxe Decade. Of course, as one of my bosses at Cartier, the brash, larger-than-life Bernard Fornas, liked to say: "Better nouveau riche than never rich." But wealth is not everything. What counts more is the psychological aspect, the feel-good factor.

Wealth creation clearly supports luxury consumption, but this consumption is more about proving a point and looking to fit in than being wealthy as such. This dynamic can be illustrated with what may seem like a counter-example: Mark Zuckerberg, the founder of Facebook and a notoriously wealthy individual (his net worth is estimated at more than USD75bn as I write this), is also known for wearing the same plain gray T-shirt or hoodie every day, a bit like Apple founder Steve Jobs with his jeans and black turtlenecks. Sure, Zuckerberg's tees are coming from Italian house Brunello Cucinelli, a seriously high-end ready-to-wear company for consumers in the know. But to anyone watching the news, it is just a plain gray T-shirt. Zuckerberg is not trying to stand out and prove to the world that he has made it; he is, rather, attempting to do the reverse by making us believe he is just like you and me. He is the antithesis of how luxury consumers approach brands: they may not be incredibly rich, but they want society to know immediately that they have succeeded. Everyone knows Zuckerberg has succeeded, so he does not have the typical luxury attitude of struggling for recognition. But he still wants to fit in.

By entering the world of luxury, you become part of the bigger story. Many of the most successful brands were founded decades or centuries ago. There is depth in the origin and story of brands, the relationship with the consumer, and passing the test of time. I believe the brand identity of family-controlled spirits group Rémy Cointreau sums it up quite well: "Terroir, people and time." The purchase of luxury tells you where you come from, which group you are part of, and offers an anchor, a reference point in an ever-changing world, an illusion that you are part of a bigger story.

As luxury brands and cultural milestones become inseparable— Cartier was the jeweler of kings, Gucci and Louis Vuitton dress Hollywood greats, Tod's is sponsoring the rehabilitation of the Coliseum in Rome, Dior held a runway show in Marrakech's El Badi palace— you are also participating in the world's culture, and in a small way, its history. After the Notre-Dame Cathedral was partly destroyed by a fire in April 2019, the owners of LVMH and <u>Kering</u> stepped forward as the major donors in an effort to rebuild this emblematic monument. Many observers were surprised, and some in the French press even suggested this was not the proper role of luxury conglomerates. I disagree. Many of the most prominent brands support arts and culture via donations or foundations: Cartier has the Fondation Cartier, a contemporary art museum created in 1984. The more recently opened Fondation Louis Vuitton is a Frank Gehry–designed cultural center and art museum. The Pinault Collection, founded by François Pinault, the founder of Kering (and father of François-Henri Pinault, the current CEO), operates two superb art spaces in Venice, the Palazzo Grassi and the Punta della Dogana. Luxury brands are natural patrons of arts and culture because they have a similar function in society. One senior executive of an affordable luxury brand once explained his company's subpar growth by telling me: we are not capturing the cultural zeitgeist. The raison d'être of luxury brands is indeed to capture the cultural zeitgeist of society and deliver it to consumers.

In reflecting on the meaning of luxury products, I often return to a popular saying: "People may forget what you said, but they will never forget how you made them feel." The utility of luxury consumption ranges from fitting into society, to simply feeling happy, empowered, or complete. That is potent. That has value. That is a big part of the reason luxury brands become legendary. It is not just that they were created long ago. That helps for storytelling and marketing purposes. It is more that when your parent, friend, spouse, or lover buys you a gift or when you reward yourself for an achievement or just because you feel like it, strong memories of those moments will endure.

THE NEXT DECADE will see strong sales growth in luxury. How do I know that? I could tell you that fitting in, moving ahead, and boasting of your success are intrinsic to human nature even after the trauma of a pandemic, and so sales of luxury will be supported forever. Or I could tell you that the CEO of the biggest luxury conglomerate, LVMH, believes that, statistically, in a ten-year period, the group's brands will experience seven years of robust growth, two years of so-so trends, and one tough year, generally in a recession, and that the latest tough year, 2020, will soon be just behind us, so we are good to go.

As this book is about predicting the future, I have taken the plunge by trying to anticipate twenty-one changes in the luxury industry that I expect will occur in the next decade. The first of those predictions is on page 31 (and all are collected in Twenty-One Predictions for '21 and Beyond, if you can't bear the anticipation). These are based on established trends and projections. But we all know that past performance is no guarantee of future results, and this book is not only about looking into a crystal ball. It is also about giving you some tangible keys to understanding the future of luxury.

By examining why luxury sales have been so strong for the past decade, we can better understand where things stand today and be on firm ground to make some useful observations about where the next decade will take us—and how the definition of luxury itself is about to change. And while the spread of COVID-19 in 2020 will undoubtedly change the way consumers approach brands, it should act as an accelerator of trends that were starting to emerge rather than a 180-degree shift.

Luxury rising: A decade of decadence

Over the past ten years, three driving forces have been behind the growth in the sector: Chinese wealth surging, the guilt factor subsiding in the U.S., and the "selfie generation" moving the needle. Over the next ten years, most of these drivers will remain relevant, but some will evolve. This will redefine who the consumers are, what brands and groups will succeed, and how they will sell products.

First, the Chinese consumer has proven to have an incredibly strong propensity to buy. The biggest growth factor in luxury for the past ten years has been the formidable wealth creation in China. Both psychologically and financially, Chinese consumers have done much better in the last decade and have rapidly replaced the Japanese consumer as the main luxury shopper. The great news for luxury is that this does not appear to be a bubble. Indeed, socio-economic factors suggest that Chinese consumer growth is firmly entrenched, and there is no reason to fear the market will burst. In hindsight, 2020's COVID-19 outbreak might be considered a short-term hurdle in an otherwise continuous expansion, and, if anything, in the spring of 2020, the Chinese consumer became the only relevant one for the sector as the West closed down.

Second, the guilt factor is subsiding, especially in the U.S. I'm French (nobody's perfect), but I grew up in the U.S., a land of wealth and opportunity where you would think the luxury sector should be supported by all of the haves. Surprisingly, it is not that buoyant, relative to wealth, especially as compared with the Chinese luxury market. In the U.S., luxury products have historically been frowned upon and associated with a guilt factor, especially in the years spanning 9/11 and the financial crisis of 2008-09. It's fine to make money, this thinking goes, but any obvious display of wealth via wearable products is either inappropriate or vulgar. Whether it is for depressing societal reasons (the media has made citizens used to seeing death, destruction, and despair) or more positive philosophical ones (you only live once, might as well enjoy life), U.S. consumers have turned down guilt. Luxury products, which historically may have been frowned upon, have become more acceptable in the U.S., and it is likely that the combination of more than a decade of strong economic growth, a Wall Street bull run, and the ubiquity of social media have helped create many new American luxury consumers. Luxury stores have developed in some areas which were wealthy but guarded, such as Boston in the U.S. or Germany in Europe, regions where wealth has developed for decades but display of wealth was seen as culturally taboo. Things are changing fast. You are allowed to reward yourself now. It's ok. You don't need to feel guilty about it. The aftermath of COVID-19 will undoubtedly rekindle some form of subtlety in the types of purchases and product designs viewed as acceptable, with many designs becoming minimalist, but the U.S. is still an underdeveloped market for luxury.

Third, the so-called selfie generation—technically Millennials and Gen Z—has supported luxury demand. With the emergence of smartphones in our lives and the fact that most young consumers spend hours browsing on social media, a "look at me" mentality has developed quickly. Instagram or Snapchat feeds are loaded with pictures of consumers trying to prove to their followers that they are worthy of mingling with. And the consumers who most want to fit in are the younger ones, who seek recognition, a new job, or a membership to a club, literally or metaphorically.

Some might find the yearning for validation sad, but it's just human nature. Equity markets, trade tensions, and macro headwinds will fluctuate; human nature, however, is unlikely to change. Luxury products are the ultimate purchase for people who wish to announce that they have arrived.

Redefining bling

My work places me at something of a cultural crossroads. Working for a bank, I spend my time with equity investors but also with consumer brand professionals. Being at the intersection of two very different worlds gives me a valuable perspective on how the respective fields think. Luxury executives tend to get carried away by their optimism, which is refreshing, and I think it is fair to say that many are dreamers. Without that capacity to dream, brands would not have been as successful in this sector. As Tory Burch put it: "If it doesn't scare you, you're not dreaming big enough."[2] Conversely, equity investors, especially those in the U.S. and London, tend to be eternal pessimists, hoping for the best but planning for the worst. The issue is not that they are a cynical bunch (though some undoubtedly are); it is more that the risks of investing demand a thorough and critical approach.

In balancing these perspectives, it's worth acknowledging that, theoretically at least, the risks for the sector to lose relevance are high. Gen Z might lack interest in the space. New entrants might come in, disrupting existing brands. Chinese consumers could stop purchasing imported brands and go domestic. In practice, however, I believe—and will try to convince you in this book—that the luxury industry has another formidable decade of growth ahead, as long as brands know how to seize the opportunity. If you don't believe me, I have included in most chapters an interview with a CEO or expert to try to help make the point a bit more convincingly!

A part of this growth will be a shift in what luxury means, away from the bling of the early 2000s, and its associations with tacky, loud, over-the-top ostentation. While flashy colors and logos will come and go as a trend, the reality of luxury in the future will be one where bling becomes the little things in your day that make it brighter. Luxury will not necessarily be ostentatious but will encompass some product or experience that makes you feel happy and, more importantly, special. And that should be less about products than about values and purpose.

As I venture to redefine bling in this book, I will take you through three distinct parts to understand how the luxury sector should evolve between now and 2030. The first part details how the consumers of luxury will change significantly over the next decade. Mostly female, Asian, and young, these buyers are supporting increasing sales of luxury brands—with no end in sight. Part two concerns the corporate and retailing landscape. For luxury, scale matters substantially, and the big groups in the sector (notably, but not exclusively, LVMH) will only get bigger. As for retailing, even though online is the fastest-growing channel for luxury today, the future of the industry will continue to rely primarily on physical stores. In ten years' time, those stores will look very different, but I do not think you will necessarily have fewer of them. The third and last part of the book explains that if consumers of luxury are changing and the corporate structure and distribution of luxury goods is evolving, this will lead to the definition of luxury itself shifting dramatically. Young, affluent consumers may eschew expensive handbags to focus on things like wellness, travel and other experiences, or art. As these sectors gain in importance, younger consumers will also question the ways traditional luxury items are produced and become more demanding. The emphasis on conspicuous consumption will subside. Environmental, social, governance, and sustainability issues are not just buzzwords anymore and could reshape the industry entirely.

As the old Danish saying goes: "It is exceedingly difficult to make predictions, particularly about the future." Yet I believe I have sufficient factual data and information to convince you that these predictions are not a shallow forecast but are grounded in measurable trends. Human nature and the need to fit in is a constant, but changing demographics, rising wealth creation, and trends in corporate structure and spending will all fuel the evolution of luxury. Disruption is certainly coming. For those brands and groups who embrace it, there are fantastic opportunities ahead. The industry has no place for complacency, and the reward for evolution can be substantial.

PART ONE

THE
BUYERS

— I —

THE FUTURE
IS FEMALE

Women hold up half the sky.

MAO ZEDONG

T HE SAYING "THE future is female" was coined in the early
1970s, as a slogan for New York City's first women's bookstore,
Labyris, which was opened in Greenwich Village by lesbian
feminists.[1] From those radical roots, the slogan has gone massively
mainstream: in 2015, Millennial British supermodel Cara Delevingne
wore a T-shirt bearing the phrase, and Hillary Clinton used it in
her first speech after the Women's March of January 21, 2017. The
popularity of the sentiment speaks to its wide relevance, including
in the luxury space. I cannot think of a better way to describe the
upcoming wave of spending that should be expected from female
consumers in the luxury space.

When equity investors search for growth potential, they often
work at the macro level, making distinctions among developed markets (Western countries, Japan), which are seen as mature if not
saturated, and emerging markets (Asia not including Japan, Latin
America, Africa), which have room to grow. This obscures the fundamental reality that growth can often be found closer to home.

Women, in whatever country they reside, are in my mind the most formidable emerging market for consumer goods in general and luxury in particular.

There are two sets of related reasons to expect women's spending to grow. One is essentially linked to "womenomics," the name of a book by Claire Shipman and Katty Kay published in 2009 but also a term popularized by Japanese Prime Minister Shinzo Abe in 2013, when he pledged to create a "Japan in which women can shine." Today, the term is used more broadly to refer to an improving economic reality for many women, one of greater financial means linked to changes in labor, pay, and marriage patterns. The other is more an awakening of consciousness around injustice, especially discrepancies in the way men and women are treated in society, and an increased willingness to speak up and change the world. And women will not just grow the market: their values and preferences will alter the nature of luxury.

Womenomics

In most countries, reports and surveys show that women already influence the majority of spending decisions.[2] Of course, women are purchasing goods and services not only for themselves but also for their entire household, including their spouse, children, and, potentially, elderly parents. Ever see a man choosing prescription eyewear or a suit on his own? Sure, but more often than not, a man will walk into a store, try something out, chat with the sales associate, and say: "Thanks a lot. I will come back shortly with my girlfriend/spouse." Whether men haven't really grown up or just need a second viewpoint, women are clearly trusted for their authority on taste, color coordination, and fit. Beyond a spouse or a partner, women are influential with a broader circle of family and friends.

The anecdotal spending power of women is supported by hard numbers. Since 2015, women have controlled the majority of personal wealth in the U.S.[3] According to the Boston Consulting Group, private wealth globally held by women grew from USD34trn to USD51trn from 2010 to 2015 and was expected to hit USD72trn by 2020, more than doubling over the decade.[4] That influence is likely to become even stronger over the coming decade, thanks to a few widespread trends: more women working, for higher wages, with fewer family members to support.

First, female employment rates are going up across the developed world. This is particularly true in countries facing demographic headwinds, such as Japan and Germany, where shrinking working-age populations have triggered more women to enter the labor force. In Japan in particular, the term "womenomics" entered the vocabulary in 2013. Until recently, Japan was experiencing a pronounced M curve in female employment: women worked until age thirty, then left the workforce to get married and/or give birth, and then returned to work a few years later (data thus drawing an "M" shape). That is no longer so pronounced, as the government has encouraged female labor participation, through a mixture of lower tax rates for married women, better family-leave policies, and better childcare availability. In June 2019, the Japanese Ministry of Internal Affairs and Communications noted a record of 30 million women in the workforce, including 90% of new workforce entrants that month.[5] With a combination of a shrinking population and very little immigration, the increase in Japanese women's participation is very welcome. Even leaving aside such an extreme demographic case as that of Japan, more women than men are entering the labor force. In the U.K., participation rates are moving in opposite directions with men decreasing and women increasing. In the U.S., while participation rates are declining across the board, the decline in female participation rates has been far more muted than the male equivalent.

Second, although OECD data still show a wide gender pay gap in most countries, that gap is slowly closing. According to the U.S. Census Bureau, in 2017, the ratio of women's to men's median annual earnings for full-time workers was slightly above 80%—but it was twenty points lower in the 1980s.[6] Advocacy groups in many countries observe an Equal Pay Day, which represents the average additional time women would have to work in the new calendar year to earn what men earned the previous year. In 2019, Equal Pay Day in the U.S. was held on Tuesday, April 2, and in 2020, it was moved up to March 31. At the rate of growth that has been observed since 1960, when measurements started, it will take until 2059 to get to parity. Sure, that's a long time, and these types of events don't solve the problem, but they do increase awareness of it. As wages inch closer to parity, women's discretionary spending grows incrementally as well, which is good for luxury spending.

Finally, families are changing. The share of women who are married has been falling, and the median age of married women has been rising.[7] Even in China, where marriage rates have been steadily rising, the UN estimates that this trend will reverse in the coming years. This lower number of marriages will mean that a greater share of the growing female income pool gets spent on women themselves, rather than on others. In the U.S., women's median age at first marriage was close to twenty-eight in 2018, up from about twenty in 1958, as the graph on page 17 shows.[8] Similarly, the marriage ages in China and Western Europe have continuously gone up over the recent period. On top of this, women are having children later in life: the average age of a first-time mother in the U.S. rose from twenty-one to twenty-six between 1972 and 2016, and this continues to move even higher.[9] In some developed markets and some U.S. states, the average age for first-time mothers is over thirty-one. Welcome to the new family: married later, fewer kids. That's a reality and a positive one for the luxury sector at least, as women can spend on themselves rather than on a household, children, and other distractions from the sector.

These trends will contribute to women dramatically increasing their discretionary spending. Globally, while women make up

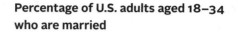

Percentage of U.S. adults aged 18–34 who are married

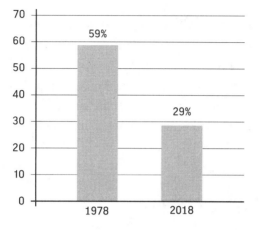

Median age at first marriage in the U.S.

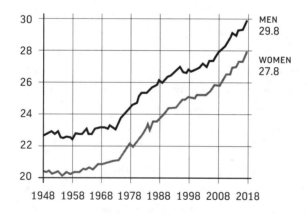

In the U.S., the proportion of married adults under age thirty-five in 2018 was about half that of 1978, and the age of first marriage had risen by about six years for both men and women.

SOURCES: "Percent Married Among 18-to 34-Year-Olds: 1978 and 2018," U.S. Census Bureau, November 14, 2018, https://www.census.gov/library/visualizations/2018/comm/percent-married.html; "Median Age at First Marriage: 1890 to Present," U.S. Census Bureau, https://www.census.gov/content/dam/Census/library/visualizations/time-series/demo/families-and-households/ms-2.pdf.

half the working population, they generate only 37% of GDP. In a groundbreaking 2015 study, the McKinsey Global Institute estimated that were women to participate in the economy identically to men, it would add 26% to GDP growth by 2025—the equivalent of the combined size of the U.S. and Chinese economies.[10] While the study explains some of the gap by the fact women are traditionally more involved in family and home-based responsibilities, it also shows that economic development and changing attitudes around gender equality in society go a long way to influencing the trajectory towards economic parity.

Profound cultural change

Womenomics will go a long way to correcting economic injustice, but less-quantitative factors are also at work. The culture is changing, helped along by the Me Too movement. The movement was founded in 2006 by Tarana Burke, but it really picked up steam in late 2017, in the wake of sexual harassment claims against movie mogul Harvey Weinstein (recently sentenced to twenty-three years in prison) when Alyssa Milano tweeted: "If you've been sexually harassed or assaulted write 'me too' as a reply to this tweet." Tens of thousands of women responded, including several celebrities, lifting the movement into international prominence and affecting countless industries aside from Hollywood.

Beyond shedding light on the misogynistic nature of parts of society, the movement was also part of a broader awakening of female empowerment and values. Whether it is a globally active movement like Me Too or local women's groups, there is clearly a growing collective conscience that should gradually give women a greater voice in all parts of society and ultimately correct economic injustices. But it takes time. So what can women do if society is too slow? Help each other out.

One example is Luminary. After a long career in finance, Cate Luzio decided to create a collaboration hub for women to develop, network, and move forward in their careers. Luminary was born in early 2018 in downtown Manhattan, with more than 15,000 square feet (including a rooftop bar conveniently covered with a glass ceiling) dedicated to private space, working space, yoga, workshops, and a whole lot more. The idea is to build the confidence of members to take whatever next steps they have envisaged and accelerate their careers. Memberships adapt to any need, whether members are light users of the club ("side hustle"), are below the age of twenty-five ("rise" member), or get a full membership. Out of the seven hundred members at the time of writing, about a third are corporate memberships, a third entrepreneurs, and another third women rebuilding, switching industries, or reentering the workforce. Luzio has also founded a dinner series called The Whisper Network, to discuss "taboo topics facing women's advancement in the workforce."[11] At the intimate dinners, difficult topics such as "how much money should I make" or "how can I help you" are perfectly acceptable.

This is one example of many. There is also The Wing (a network of women's clubs and community spaces), CREW Network (for women in the commercial real estate industry), Well Women Network and The Assembly (focusing on health and lifestyle choices), The Coven (a community and work space in Minneapolis), Chief (a private network supporting female leaders), and many more in the U.S. and abroad.

The common thinking is that it's great to talk about advancing professionally, "leaning in" as Facebook's Chief Operating Officer Sheryl Sandberg would say, but these initiatives should help move from good intentions to concrete actions. The thinking of Luminary's founder, from our most recent discussion on the topic, was for her to say to members: "Don't hide behind stats. Don't make up excuses. Just do it!" In France, a female group of entrepreneurs and investors called Sista was founded in late 2018 and highlighted how low funding is for female business founders, who receive only 2% of global venture capital funding.[12] By working to limit unconscious biases, Sista aims to have 50% of start-ups by 2025 be founded or cofounded by women.

In late 2019, Tadashi Yanai, the billionaire founder of Fast Retailing (owners of giant casual brand Uniqlo as well as GU, Theory, and many more) said that his job would be more suited for a woman because women are persevering, detail oriented, and have a better aesthetic sense, and he wanted a female to replace him when he retires. He's not alone in his thinking. For their book *The Athena Doctrine: How Women (and Men Who Think Like Them) Will Rule the Future*, coauthors John Gerzema and Michael d'Antonio conducted surveys across thirteen different countries in order to verify their assertion that feminine leadership qualities are likely to solve tough problems, create a better world, and build a more prosperous future. Recent events seem to confirm this: an April 2020 *Forbes* article discussed the effectiveness of leaders in New Zealand, Taiwan, Germany, Iceland, and Scandinavian countries under the headline, "What Do Countries with the Best Coronavirus Responses Have in Common? Women Leaders."[13]

Gerzema and d'Antonio also make the case that women have higher expectations as consumers, leading to better service and benefiting all consumers as these higher expectations keep brands on their toes. Environmental and social considerations are also more prevalent amongst female shoppers. Surveys suggest that more than half of female consumers say they go out of their way to ensure that they and their families eat healthily, while research from Insights in Marketing shows that a majority of Millennial women do a considerable amount of research before buying beauty products.[14]

As female spending power rises and a greater share of that consumption is spent on products for women themselves, the slightly different female shopping habits become increasingly important. Female shoppers are more willing to shop online, are savvier when it comes to comparing prices, and are more likely to embrace mobile shopping—meaning these separate trends should increase even more. The younger generation is more active in this regard, with Millennial women recognizing that recommendations from friends, relatives, coworkers, and social media influence their consumption more than TV programming, advertisements, or celebrity endorsements.

What does this all mean for luxury subsectors?

While female purchasers should lift all premium categories in terms of sales support, some quintessentially female-dominated categories should see particularly strong growth in the years ahead, supported by female wealth creation: jewelry, cosmetics, and handbags.

Why jewelry is bound to be brilliant

According to De Beers, Millennials (born between 1981 and 1996), combined with Gen Z (born from 1997 onward), account for two-thirds of the total spending on diamond jewelry in the four largest diamond-consuming countries. While most jewelry is unbranded and many countries have local champion brands (e.g., Titan in India or Chow Tai Fook in China), very few global brands exist in this space. When leaving aside the more affordable brands (Swarovski, Pandora), luxury names that are big and relevant for consumers around the world are few and far between: Tiffany, Cartier, Van Cleef & Arpels, and Bulgari are the four key names. Each has a distinct positioning: Tiffany, the iconic New York jeweler (which LVMH has bid for), is well known for its diamond and sterling silver pieces and tops consumer brand preference surveys in the U.S. Cartier, the prestigious French brand (part of the Richemont group) known as "the jeweler of kings and the king of jewelers," is preferred in China. Van Cleef & Arpels (another French Richemont asset) is known for its romantic femininity and its pieces shaped like animals or floral designs. And finally, Bulgari (part of the LVMH group) is an exuberant Roman jeweler.

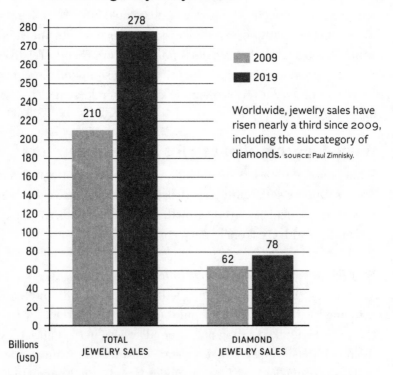

The rise of global jewelry demand

Legend: 2009, 2019

Worldwide, jewelry sales have risen nearly a third since 2009, including the subcategory of diamonds. SOURCE: Paul Zimnisky.

Total Jewelry Sales: 2009 = 210, 2019 = 278
Diamond Jewelry Sales: 2009 = 62, 2019 = 78

Billions (USD)

TOTAL JEWELRY SALES   DIAMOND JEWELRY SALES

There are more competitors, but they are smaller and less global in terms of their retail footprint (Harry Winston, Boucheron, Chaumet, FRED, Graff, Buccellati, Chopard, Damiani, David Yurman) or are not purely jewelers (Chanel, Louis Vuitton, Christian Dior).

As we saw, women are getting married at a later age, which technically should put pressure on the jewelry segment as traditional bridal jewelry suffers. The reality, however, is that more than 50% of women are buying jewelry for themselves either as a celebration of an achievement at work, as an indulgence to treat themselves (do you always need a reason?), or as an investment that they can pass down to their own daughters, according to MVI Marketing, a jewelry consulting firm.[15] The graph above shows the increasing global demand for jewelry, including diamond jewelry.

This shift in women's purchasing habits is already being reflected in the hard luxury sector. *Vogue* recently highlighted the versatility of Chanel's pearl and camellia collection, for which adjustable pieces adapt from office appropriate to something more glamorous for the evening.[16] Other brands have launched playful collections that surprise either by their color (think Bulgari stones) or by their design (e.g., the Clash de Cartier product range, which has mobile parts). Early in 2019, Real is Rare, Real is a Diamond, an important communication platform from the Diamond Producers Association (DPA), an alliance of the leading mining companies, launched a series of films with women rewarding themselves. Having sensed how dominant self-purchasing had become, the association had all films end with the tag line "for me, from me," a telling message to attract female consumers directly to the products. Forget the spouse—self-purchasing is the future.

HARD/SOFT LUXE

"Hard" and "soft" luxury: Hard luxury is a generic expression that traditionally refers to watches, jewelry, and pens, but people don't write with pens much anymore, so today, it refers primarily to watches and jewelry. Soft luxury encompasses leather goods, apparel, and footwear.

How beauty will thrive

Over the past few years, the fragrance, skincare, and makeup industry has seen strong growth from international groups such as American powerhouse Estée Lauder and French conglomerate L'Oréal. The growth is not equal within the categories, however. Makeup accelerated from 2010 to 2018, while the current growth seems to be more skincare driven; in 2020, skincare clearly outperformed makeup because COVID-19 had many consumers staying at home. Fragrances, the third pillar, is more of a low-growth segment as it is saturated (do you know a luxury brand that does not have a fragrance?) and not getting much traction with the up-and-coming Asian consumer. Leaving aside the bigger diversified groups, the sector has seen many new entrants (e.g., Drunk Elephant, FENTY) and online concepts which have awakened consumers' interest. Outside of international Western brands, South Korean companies such as LG H&H and Amorepacific or Japanese ones such as Shiseido have captured parts of the growth as well. From a distribution perspective, the biggest changes have been the shift in the U.S. from department stores to specialty retailers (e.g., Sephora, Ulta Beauty, Bluemercury) and brand retail (e.g., Kiehl's, MAC, Atelier Cologne, Dior).

The beauty sector shows an abundance of creativity, and while some clients may question the actual technical efficiency of some skincare products, these remain in general a relatively affordably priced luxury. With women focusing more and more on natural, "green" beauty, many new brands have emerged on the scene, such as Herbivore Botanicals ("the ingredients are so natural that sometimes they run out"), Kopari (a coconut-based brand "unnaturally obsessed with all things au naturel"), Tata Harper non-toxic skincare, and KORA Organics. The trend is so entrenched that French group L'Occitane, owners of the eponymous brand as well as Melvita, Erborian, and Elemis, has the stated ambition to become the market leader for natural cosmetics, and its key shareholder, billionaire Reinold Geiger, is obsessed with sustainability, in a good way!

Handbags: No better personal branding

In terms of rewarding yourself and seeking social status, wearing a piece of jewelry or a particular skin cream won't necessarily be noticed, but a handbag? For sure! Over time, logos on handbags go in and out of fashion, but never believe someone who tells you "logos are dead." Every time I hear that assertion, it's déjà vu all over again (as Yogi Berra said). We've been through many phases before when logos are in, and suddenly, they are out, but they never die completely. When stress is high and consumers might feel guilty about purchasing labels, like in 2020, logos might be discreet or disappear completely. When confidence is high, female consumers have no better way to tell those around them that they have arrived. This, along with the price point, is likely the reason the largest brands by sales in the luxury industry are handbags and accessories companies. The current leaders are Louis Vuitton, Gucci, and Chanel. While market shares might evolve over time depending on fashion trends or management changes, the category itself should continue to be a strong growth segment as more women enter the space and reward themselves.

INTERVIEW: On women ruling the consumer world

I will not go through all the discretionary subsectors for which women will significantly move the needle, as there are countless examples. One segment that is counterintuitive, as historically it developed by men for men, is spirits. And to illustrate this, I will let Nicola Nice, founder and CEO of gin liqueur start-up Pomp & Whimsy, do the talking.[17] (For an example of one of Pomp & Whimsy's sophisticated products, see the photo on page 29.)

ERWAN RAMBOURG: Describe your initial assessment of how spirits remains a very male-dominated, macho industry in the products and the communication.

NICOLA NICE: After initially training as a sociologist (I have a PhD in sociology of science from Imperial College London) and spending some time in social research, I have spent the bulk of my career in the field of consumer insights and brand strategy. I have worked across a wide range of industries globally in my career—from fashion to beauty to alcohol—but have always specialized in advocating for the female consumer. In consulting for the large spirits producers, I was always struck by the way women seemed to be treated as second-class consumers when it comes to the branding and marketing of spirits. This is evidenced by the extremely small number of successful spirits brands that are actively targeted towards women or have women's needs at the heart of their DNA.

Luxury spirits have always been marketed as aspirational lifestyle brands but positioned around what can only be described as a proportionately male view of success. If we were to close our eyes and imagine a typical whiskey or vodka advertisement from the last twenty years, the chances are we would all conjure a similar image: a well-dressed, successful guy surrounded by a bevy of beautiful women. Women are portrayed as the accessory to this man's success, a trapping that comes with his wealth and status. In this way, luxury spirits are presented to women like a diamond ring, expensive fragrance, or designer purse—as something a man buys for you.

In contrast, spirits that have been marketed towards women are usually reductionist, positioning around a one-dimensional view of femininity, often talking down to women and the female experience. This is evidenced by brands that focus solely on diet/calorie counting, are overly sexualized, or push women to drink as an escape from the boredom and monotony of their domestic lives.

This is hardly aspirational or what one would expect from a category that is all about selling lifestyle and luxury! In short, it is clear to me that women are not being taken seriously by this industry, and in my opinion, this is a huge missed opportunity.

ER: You launched a gin liqueur in 2017 by women for women. What are the insights you had of the spirits industry that led you to believe there was an opportunity in the market for this product?

NN: Unfortunately, there are a lot of myths and stereotypes about women as spirits drinkers that have been hard to shake. For example, that women do not like spirits, only wine. Or that they will drink the brands that men buy for them. Women control 70% of the household spending on liquor. And add to this the fact that according to research by Berlin Cameron, 83% of women want to buy products from companies that are founded by women, and you have a perfect storm of opportunity for spirits that are about women, by women, for women. I estimate that conservatively the market size for spirits for women in the U.S. is in excess of USD4bn.

ER: How do women approach drinking occasions differently, and what does it say about differences in personalities between genders?

NN: Drinking is fundamentally a social occasion, and it's easy to assume that the experience of drinking must be universal. However, our research shows that there are specific occasions for spirits that are significant to women specifically. In developing Pomp & Whimsy, we have focused on three of these occasions:

1. "The me moment"
Alone or with significant other, this is the transitional moment in the day when women stop playing all their other multiple roles (mom, wife, manager, chauffeur, chef, teammate, etc.) and they become ME again. A moment to host herself, check back in, and reconnect with her thoughts. This type of introspective occasion is a classic neat spirits moment, when consumers look for the weight and sophistication that a luxury spirit can give them. Currently, for the women who do not like drinking neat spirits, this moment is probably filled by wine.

2. "The girls' night celebration"
I say girls' night, but this could equally be date night. Moments when

women are able to let loose and dial their energy up. A celebratory moment that calls traditionally for champagne, sparkling wine, or spirits that mix well with sparkling wine in a cocktail. Brunch would be a low-key weekend version of this moment or need.

3. "The hosted event"

Women are by nature hosts and entertainers. Their regular hosted events could be as casual as weekend barbecues or weeknight book clubs, or they could be as formal as a baby shower or bridal shower. These moments call for liquors that can be mixed into a simple cocktail, a signature drink that defines the moment and integrates easily into the vibe of the occasion.

It's also worth noting that in general women are also often looking for lower ABV [alcohol by volume] cocktails. I believe women are more conscious about the need to stay in control and tend on average to be more responsible drinkers.

ER: Explain why spirits for women by women can also appeal to men and how women are decision-makers for most purchases a couple or a family makes.

NN: I think it is overly simplistic to assume that because we are taking a female-led approach to innovation that we are either "gendering" spirits or excluding men. Certainly, in creating P&W, we believe we are no more exclusive of men than a brand like Jack Daniel's or Johnnie Walker would say they are of women. Certainly, from a product perspective, we have created a liquid that appears to have universal appeal, and this has been demonstrated many times over by the slew of gold medals and 90+ ratings that we've received from both industry and non-industry competitions, which are usually composed of mixed panels of judges.

Pomp & Whimsy is an award-winning gin liqueur on a mission, says founder Nicola Nice, "to give women back their rightful place in the history of gin and the cocktail." CREDIT: Courtesy of Pomp & Whimsy.

From a design and branding point of view, our intention from the beginning was to create a brand experience that women would instantly recognize was for them but at the same time, would not necessarily send a signal to men that it is not ok for them to like it too. Getting this balance right turned out to be the most challenging part of the brand development process. As women, we are used to purchasing brands that are not targeted at us; however, for many men, this is an alien concept. Based on the feedback we receive from male consumers, however, we believe that we have achieved this balance in our design aesthetic.

Finally, it is not only the taste and packaging but also the authenticity of the brand story that is important in forming a connection to our consumer. Pomp & Whimsy is not just for women, but it is also by women and inspired by women's stories and the role that women have played in the history of gin and the cocktail. Our mission as a brand is to inspire women to take back their rightful place in this story, and we have found that this is something that both men and women are able to get behind.

ER: Have you encountered other female entrepreneurs in the spirits industry, and how do you think their presence can change the industry?

NN: The final piece in the story of creating a spirits company for women has been in connecting with other female founders. At the end of 2018, we launched a network with other women entrepreneurs in the spirits, wine, and beverage industries under the banner of the Women's Cocktail Collective. Our mission is very simple: to diversify the back bar. Under the belief that a rising tide lifts all ships, we are using a cooperative approach to promote each other's businesses and add value for distributors, retailers, and consumers, while simultaneously amplifying the voices of women in general in our industry. Ten years ago, you could count the number of female entrepreneurs on one hand. Today, we have twenty members and are growing. Our success is proven in the innovation that is being brought to market and the value that is being generated for investors, retailers, and end consumers alike.

Summary

Women are already the key decision-makers for households across the planet. Yet with greater financial autonomy and higher employment participation rates, the female spending power is on the cusp of becoming much greater. As women get married later and have fewer children, the higher disposable income, notably at a young age, will also support increased luxury spending. While economics will support female-driven consumption, societal change around gender inequality seems to have accelerated recently, and many initiatives are under way to improve the economic position of women. Women should greatly influence spending in jewelry, cosmetics, handbags, accessories, and much more.

PREDICTION #1

Because luxury sales are essentially driven by female purchases, the limited number of top female executives in the sector is fast becoming an embarrassment—or if it is not, it should be. Luxury has long been driven by a macho culture, but there is no scarcity of female talent in the industry. In the next ten years, I predict that the majority of board members and at least 25% of brand CEOs will be female.

2

ALL POINTS EAST

Opportunities multiply as they are seized.

SUN TZU

THE COUNTRIES WITH the highest potential growth rates over the next decade are overwhelmingly in Asia. Incomes in Asia will see a sharp rise, especially when compared with those in other emerging markets and the developed world. In 2019, China added more to global economic growth than the U.S., and India added more than the eurozone, and while 2020 remains uncertain at the time of writing, the COVID-19 consequences will widen the gap much further. Emerging markets in Asia will contribute 55% to global growth over the next ten years, more than twice as much as the entire developed world combined. By 2030, those markets should account for over a third of global GDP in USD, up from slightly more than a quarter now. The future direction of the global economy is being decided in Asia.

The Asian consumer will play a greater role in the luxury sector as rising incomes affect not just how much they spend but where they spend it. Even though working-age populations have started to shrink in China, South Korea, and Thailand (joining Japan),

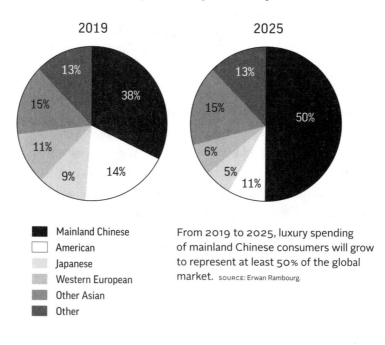

Share of global luxury market by nationality of consumer

2019

2025

Mainland Chinese
American
Japanese
Western European
Other Asian
Other

From 2019 to 2025, luxury spending of mainland Chinese consumers will grow to represent at least 50% of the global market. SOURCE: Erwan Rambourg.

Asia's consumers are aging into prime consumer groups. The rise in growth will usher in a fresh generation of middle-class consumers across Asia. The share of the population defined as middle class should double over the course of the next decade. By 2030, the Asian middle class will be made up of 3.5 billion people, up dramatically from 1.4 billion in 2015, and will account for 65% of the world's total.[1] This means that a staggering 88% of the next 1 billion people to enter the middle class globally will be Asians! This higher income will change the shape of consumption, with spending shifting away from primary needs like food and shelter towards high-end products and services, including entertainment, restaurants, holidays, and luxury purchases. Mainland Chinese consumers in particular will account for an increasing share of global luxury spending, as detailed in the charts above. For an overview of the changing middle class in China, see the table on page 38.

The "bling dynasty" lives on

Chinese consumers are drawn to harmony, which is characterized by order and stability. The fact that China removed term limits in 2018 to allow Xi Jinping to remain "president for life" drew criticism from the Western press. The move likely reassures the Chinese consumer, as it lifts uncertainty about the future and plays into the stability of the country. Just before the COVID-19 outbreak in January 2020, Chinese consumer confidence was at a thirty-year high.

Despite a slowdown in the mid-2010s, there are many reasons to still be optimistic about Asian consumption of luxury in general and Chinese demand in particular. Most of those I detailed in my previous book, *The Bling Dynasty*, remain valid:

- A multifaceted shopper (versus a monolithic office-lady type in Japan twenty years ago that society harshly nicknamed the "parasite single")

- A Confucianist culture which has you develop relationships ("guanxi") with your family, friends, and coworkers, and for which luxury items serve as a validation point

- A fascination for travel and for becoming a cosmopolitan consumer, not for comparing yourself to other Chinese citizens

- A culture of success and moving ahead which resonates with Deng Xiaoping's "to get rich is glorious" motto, which seems contradictory within a socialist regime but has become very widely accepted in China

- An absence of local Chinese brand alternatives and a lack of trust in products made by Chinese brands

The risk for Western luxury is for a new Chinese generation to look inwards and seek local brands rather than Western ones. While it is true the younger Chinese generation has developed a relatively new sense of pride in their nation, recently boosted by the rapid containment of the COVID-19 outbreak relative to the rest of the world, that is not necessarily an issue for luxury consumption. It may be a factor for smartphones (Huawei versus Apple) or staples (local versus imported beer, yogurt, etc.), but I continue to see for some of the premium subsectors either a clear preference for imported brands (think sporting goods with the success of Nike and adidas) or simply no credible local alternative (as with most luxury products).

The threat of Chinese brands is still remote, given the lack of Chinese luxury powerhouses and Chinese consumers' cosmopolitan appetites. In fact, for various reasons, luxury spending in China can be expected to grow.

PREDICTION #2

While credibility and sales of Chinese brands should increase dramatically in subsegments such as consumer staples or electronics, I project that in ten years' time, Western brands will still dominate in the traditional luxury segments such as high-end leather goods, watches, and jewelry, as well as in sporting goods and cosmetics.

From male gifting to women taking over

One reason is linked to the topic I just discussed in the previous chapter: women. While luxury consumption in Western Europe, the U.S., and Japan has long been dominated by female purchases, this is a relatively new development in China. Indeed, up until ten years ago, the Chinese luxury market was male driven and notably influenced by graft. Government officials, mostly men, would at times accept a watch as a gift in exchange for a favor. This led Xi Jinping, who assumed the office of general secretary of the Communist Party of China in 2012 and became president in 2013, to embrace an expansive anti-corruption campaign early in his time as "paramount leader." Xi listed an eight-point guide in order to make clear what behaviors were seen as unreasonable. While some high-profile arrests took place, the campaign was focused on not only higher-rank individuals but also corruption at all levels, the stated target being to get rid of "tigers and flies."[2]

As far as luxury consumption is concerned, the administration's actions led to a sales hit in the sector that leveled off in 2015, and a reset in categories that for structural reasons had been male driven, such as watches and Baijiu, the world's best-selling spirit by far (11 billion liters sold every year), often consumed at fancy banquets. As gifting decreased, China gradually became a female-driven luxury market like any other. Today, the young, affluent female Chinese consumer is by far the most relevant demographic for the sector.

A rising tide

One element that investors have found hard to understand is that luxury is predominantly a recruitment rather than a repeat purchase business. Since 2015, most of the sales growth in China observed by the bigger brands in the industry, the likes of Louis Vuitton, Gucci, and Moncler, has been volume driven with very limited growth coming from mix (i.e., consumers buying higher-ticket items within the brand) or price. In 2019, more than 70% of global Moncler sales came from first-time purchasers. That same year, more than 60% of Gucci sales also came from newcomers to the brand.

Why? Because even though the Chinese are by far the dominant nationality of consumers for the brands, accounting for roughly 40% of sales in 2019 and even more in 2020 (versus less than a third when I published *The Bling Dynasty* in 2014), the potential for recruitment with the Chinese consumer still remains phenomenal. The Chinese luxury target market is bound to expand at a very fast pace in the years ahead.

ASPIRATIONAL LUXURY

Think of this segment as being neither too affordable nor completely over the top. Even though this category is stuck in the middle (between the higher end of "absolute luxury" and the "accessible" or "affordable" market), it is probably the one that has seen, at least in handbags, the strongest growth over the past few years, with a noticeable outperformance of the likes of Louis Vuitton, Gucci, and Christian Dior for instance. Typically, as their wealth builds, consumers will skip the affordable luxury brands and jump directly to aspirational brands, which will help them more in terms of fitting in.

In September 2018, management at Louis Vuitton made a presentation to analysts like me in China, telling them that the brand's target market in China was made up of 13 million people but that the brand was selling to 1.3 million only. So basically, the brand had a penetration rate of its target audience of roughly 10%. Immediately, some financial analysts like me started asking themselves how the brand could increase its penetration rate from that 10%. In hindsight, that was not the right question. More important is how large that 13 million target market would become over time—and the answer was 24 million, only four years later. In other words, even with Louis Vuitton not increasing its penetration rate, sales of the brand could almost double in four years with Chinese consumers. This is a stunning projection and at the same time quite consistent with estimates from McKinsey that project a doubling of affluent Chinese consumers (those earning over USD35,000) from 18 million to 38 million between 2020 and 2025.[3]

The difficulty when measuring potential for luxury consumption is that wealth seems to be a lot more relevant than income in China, as illustrated by the emergence of so-called seven-pocket consumers, who benefit from wealth passed on by four grandparents and two parents, in addition to their own income stream. Equity markets? Consumer confidence? Property prices? Tariffs and trade? Sure, all of that should affect luxury consumption. Some will also question whether COVID-19 will impact wealth, and it certainly should, given the softness of Chinese GDP in the first quarter of 2020 and the subsequent nosedive in Western markets that China sells to. But come hell or high water, the number of Chinese consumers being able to purchase luxury is bound to grow dramatically over the next decade.

Affluence of urban households in mainland China

Household class by annual disposable income (RMB)	2010	2018	2030 (est.)
Mass affluent (200–300K)	4 (2%)	26 (9%)	162 (45%)
Affluent (300–390K)	1 (0%)	4 (1%)	36 (10%)
Global affluent (>390K)	3 (1%)	8 (3%)	22 (6%)

MILLIONS (PROPORTION OF TOTAL)

The middle class is booming in China, with the proportion of urban households with annual disposable income over RMB200,000 (about USD29,000) set to increase dramatically between 2010 and 2030.

SOURCE: "China and the World: Inside the Dynamics of a Changing Relationship," McKinsey & Company, June 2019, https://www.mckinsey.com/featured-insights/china/china-and-the-world-inside-the-dynamics-of-a-changing-relationship.

Spending comes HOME

The key change since I published *The Bling Dynasty* in 2014 is the fact that Chinese consumers will now be purchasing luxury goods increasingly in mainland China rather than outside. See the charts on page 40 for a projection of how Louis Vuitton's sales to Chinese consumers will change to reflect this phenomenon. In 2019, domestic Chinese travel reached over 6 billion trips, and China itself was one of the top five countries where Chinese consumers preferred to buy luxury products that year. Local spending grew twice as much as spending abroad in 2019.

In 2019, many factors contributed to accelerating this phenomenon of repatriation. A combination of currency fluctuations (a weak RMB to the USD) and tensions around tariffs and trade between the U.S. and China have meant that tourism flows from China into the U.S. gradually dried up starting in the spring of 2018. Of course, in the very short term, the spread of COVID-19 around the world has been a great incentive for Chinese to stay at home whether by regulation or by choice, as fears around health and safety weigh heavily on the minds of potential travelers. Separately, the Hong Kong protests that began in March 2019 started to have a big impact by early August, as Chinese travelers became concerned about security issues and either traveled to other markets or stayed at home. While politics, regulation, currency fluctuations, security threats (terrorism, viruses, etc.), and fashion trends will influence the relative success of various travel destinations (as I discuss in chapter 9), several fundamental reasons suggest that wealthy Chinese individuals will incrementally purchase luxury products at home. This is a long-term trend, not a blip, and a move that is not too dissimilar from what happened in terms of travel patterns with the Japanese in the late 1990s and early 2000s, when Japanese consumers dominated the luxury sector.

PREDICTION #3

One impact of COVID-19 in 2020 will be to accelerate the shift of consumption of Chinese consumers back to mainland China. The year 2020 should prove to be a bit of an exceptional year for luxury, with Chinese being wary about traveling. Still, in ten years, I believe that more than 75% of luxury sales to Chinese citizens will occur in their homeland.

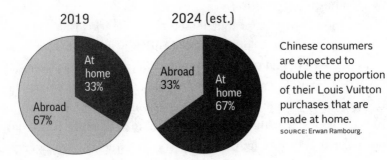

Louis Vuitton sales to Chinese consumers at home vs. abroad

2019

At home 33%

Abroad 67%

2024 (est.)

Abroad 33%

At home 67%

Chinese consumers are expected to double the proportion of their Louis Vuitton purchases that are made at home.
SOURCE: Erwan Rambourg.

For four reasons, Chinese citizens will stay and spend at HOME:

HARMONIZATION Price points are more similar than they used to be, notably for premium products. This is linked to the currency (weakness of the RMB), brand policies targeting more subtle price gaps between markets, and measures by the Chinese administration to lower import duties. In 2019, the standard VAT rate was cut from 16% to 13% in order to boost the economy. As the price premium in China approaches VAT and falls more in line with the prices Chinese consumers pay for luxury goods abroad, the appeal to shop abroad falls. In 2014, it cost an average of 45% more to purchase in Shanghai than in Milan or Paris; nowadays, price gaps are about half that and likely seen as acceptable. One of the reasons to purchase abroad, getting a deal, is suddenly not as compelling.

OMNICHANNEL With the explosion of e-commerce and the rollout of omnichannel strategies, shopping is easier than ever. Unless you're thinking of trekking, skiing, or visiting museums abroad, why not enjoy the comfort of shopping in China? Furthermore, newfound collaborations have ushered in a seismic shift in how luxury brands approach e-commerce in China. In the past, brands didn't seem to trust third-party platforms. Most of the luxury brands had their own ".cn" websites and their own WeChat mini-programs (a "sub-app" within WeChat to sell products), and they generally stayed away from the high-traffic e-commerce platforms. This is no longer the case. Now, only two platforms remain (with VIPLUX having lost relevance), and the Western brands seem to trust the Chinese operators more than before. You can basically choose between JD.com's Farfetch on one side and NET-A-PORTER on Alibaba's Tmall Luxury Pavilion on the other. In a country like China, where, according to McKinsey, 75% of the potential customers live outside the top fifteen cities, companies face the challenge of building enough brick-and-mortar stores to reach them all.[4] E-commerce enables brands to have a wider reach and is often more convenient for consumers as they can purchase goods wherever they are, whenever they want.

MONITORING Since April 2016, checks at the border and risks of increased customs taxes have increased, encouraging a slowdown of haitao (bulk purchasing from resellers) and daigou (Chinese tourists purchasing products abroad on behalf of others). Fines have been a very efficient deterrent. As a consequence, brands have better control of whom they are selling to, and products are being purchased locally more often than before.

EDUCATION In the past, the average Chinese tourist was unable to tell whether the luxury good they were purchasing in mainland China was in fact a reproduction. But after having traveled, this tourist is now savvier and knows the difference between legitimate retail operators and locally produced knockoffs. This should give Chinese tourists greater confidence in shopping locally.

For all of these reasons, I believe this trend should continue, with global luxury sales growing around 6% per annum and sales to Chinese consumers growing at around twice that pace for the next ten years. Consultancy firm Bain & Company estimated that Chinese consumers will make 50% of their luxury purchases at home in China by 2025.[5] I think that shift has occurred already, partly thanks to all the aforementioned reasons, and in 2020, as a consequence of COVID-19 forcing or incentivizing consumers to stay at home. Even if 2021 and beyond are more normal years in terms of travel patterns, the shift has taken place.

As Chinese consumers purchase more at home, the profitability of retail stores picked up dramatically in 2018 and 2019. Luxury stores in China used to be empty showrooms in which consumers browsed and ended up buying products abroad. At the peak, before the corruption crackdown (i.e., around 2011-12), I believe luxury businesses in China were above the global average in terms of profitability. There is no such thing as a typical luxury P&L, as this will vary greatly from one subsector or one brand to another, but in general, gross margins were higher (prices were a lot higher) and store expenses to sales were lower, and that more than compensated for the need to invest in infrastructure (general and administrative costs) as well as communication. Luxury sales took a hit in the midst of the anti-corruption campaign, in 2014-15. Gross margin had come down already, with prices less disconnected from Europe, and the selling and administrative cost part of the P&L suffered from strong de-leverage. Since late 2015, however, profitability in China has gone up, and it is now likely that for all brands, China is one of the most profitable markets, alongside Japan.

Store expenses in China are still moderate as staff costs are in check, store rents are mostly variable, and brands have likely managed to leverage general and administrative as well as communication costs (despite both being higher than in the West). Sales densities are high, especially compared with the overabundance of retail space in the U.S. Today, stores have gained tremendously in traffic and conversion. Consumers and retail executives I meet with share a view that we could call "1-2-4": if you sell 1 in the U.S., then you sell 2 in Europe and 4 in Asia.

Unforeseen hiccups along the way

In late 2019, a novel coronavirus, COVID-19, started to develop in China's Hubei province and its capital city, Wuhan. For the first few weeks of January 2020, the outbreak was under the radar, but on March 11, the World Health Organization declared a pandemic. With the exponential spread of the virus, the number of cases rapidly accelerated. For several reasons, this pandemic is highly significant for the luxury sector.

First, at a time when Chinese consumers account for close to 40% of luxury sales, having the Chinese economy slow dramatically—due to factories and stores being shut, movement restricted, and the national psyche affected—is not great. In mid-February 2020, mainland China saw the peak of the spread, and thereafter, economic activity started to gradually recover. The issue of course is that as the virus spread way beyond mainland China, some luxury markets traditionally driven by Chinese outbound travel flows, such as South Korea, continental Europe, and the U.S., started to get hit. I have spent the past ten years advising investors to buy luxury stocks because they are pure plays on the compounding nature of the Chinese traveler. Of course, in late February 2020, that traveler pretty much disappeared.

Second, as cases started to develop in the Western world, a contagion of fear seemed to catch on more quickly than the virus itself, and equity markets globally took a big hit. While I believe that fewer luxury consumers are driven now by equity markets than they were before, clearly wealth destruction will prove not to be good for luxury consumption.

Finally, both consumers' adoption of a wait-and-see attitude and the spread of fear affect broader economic growth. The U.S. administration cut interest rates by 50bps on March 3, 2020, but much of the initial reaction was along the lines of "we don't need lower rates, we need a vaccine," as investors doubted that lower rates would really motivate consumers, given their nervousness. On March 25,

2020, President Donald Trump signed a historic USD2trn biparti-san stimulus package, but again, the jury is out on whether this will mitigate for all the job losses brought about by a stalling economy. Two months later, the U.S. had lost more than 25 million jobs, the largest decline since tracking began in 1939, and unemployment was above 16%.

COVID-19 has had meaningful consequences for how luxury sales have developed in 2020. The key question in terms of project-ing the next decade, however, is whether this virus will structurally affect the appetite of Chinese consumers for luxury products. All luxury executives I have interviewed since the outbreak think not, and I agree with them. Chinese have come back to the bigger brands and the "hero" products first, but the recovery has been swift. The events have been painful but should be seen in hindsight as a blip in a continuous growth phase. While luxury sales should rebound from the 2020 slump, the values of consumers will likely also have shifted. In March 2020, trend forecaster Li Edelkoort predicted that the virus would have a silver lining, as the "quarantine of consump-tion" will force consumers to go without, ultimately leading to less waste, to the benefit of the planet.[6] More thoughtful consumption will emerge no doubt, and habits of buying less but better and buying more locally produced goods are bound to develop and stick.

What about the potential of Asian markets outside mainland China?

The Japanese were the key luxury consumers twenty years ago and in 2003 accounted for more than half of Louis Vuitton sales. But with Japan's aging population and predominantly young female consum-ers who are not being replaced, the prospects do not seem positive for the long term. However, two reasons offer optimism in the short term. First, this is a country where female labor participation has ramped up dramatically since Shinzo Abe's womenomics kicked in.[7] Second, retirees are leaving work with relatively high amounts of money. Both realities likely explain why Japanese luxury demand was stronger than expected in 2018 and 2019.

Elsewhere in Asia, Taiwanese consumers seem to have hit a level of maturity or even saturation that means growth there is capped. In South Korea, whilst the cosmetics market has been very well supported, some potential for growth in luxury likely remains, notably with the emergence of a male consumer who is also starting to gain interest. South Korea is maybe the only country where male-driven consumption could outpace female growth.

Real hopes for luxury exist in Southeast Asia, with Vietnamese consumers already very influential in imported spirits such as cognac and scotch and Indonesia boasting a dynamic youthful population. The issue is that upper-middle-class numbers are not at all comparable to those out of China, and while growth potential might be there, it likely will not move the needle for some time.

High-end consumers in India have been a case of "jam tomorrow" for the luxury industry, with meaningful growth remaining wishful thinking. Obstacles for the sector have included insufficient wealth, import tax difficulties, unorganized retail, and fundamental tastes of consumers, which tend to focus on the intrinsic value of products rather than branding per se. Fourteen years ago, I started writing a report called "Big Bang Galore? Can Luxury Make It Big in India?" but I never ended up publishing it, as I thought we had time on our hands before investors would have interest. Fourteen years later, nothing has changed much, yet. However, now more than a glimmer of hope has appeared. Some first-generation wealth (as opposed to inherited wealth) is emerging, and it will likely want to get noticed. Indian consumers may well help support growth in the sector once Chinese start to plateau, and I see this happening gradually over the next ten years. Let's wait and see.

PREDICTION #4

The Indian consumer, while still a marginal contributor to luxury sales overall, will become a key contributor to the sector's growth, giving some hope as Chinese growth gradually slows between now and the late 2020s.

INTERVIEW: On the outlook for Chinese luxury consumption

In the meantime, here is Cyrille Vigneron, the CEO of Cartier, talking about prospects of Chinese luxury consumption.[8] (For an image from the Clash de Cartier campaign, see page 50.) Vigneron has a unique perspective: he was based in Tokyo for many years, where he experienced the emergence of Japanese luxury consumers, and now, he runs a global business that relies on Chinese consumers.

ERWAN RAMBOURG: You have spent part of your career developing luxury brands in the Japanese market. How do you perceive the main differences between Japanese and Chinese consumers of luxury? Is there a risk China becomes like Japan and offers less growth than what many hope today?

CYRILLE VIGNERON: In essence, the Chinese market for luxury is a lot more diverse than the Japanese market ever was and evolving at a much faster pace.

The appetite to purchase wearable products developed in Europe initially in the 1970s and 1980s with European and American clienteles, and in the 1980s and 1990s, the Japanese became the first growth driver for the luxury industry both at home and abroad, with spending in Europe but also closer to home in Asia, with Hong Kong, Guam, and Saipan playing important roles. The Baby Boomer generation in Japan was very pragmatic, focused on rebuilding the nation after the Second World War and having a keen emphasis on values such as education, work, and family. Men worked and women took care of children and their education. As discipline and work ethics brought about much prosperity, the following generation of Japanese consumers really took advantage of the country's great economic growth linked to industrial developments; [they] opened to the world and embraced luxury consumption. A young generation of twenty-five-to-thirty-five-year-old females emerged, living at their parents' until they got married and having substantial disposable income. Out of the 125 million Japanese citizens at the time, more than 10% were very wealthy and would have pocket money of JPY5-10m, the equivalent today of EUR50-100k [USD55-110k], and that was obviously incredibly supportive to the luxury sector.

Separately, Japan saw the emergence then of very strong department stores, accompanying this new generation of buyers and finding ways to attract some imported premium brands to increase their sales productivity. Japanese department stores were bearing the investment capex and charging variable rents based on sales. The commission rate was high, but the retail prices were higher than elsewhere in the world. This allowed a fast-track expansion for the brands even if they did not have a lot of cash. The price gaps between Japan and abroad rapidly led to Japanese consumers heading out to Hong Kong with shopping as their key motivation and to a culture of "shop till you drop." The Nikkei 225 equity market index peaked [in] late 1989 [to] early 1990 at close to 40,000 points, a level roughly twice what the market is trading at now, and there was a substantial property market bubble at the same time.

Whilst European consumption of luxury was about differentiation, Japanese consumption was about assimilation, fitting in, a bit like the cinema box office today: if others see the same movie as you, that's reassuring; if others purchase the same handbag as you, that's what you want. Owning a Mercedes car, an Hermès bag, a Cartier watch—these were enablers and brands that were worn by the stars.

The generation who was hungry for luxury then aged, and after excess consumerism led to a feeling of saturation, Japanese consumers took a step back, were not as willing to go abroad, became less obsessed about their careers, and gradually grew less hungry for luxury. The new Japanese generation enjoys luxury goods, but frenetic consumption has subsided.

After aspiring to access parts of Western culture and artifacts, Japan itself has now become a source of inspiration for many consumers globally, with attributes of safety, cultural wealth, limited pollution, service, and more starting to appear as fascinating elements for tourists. In 2018, Japan welcomed more than 30 million visitors, triple the amount of 2013 and way above the stated target of 20 million by 2020, with Chinese now the first nationality to visit the country ahead of South Koreans.

By contrast to Japanese luxury consumers, Chinese luxury consumers are not a homogenous clientele. With the opening of the economy under Deng Xiaoping, wealth developed rapidly in the cities within the coastal areas, giving way to the emergence of a very large number of clients with various types of backgrounds. China is really more of a continent than a country, with a kaleidoscope of cultures. There are as [many] differences between Shenzhen's high-tech city dwellers who project a cosmopolitan lifestyle and wealthy consumers from third-tier cities who may respond to more regional triggers than there are between citizens of different countries. Besides, unlike the Japanese approach to luxury, Chinese consumption of luxury can be about assimilation for certain attributes but differentiation for others. This has meant that to approach Chinese consumers, marketing strategies are significantly more complex. What also makes the China market difficult is the speed of change. Whilst Japanese attitudes to luxury were really driven by a generational approach, changes in China will come about in ten years rather than over a full generation. Social relations and attitudes will shift very quickly. Wealth creation can also be very quick with the emergence of very young consumers in China, so-called seven-pockets consumers, first-generation achievers who may have very quick access to wealth and will be willing to trade up rapidly instead of gradually going through a premiumization phase. It's a bit like a Silicon Valley entrepreneur who would have made a lot of money in a short period of time and would be willing to buy the best brands at the very high end of the luxury pyramid without having spent the time sifting through all available options.

ER: How is the Chinese Cartier consumer different from other consumers of the brand? Is there a specific Chinese taste that would have you develop particular products to attract and retain these consumers, and what are ties of the brand to China?

CV: Gender equality in China was promoted very early on by the administration, unlike in Japan, where the role of women and wives in society remains quite different. Social relationships are very different in China as gender equality is very entrenched. The key difference is that Chinese consumers are significantly younger than consumers from other nationalities and will start buying at lower levels of income as luxury is used for fitting-in purposes. In terms of products Chinese purchase, there aren't meaningful differences. Eighty-five percent of watches sold globally are round shaped. This could be even marginally more in China as an angular watch shape does not come across as harmonious. Color preferences are also more skewed towards red (a bit like Middle Eastern clienteles would prefer green). But at the end of the day, wealthy Chinese consumers aspire to be cosmopolitan, display international taste, not Chinese specific, so I wouldn't say that product preferences are incredibly different from what we observe with other nationalities.

There is a growing interest for Chinese sources of inspiration, a genuine reappropriation of historic codes, designs, and culture, not something gimmicky. For instance, Cartier has a legacy of getting

CLASH DE *Cartier*

English actress
Kaya Scodelario for
Cartier's Clash de
Cartier jewelry line.

CREDIT: Courtesy of Cartier.

inspiration from China in a very respectful manner, and it is certainly one of the reasons our recent Cartier exhibition (Beyond Boundaries) within the Palace Museum, in the heart of the Forbidden City in Beijing, has attracted so much enthusiasm and [many] visitors. The exhibition took place over June and July 2019 and welcomed more than 600,000 visitors. Jacques Cartier, one of the grandsons of the founder of the Cartier brand, traveled extensively in the early 1900s to the Middle East, India, and China and took inspiration from the shapes of dragons [and] phoenixes and also worked with local materials such as ancient jade, and it is believed that the work on coral was what led to today's Cartier red, the emblematic color of the brand. The Beyond Boundaries exhibition is inspired by China but also likely inspiring for Chinese, given the role of jewelry as a symbol of power and the recognition of China's role on the international stage.

ER: How do you approach social media and online sales in China? Do you use local ambassadors and other China-specific actions?

CV: Here is another key difference between Japan and China. In Japan, luxury relied on a very dense network of powerful department stores and a very concentrated number of cities, mostly part of the Tokyo-Osaka-Kobe megalopolis. As a consequence, e-commerce of luxury has been quite slow to develop in Japan, given luxury products have been relatively easy to access physically. China on the other hand is very spread out geographically, without such a powerful department store footprint at the national level, and within some of the bigger cities such as Beijing, traffic has become problematic. As a consequence, e-commerce has a very important role to play, and some consumers have made the leap directly to online purchasing without ever experiencing department store shopping. Furthermore, the online offer in China is very rich and diverse, with the likes of WeChat, Alibaba, and JD.com platforms offering convenience that has no equivalent anywhere else in the world.

The question is not whether to use these platforms; they are unavoidable as the basis for China's online ecosystem. It is more how to create a safe and healthy environment for the brands on these platforms. WeChat mini-programs are complimentary to brick-and-mortar sales, and the joint venture the Richemont group (owner of Cartier) has signed with the Alibaba group to develop NET-A-PORTER in China can be incremental in terms of sales. Online in China is about convenience, but it is also important to bear in mind that the physical contact with products and in-store experience is also very much appreciated by Chinese consumers.

As far as brand ambassadors go, we do not use an ambassador for the brand at a global level. It is not in our culture. We have an approach that relies more on content, and when we look at personalities, they will be specific to our brand and for dedicated projects.

For example, we have worked with Lu Han, the face of the new Chinese generation, for a campaign on our jewelry range Juste un Clou, and we developed a Panthère campaign with British rapper Tinie Tempah. These representations of the brand are unexpected and are developed to surprise and delight consumers.

ER: How do you project where Chinese will purchase Cartier products in the future? Accordingly, how do you plan your pricing architecture by market and your physical store presence in China and abroad, in downtown areas and airports?

CV: Our price points were harmonized a few years ago, and as far as Chinese luxury consumption is concerned, it is not a zero-sum game. You can sell more to Chinese consumers abroad, and you can also sell more at home. With Japanese consumers initially, 20% of luxury purchases were done at home and 80% abroad. That has now more than reversed, as close to 90% of Japanese spending on luxury takes place locally in Japan. It is thus only natural for other countries, of which China [is one], to go through this same trend of localization of consumption. More than half of our sales with Chinese consumers [take] place at home, but there can be growth everywhere. We have the store network we need in China today to capture the growth. Maybe we just need to have slightly bigger stores in the future, and e-commerce will obviously play a bigger role as well. Following the Japanese example, it would not be surprising if in five years' time, 75% of the business with Chinese is driven by China domestic sales. Brands have made an effort on price points, but the Chinese administration has also been instrumental in sales taking place in China by lowering VAT in April 2019 and also clamping down on cross-border sales.

ER: Chinese have been buying gold- and jade-based jewelry items from local Chinese retailers for ages. What do Cartier and other high-end Western jewelry brands bring to the table, and are they suited for different occasions?

CV: I would look at this in terms of style rather than nationality. Western brands offer a different take on style and status, while local brands are relatively far from today's open world; they are very local in nature. Our brand is valued by consumers around the world, and that is why it is always important in design to avoid developing products that look too Chinese as again wealthy Chinese are cosmopolitan consumers above all.

ER: Who are the next Chinese for Cartier?

CV: Theoretically, on paper, India, given its size, could be the next country to move the needle for luxury, as it should rapidly become the third most important economy in the world, and one could make a case for 50 to 100 million additional first-time purchasers in luxury ahead. The reality for now is that average purchasing power remains low, import duties in India very high, and local jewelry is very different in terms of tastes and designs. Pragmatically, it could well be that the next Chinese over the next ten years could simply be more Chinese. Visibility on GDP growth and income is still very strong, and there is still a substantial reservoir of growth to tap into. Chinese luxury consumption could well plateau at some stage, but we are far from that day. Japan's population is equivalent to that of the Shanghai region, and this implies that as GDP per capita continues to develop, the luxury market of China could be the equivalent of the Japanese luxury market in the very early 1980s. Another ten years of solid growth in China is a distinct possibility.

Summary

Six years after the publication of *The Bling Dynasty*, China has become even more important for the luxury sector in terms of contribution to sales for all brands. We are by no means at the end of the journey. I remain convinced that Asia will continue its strong support of the luxury sector, with China as the main driver of growth over the next decade. Four main trends will be associated with this growth:

1. Wealth creation will continue to fuel the next generation of Chinese shoppers, with the number of potential luxury clients close to doubling over the next five years.

2. Chinese travel is supported by wealth, regulation, and infrastructure, while bragging rights from purchasing remain a factor. However, the bulk of growth should come from China itself with four good reasons to shop at HOME: Harmonization of prices, the rapid development of Omnichannel buying, the administration's Monitoring of consumer spending, and increased Education about where to purchase genuine luxury products. Short term, COVID-19 has been an accelerator of this repatriation of growth in the mainland.

3. China's luxury market is becoming one of the most profitable on earth after having been margin dilutive for years.

4. Finally, adoption of luxury in other Asian markets is either reaching a ceiling (Japan, Taiwan), getting mature (South Korea), or too small to move the needle for now (India, Indonesia).

— 3 —

THE POWER
OF YOUTH,
INCLUSION, AND
DIVERSITY

Youth is easily deceived because it is quick to hope.

ARISTOTLE

IMAGINE YOU ARE a young female employee in South Korea, you just graduated from university, and you are about to start your first day at your first full-time job. You have been successful in your studies, but now, you want to prove to the world (your friends, peers, parents, coworkers) that you are worthy of doing business with, possibly worthy of a promotion. Projecting an image of success will inevitably put you in a better position to indeed be successful. If you arrive at the office wearing a Cartier Ballon Bleu watch, a Louis Vuitton Neverfull handbag, and some Christian Louboutin heels, it sends a strong message to your employers and coworkers: you are ready, you belong, and you will be going places.

This urge for recognition and integration is what makes luxury products compelling for every age group, but they exert a special pull on the young. They enhance your appeal, increase your visibility and acceptance level, and create a feeling of hope. When you are young and your list of accomplishments short, there's no better way to say "I've made it in life" than to look good. Some of that comes down to physical attractiveness—witness the massive growth of cosmetic surgery clinics in Seoul, which are popular with South Koreans and Chinese tourists alike—but it can also be achieved by wearing the right brands.

I am not trying to be excessively cynical here. It is nothing more than human nature, as timeless as Aristotle's quote about youth. Importantly, as this cohort ages, it moves into a bracket of higher incomes and higher spending. Of course, over time, some of the wealth held by this generation's parents—either housing or financial—may be passed down to this generation, amplifying financial gains. So we should start to see even more spending from this group. The youth of the world today will become the world's consumers over the course of the next decade and beyond, and their differing tastes will matter.

As their economic power and social and cultural influence grows, today's youth will play a large role in reshaping the luxury sector. This will not come as a surprise to that generation, but it does consti-tute a shift in terms of who the core buyers for the sector are. When I was based in Hong Kong in 2015, Asian luxury executives were telling me that for the previous three years, the average age of consumers in China for their brands had come down on average by one year every year! Obviously, there is a limit to where that can go, but the gap between the age of the managers who are running the brands and that of the end consumer has increased dramatically. This of course feeds into the need to refresh elites in the business.

Beyond age itself, ethnic and cultural diversity will become more visible and influential. Casual wear will continue to spread. Social media will only gain in importance, even as consumers expect authenticity from brands. And young consumers will favor companies that reflect their values of environmental awareness, ethical production, and inclusivity and respect for people of color and other historically marginalized groups. These are the values youth are adamant to defend—and which brands have repeatedly faltered on with fashion missteps.

PREDICTION #5

Founders of Kering and LVMH have given some of their children management responsibilities. Because the average consumer of luxury is young, so should the managers be. Not all young managers have the bandwidth to become a CEO of a luxury brand, like Alexandre Arnault, heir of LVMH's Bernard Arnault, born in 1992 and running RIMOWA since age twenty-five in 2017—but a new generation is coming. At the end of the 2020s, it should not be surprising for brand CEOs to be in their thirties or forties rather than fifty and older, as they are today.

Youth demographics and luxury brands

Today's "digital natives," often referred to as Millennials, consume differently. Having grown up at a time of rapid IT development, they are more likely to adopt disruptive technologies. Digital natives accounted for around 9% of the world's population in 2016, and this is set to rise to 30% by 2030.[1]

In South Korea, China, Japan, and most Western countries, the population is aging, with median ages creeping up to thirty-eight in the U.S. and China, forty-two in South Korea, forty-six in Germany, and forty-eight in Japan, the oldest country in the world. In all of these countries, birthrates are quite low, even falling below 1 birth per woman in South Korea, with Japan at 1.3, Germany at 1.6, and the U.S. at 1.8—all below the rate of 2.1 that is considered necessary in developed markets to maintain a population, suggesting that even in advanced industrial nations, the hope that Aristotle spoke of has faded somewhat.

Looking at the two global consumer powerhouses, China and the U.S., the modal age of their respective population (i.e., the age that holds the greatest number of citizens), is thirty-one for China—with a large cohort of people around that same age—and twenty-six in the U.S. Importantly, that number changes dramatically if you break it down by race and ethnicity: for Hispanics in the U.S., the most common age is eleven; for blacks, it's twenty-seven; for Asians, twenty-nine; and for whites, fifty-eight.[2] In most emerging markets, the modal age is usually lower than it is in developed countries, with India for instance being at twelve only and the country having half of its population aged twenty-seven or younger. The graphs below give a visual representation of modal ages in the U.S. and China.

Modal age in U.S. vs. China

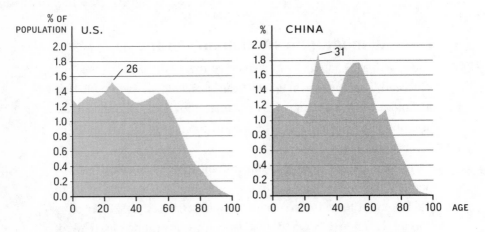

As of 2019, the modal age—the age that is most common among the populations—was twenty-six in the U.S. and thirty-one in China.

SOURCE: "World Population Prospects 2019," United Nations, Department of Economic and Social Affairs, Population Dynamics, n.d., https://population.un.org/wpp/.

In China, the sheer size of the population means that even as growth slows, there will be huge population increases in absolute numbers. For places like Germany and the U.S., however, the pressure that a low birthrate exerts on the labor markets is alleviated by immigration. In Germany, the second most popular migration destination in the world (after the U.S.), immigrants now account for more than 15% of the population. Immigration, after a generation, can also prove to support luxury demand. In the U.S., immigration will continue to contribute to demographic change that will see the proportion of Americans that are Hispanic or Asian increase.[3]

SO HOW WILL all this affect the luxury sector? Well, for one, the global luxury consumer will be even more likely to be Asian or Hispanic.

As I discussed at length in *The Bling Dynasty*, the luxury market in the U.S. has been driven in great part by the propensity to buy of second-generation Hispanic consumers as well as Asian Americans. Numerous articles and surveys from advertising agencies and marketing blogs detail how to target the affluent—and influential—Latino community in the U.S. These consumers are upscale, young, bicultural, and enthusiastic shoppers who, along with Asian Americans, spend significantly more on premium goods and experiences over their lifetimes than does the average non-Hispanic white American. In 2018, U.S. Hispanic buying power was USD 1.5 trillion—larger than the GDP of Australia.[4]

Louis Vuitton understood this early on. It signed Jennifer Lopez as the face of its nationwide U.S. ad campaign in 2003. The then-thirty-four-year-old had found success in both the music and the film industries and represented the face of the new generation of future U.S. consumers. In early 2020, J.Lo was front and center of a Versace ad campaign celebrating the twentieth anniversary of the 2000 Grammy Awards, when she wore a green Versace dress that attracted so much attention it inspired Google to create its image search function.[5] The star and with her, the American Hispanic luxury market remain essential.

The increasingly diverse nature of luxury consumption is not just a U.S. theme; it is one of global integration. In discussions with luxury executives running the French and the German markets, I quickly get a sense of the importance of second-generation North African descendants in France and second-generation Turkish descendants in Germany. Again, it is quite intuitive that consumers from a nation's minority ethnic or cultural groups would look at ways to fit in to the dominant society, and even beyond the country they are in, to feel connected to a more global, cosmopolitan lifestyle.

When luxury items are used to fit in (which is especially common at a young age), consumers tend to trade up quickly to the higher-end, more desirable brands whatever the category, as those will enable them to obtain instant validation from peers. For example, I have heard a few times from Chinese consumers that French absolute luxury brand Hermès was "value for money." It is not exactly cheap, so I believe the meaning is that even though you are spending significantly more for an Hermès handbag than for alternatives, what this gives you in terms of immediate recognition is well worth the money.

ABSOLUTE LUXURY

This expression, coined by consultancy firm Bain & Company, describes the very high-end brands in the sector. Brands with this positioning would include Hermès in handbags or Patek Philippe in watches.

The spending habits of youth and people of color support the luxury industry not just in terms of the value of their purchases, but also by influencing other consumers. Why do older, whiter consumers want to emulate them? Well again, this is relatively straightforward. Youth is associated with positivity and freshness, and older adults want to think of themselves as still being young. One of the most successful French ready-to-wear brands, Comptoir des Cotonniers, which in 2005 was bought by Fast Retailing, the Japanese owners of Uniqlo, had a very authentic mother/daughter advertising campaign for more than twenty years. The idea was obviously not that the daughter would want to buy the same clothes as her mother. The explicit message was that the stores had something for both of them—and, implicitly, that the mother was still youthful enough to shop at the same store as her daughter. I actually think that the risk of this campaign now would be that mothers would want to buy the same stuff as their daughters to feel like they are still young, so you would not need a broad assortment of products in stores.

In many countries, ethnic and cultural minority groups are often seen as early adopters of cool trends and are among the strongest influencers. One of the biggest assets for luxury in recent years has undoubtedly been American rapper Kanye West. He is possibly the first man to have made luxury products cool while being embraced himself by the luxury sector. Indeed, rappers had adopted luxury brands in their lyrics and their wardrobes in the 1990s, but the luxury sector was not necessarily embracing the demographic change. Today is completely different. Kanye has participated in the design of some adidas Yeezy shoes retailing for several thousand dollars, with a collaboration starting with the German brand in 2016 and still going strong today. Virgil Abloh, the Louis Vuitton menswear designer and a friend of West's, has amplified the movement with inspiration taken from the music scene, rap culture, sports, and the street. In early 2020, Louis Vuitton announced a long-term partnership with the NBA. This would have raised a few eyebrows ten years ago, but it's completely natural today.

In the next decade, the influence of these luxury consumers will contribute to several changes in the industry, both aesthetic and structural. The danger for brands lies in not adapting fast enough and in committing embarrassing or offensive blunders—some examples of which we'll see near the end of this chapter.

A "chill" attitude

I often get the question "is casualization a fad?" I have been watching sporting goods companies such as Nike, adidas, and PUMA become increasingly popular over time. Now, some luxury brands are moving onto their turf: Gucci, Balenciaga, Prada, and Moncler have developed reputations for slick sneakers, while Tory Burch and Celine have developed activewear ranges. German brand Hugo Boss was once known for formal attire, shirts, suits, and black shoes. Today, the dominant part of its assortment and sales are with casual wear. The way I look at it is that fads do not last for decades. The fact is that people dress in more relaxed ways, and I do not believe that is linked to a particular short-term trend.

CASUALIZATION

This describes the evolution of the luxury goods industry towards products that are worn in a more relaxed way. The trend has led to formal suits and ties not being strong growth markets and also to the emergence of athletic footwear ("sneakers" in the U.S. or "trainers" in the U.K.) and "athleisure" in general as an important category for some of the existing luxury brands. This evolution is obviously driven by the emergence of a younger consumer. Media outlets have used terms such as "sneakerization" to describe the same phenomenon.

For me, it is more of a generational shift. I meet with investors who are starting their careers, are in their late twenties and early thirties, and wear tracksuits and sneakers at work. Of course, the sneakers are not just any piece of athletic footwear; they're the latest limited-edition Nike or high-top Dior B23 sneakers going for more than USD1,000, but they are sneakers nonetheless! Sporting goods are seen as being comfortable and looking cool, and once male consumers stop wearing ties and gradually move to stop wearing suits, they are unlikely, in my view, to go back. The younger generation of professionals wants more flexibility at work, the start-up culture is aspirational but casual, and consumers do not want to take themselves too seriously. The habits developed from consumers' working from home during 2020's COVID-19 outbreak will support the shift as well. The chill factor is bound to last.

The selfie generation

The younger generation of consumers are digital natives, and this continues to change just about everything. Smartphones have become ubiquitous around the world, with around 1 billion iPhone users, while more affordable brands, notably what I would call the "Chinese quartet" (Huawei, Xiaomi, OPPO, Vivo), equip many other consumers. This has had some unexpected consequences, including adapted products and designated walking lanes in China for texting pedestrians. Ever wonder why the backpack has become the frenzy from TUMI to Louis Vuitton? Exactly: because it is the best bag to allow both hands free to use your phone if you are a member of the "heads-down tribe." This is a trend that Korean-owned brand MCM picked up on very quickly, and the majority of its sales come from its colorful studded backpacks featuring the brand's logo.

I have had many arguments with investors who were convinced that the younger generation would turn away from luxury consumption because they had other interests, such as spending on travel, entertainment, or experiences generally. But the emergence of what some brand consultants have called the "selfie generation," young people around the planet using mostly pictures and videos of themselves to connect with their friends, is a fundamental positive for luxury. With this constant visual representation, how you look and what you wear is paramount. Apple's iPhone 11 launch from September 2019 seemed relatively boring in the eyes of a consumer in his mid-forties (me!) as the product has very few value-added functions. Yet the presence of three cameras (ultra-wide, wide, and telephoto) and the invention of a slow-motion selfie (or "slofie," a horrible word Apple tried to trademark at launch) for the iPhone 11 Pro has seemed to motivate many consumers to trade in their existing Apple product and trade up. The elevated role of the cameras reflects the predominance of image, which helps keep brands at the center of the conversation. Obviously, spending hours on end on screens also has implications in terms of adapting the online content of the brand, and learning how to work with different e-commerce ecosystems and apps, as we will see later in the book. It also means that given consumers' easy access to information and exposure to an incredibly large number of brands, these need to be smart in finding ways to capture consumers' attention without their feeling harassed.

Brands must be authentic

Constant exposure to social media has made youth savvier and wary of mass communication. Occasionally, social media blowups play a big role in pushing young, formerly credulous consumers to look at brand messages closely. One such scandal was the fraudulent Fyre Festival, which was meant to take place in April–May 2017 in the Bahamas. The story of the festival is so incredible that it was made into two documentaries in 2019. Netflix's *Fyre: The Greatest Party That Never Happened* describes how the festival's founder (Billy

McFarland) and rapper and co-organizer Ja Rule paid Kendall Jenner, Bella Hadid, Emily Ratajkowski, and other influencers hundreds of thousands of dollars to promote the festival by posting pictures of themselves on beaches and at parties. In the end, no celebrity attended the event, no music was played, and thousands of people were stranded on an island, sleeping in makeshift tents instead of the fancier accommodation they had paid for. McFarland pleaded guilty to fraud and was sentenced in late 2018 to forfeit 26 million dollars and spend six years in federal prison.

Debacles like this are part of the reason the bigger brand influencers on social media are bound to lose relevance and gradually be replaced by some having fewer followers but a more genuine message to share. This unfortunate project led some influencers to apologize to their followers for misleading them, and Instagram has since imposed rules to clarify when posts are paid for by brands. In the U.S., the Federal Trade Commission has been very consistent in reminding influencers and brands to clearly disclose their relationship, and this goes a long way in protecting consumers. The younger generation is expecting radical transparency, and it is interesting to see the fast emergence of an Instagram account such as Diet Prada (1.8 million followers), which calls out copycats, disingenuous products, and ad campaigns that brands have taken from others, beyond a simple "imitation is the highest form of flattery" approach. All of this is feeding into the perception that micro-influencers are more effective for brands because they are highly engaged, trustworthy, and targeted, and the smaller number of their followers implies the relationship is more genuine.

Beyond the logos: Winning with values

Claude Lévi-Strauss once wrote that "the world began without man and it will end without him."[6] Without being too depressing, let's just say that there are many societal topics such as gun control in the U.S., or environmental consciousness or social welfare globally, which are spun as political issues when I believe they are fundamentally split along the lines of a generational divide. It is clear from their dedication to environmental, social, and governance (ESG) issues that Millennials and Gen Z are more progressive than their elders. This is essentially a generation defending a future that they believe their parents or politicians did not manage to defend.

This youth movement has manifested in ways that earn extensive media coverage and are highly visible: the big youth-organized demonstrations, such as the March for Our Lives in March 2018 against gun violence in the U.S.; the various speeches of teen Swedish environmentalist and *Time*'s 2019 Person of the Year Greta Thunberg, whether at parliaments, the World Economic Forum in Davos, the UN, or elsewhere; or the advocacy work of U.S. congressperson Alexandria Ocasio-Cortez, a very popular politician and activist with more than 4 million Instagram followers. AOC, as she is often called, is the youngest woman ever to serve in the U.S. Congress. She's also the coauthor and continued champion of the Green New Deal, a ten-year plan to counter climate change and economic inequality by eliminating greenhouse gases from electricity, transportation, manufacturing, and agriculture and switching to 100% renewable energy. The proposal quickly gained support from many organizations and politicians, including virtually the entire field of the Democratic presidential primary in 2020, highlighting a broad will to tax the ultra-rich for societal benefit.

These issues are already entrenched in mainstream culture. In Sweden, for example, there is now a word, "flygskam," which literally translates to "flight shaming," to describe the feeling of being embarrassed or ashamed to take the plane because of the environmental impact. There has even been a trending hashtag on social media which in English translates into #stayontheground and is used to extol the advantages of taking the train. In a post-COVID-19 world, I am not sure people who were flying around the world for work more than half of the year will be as vocal about it; hopefully most, including myself, will be more measured and thoughtful, limiting trips. *Collins Dictionary*'s Word of the Year 2018 was "single-use" (a reference to plastic that is disposed of after it has been used only once), and for 2019, it was the expression "climate strike," a form of protest demanding action on climate change, initiated and inspired by Greta Thunberg. In the U.S., obesity rates related to fat, salt, and sugar have led to campaigns around healthier eating habits and certain initiatives such as Meatless Monday, started in 2003. *The Economist* named 2019 the Year of the Vegan. Clearly, these are the issues that are dominating airwaves today—and likely will be tomorrow.

The values and ideals of this younger generation are not just about public consumption. Surveys suggest that they care more about themselves, health, and environmental issues, and it is reflected in their personal and consumer choices. They smoke less, drink less alcohol, exercise more, are more likely to be vegetarians and vegans than are other age groups, and prefer electric vehicles over regular cars. They are willing to spend more for products advertised as sustainable, whether these are organic, antibiotic free, fair trade, or cruelty free. According to McKinsey, 66% of global Millennials would pay a premium for sustainable fashion brands, and 90% of Gen Z believe that clothing brands have a responsibility to address environmental and social issues.[7]

So what does it mean for brands? It is crucial to understand that these views are influencing all other consumers, and the implications of this influence are vast. In the short term, today's younger populations may be a small share of the population who cannot afford to shift to more ESG-focused products. While many consumers intend to have more sustainable consumption habits, those products cost more (for now), and as some argue, sadly "price eats sustainability for breakfast." However, as interest for sustainable products grows and sales rise, prices should come down. That is what is happening for the Whole Foods chain in the U.S. ever since it became part of the Amazon group in 2017. Also, luxury consumers by essence are wealthier than the average consumer, and over the next decade, Millennials will get richer and form a larger proportion of the consuming public. As they gain wealth and their views become even more mainstream, a much greater proportion of the luxury market will likely be willing to spend more on items that are seen as environmentally friendly. Producers will need to be more aware of their production processes, and supply chains and retailers will have to adapt to the changing tastes of their customers.

One of the most visible and talked-about deteriorations of the environment has been the proliferation of plastic. The datapoints are properly scary: Plastic bottles take 450 years to break down. Ten percent of all waste is plastic. The weight of plastic produced each year is roughly the same as the entire weight of humanity. Plastic production uses as much oil as the global aviation sector. One of the most widespread predictions nonetheless remains shocking: by 2050, there will be more plastic in the sea than fish, by weight.

The final episode of BBC's *Blue Planet II* documentary illustrated this grim state of affairs with footage of albatross feeding plastic to their chicks. A year after it aired, one survey showed that 88% of people who saw it had changed their lifestyle to reduce plastic waste. According to that survey, "A new era of environmentalism has taken hold, and attitudes towards single-use bags, disposable plastic straws, and packaging will never be the same."[8] Eliminating plastic is something of a luxury in itself, as plastic keeps costs low in many industries. For instance, the plastic packaging on a cucumber in a grocery store extends the life of the vegetable by four-and-a-half times, from three days to fourteen. Eliminating it puts stress on the supply chain and may increase food waste. For many, the trade-off is worth it: according to the UN, at least thirty-four countries, across both emerging and developed markets, had some form of restriction on plastic bags in 2018. The first country to introduce a tax on plastic bags was Denmark, in 1994. Since then, the EU has led the way, with policies to reduce plastic bag use in the hope that all European countries will soon have some form of ban or charge on plastic bags.

This sea change (pun intended) has led many fashion and luxury companies to announce initiatives to reduce plastic usage. L'Oréal, a leader in the very polluting cosmetics industry, took steps for all plastic packaging used by the company to be rechargeable, refillable, recyclable, or compostable by 2025. adidas has collaborated with Parley for the Oceans, an environmental organization and as early as 2017, had sold more than 1 million pairs of shoes made out of ocean plastic. Prada's nylon collection has been revamped by using 100% recycled ocean trash, with an aim to replace the entire nylon collection from the luxury Milanese brand by 2021. Luggage brands Samsonite and TUMI have developed collections of luggage made out of ocean plastics and other recycled materials. While for the time being, ocean plastic and recyclable materials have been used in specific ranges or collections, a case could be made for some brands to use such initiatives broadly across their portfolio. The younger generation would value that approach.

Luxury's "Ok Boomer" moment

In a sector whose consumers have new values, companies have been making old mistakes. Younger, more diverse consumers require different advertising strategies. Messaging that may have been seen as edgy in the past is increasingly seen as offensive. This has created a landscape that brands have not been very effective at navigating. As a consequence, many scandals have hit the luxury industry recently.

Dolce & Gabbana

D&G is the poster child for how not to address the young Chinese consumer. In November 2018, the fancy Italian ready-to-wear brand launched three short videos to advertise its upcoming Shanghai runway show. Each video featured an Asian woman struggling to eat

Italian food with chopsticks while a narrator mockingly encouraged her. The outrage was immediate, with the ads seen as pandering to stereotypes and blatantly condescending. A state-run newspaper wrote about the brand affecting Chinese dignity. Then, the day before the runway show, founding partner Stefano Gabbana was caught writing inappropriate Instagram messages about China and Chinese people. He argued his Instagram account had been hacked. Calls to boycott the brand multiplied, Chinese models recruited for the runway show canceled, and the show never took place. Chinese consumers returned their goods to the stores. Mainland Chinese online giants Alibaba and JD.com stopped selling the brand, and Hong Kong retailer Lane Crawford did the same. Former fans were seen burning their products or throwing them in the trash. Some storefronts got covered with "Not Me" signs mocking Gabbana's reaction to the events. D&G, a brand known for bold designs and political incorrectness, went too far with the wrong consumer: young Chinese, who dominate growth for the industry. Today, two years after the event, the brand has closed some of its flagships in China and clearly has significantly underperformed in terms of sales relative to peers.

While D&G's scandal has been the most extreme and obvious case of insensitive brand actions, examples abound of campaigns or products that have ruffled the feathers of a growingly aware young consumer. This has been the case for some of the bigger, most successful brands in the luxury sector, showing that no one is immune from mistakes.

Christian Dior

Also in November 2018, the LVMH-owned French couture icon Christian Dior launched an advertising campaign for its 2019 Cruise collection, which aimed to celebrate Mexican culture and especially the influence of "escaramuzas," skilled Mexican horsewomen. For the face of the campaign, it chose Jennifer Lawrence, a white actress with no Mexican heritage. Angry social media users also noticed the campaign was shot in California, not Mexico. Dior was accused of "cultural appropriation," a concept developed in the 1980s to describe the practice of dominant groups misusing cultural elements from historically oppressed groups.

Cultural appropriation is a contentious topic, notably with younger consumers. Kim Kardashian West, the American businesswoman and socialite, launched a shapewear (also known as foundation garment) brand called Kimono in June 2019. She has no Japanese background. This instantly elicited pushback from her many Twitter fans—she has more than 60 million—as well as from the mayor of Kyoto, Japan, who has been working hard to register "Kimono Culture" on UNESCO's intangible cultural heritage list. By August 2019, Kim's brand had been renamed.

Prada

Pradamalia, a range that launched in December 2018, included EUR550 (USD604) charm figurines that resembled a Golliwog, a nineteenth-century anti-black caricature. The figurines, which were shaped like a monkey with oversized red lips, were widely seen as racist and prompted outrage on social media. The brand apologized and pulled them from the line, though denied they referenced blackface (the style of makeup first used around 1830 to caricature black persons, and now considered blatantly racist). In February 2020, the company announced that top management would be getting some sensitivity training as part of the settlement with the New York City Commission on Human Rights and had 120 days to appoint a diversity and inclusion officer. Swift corporate accountability!

Gucci

In February 2019—Black History Month in the U.S.—a black wool "balaclava" sweater that had been on Gucci shelves for months blew up on social media. The sweater had a polo neck that rolled up to cover half the wearer's face, and a cutout for the mouth with a wide, bright red outline, again evoking oversized lips. The sweater was seen on social media as a direct reference to blackface. Gucci was clearly troubled by the mistake, especially as the brand had long been seen as a strong proponent of racial diversity under designer Tom Ford, who was known for using more diverse models than were many players in the industry. In the aftermath, current Gucci designer Alessandro Michele told the *Washington Post*: "When you think about Gucci, you imagine the jet set, bourgeois, rap and black people. That's the story of the brand. Gucci is half black."[9] Marco Bizzarri, Gucci's CEO, decided that creativity should not be constrained, but mechanisms must exist internally to ensure products and communication are not seen as offensive. Unlike the unconvincing response by D&G to their Chinese blowup, Gucci put in place many costly but necessary actions to meaningfully address the issue, hiring a global director for diversity and inclusion, forming an advisory council including black supermodel Naomi Campbell, working with a lecturer on "fashion and race" at Parsons School of Design in New York, and investing in community programs in ten cities in the U.S. and Canada.

Burberry

For his second high-profile collection with Burberry, Riccardo Tisci presented Tempest in February 2019. The collection was a tribute to youth, and the name a reference to "contrasts in British culture and weather," a wink to the political, not just the environmental, climate in the U.K. following the Brexit vote. Amid the collection's allusions to marine discovery and knots, one item was a tan hoodie with rope hanging from the neck in the shape of a noose. One model who walked that show said afterwards she was ashamed to have been a part of it. She expressed her outrage at the brand and its designer in an Instagram post, arguing that it was inappropriate for a youth-inspired collection to feature a noose, especially given the rise of suicide rates worldwide, and that "suicide is not fashion."[10]

What all these examples show is that youth and social media have made information travel very fast, and all fashion is now global. What could be seen as appropriate or minor in one location could well be interpreted as incredibly inappropriate elsewhere. As a result, recruitments of "heads of diversity and inclusion" have multiplied in the branded space. No doubt this is a good thing both in terms of the projected image of brands, and, importantly, of driving real diversity within the brands' management itself. Here again, COVID-19 has been an accelerator as it enhanced consumer perception of which brands were doing good—repurposing production sites to manufacture hand sanitizers or masks, making donations to hospitals or charities, cutting management pay and dividends—and which were simply not part of the conversation, or came across as untrustworthy.

Luxury consumer changes seem to have been exponential, whilst change from the companies has been logarithmic in comparison. It is key that the latter pay close attention to what youth want, and do not relax their efforts.

As this book was being completed, mass protests were taking place in the U.S. as citizens demonstrated against police brutality and race inequality following the killing of George Floyd and many other African American citizens. Consumer companies from Nike to Kering immediately understood that events were a wake-up call for them to address any type of complacency or past failures. Female representation in top management roles in luxury is limited; minority representation is appalling.

INTERVIEW: On creating content and excitement for a new generation of consumers

One brand that has captured the attention of a younger generation and found ways to constantly keep the attention high is Moncler. (The photo on page 76 provides a striking example of the creativity of Moncler's designs.) Here to explain what is unique about the brand's business model is the man who took charge of it in 2003 and reinvented it: Remo Ruffini, chairman and CEO of Moncler.[11]

ERWAN RAMBOURG: You were very successful at repositioning what was an outerwear company into a fashion-forward luxury brand. You had a classic two-season model and that was enough for good growth, but now you have moved to a monthly model. Why did you need this new approach for growth?

REMO RUFFINI: Moncler is a brand that I consider unique. I have been in love with the brand ever since I was a child. Even today, I can remember very well how proud I was when my mother bought me my first Moncler to wear as I went to school on my bike.

When I acquired Moncler in 2003, I had a clear project in mind. I wanted to create a global brand with no filters with the market and high-quality products. This is what we have been working towards during the past fifteen years. To remain successful and relevant to consumers today, however, you cannot rest on your laurels and just simply do fantastic products.

The world is changing at an unprecedented pace. Clients need newness, innovation, experience, and to feel part of a community. Companies need to recognize these needs and be ready to explore new ways of thinking. The challenge is to be flexible and agile whilst remaining faithful to their own DNA.

A couple of years ago, we started to imagine what we could do to evolve and interpret the spirit of the time, establishing a direct and frequent dialogue with consumers, communicating with new consumers, particularly the youngest ones, continuously delivering newness in store, and efficiently using the language of digital. We came up with the Moncler Genius idea, an approach that is simultaneously a digitally native communication project and a new business model that passed from a classic two-season model to a monthly collection delivery approach. Moncler Genius is a platform of innovation and creativity. Different designers are called to interpret

Moncler's identity according to their vision, each one talking to different audiences.

The project was designed to create buzz around the brand, to make the store come alive with new and unexpected products, and to use digital technologies as a tool for communication. With Genius, we aim to talk to multiple types of customers from different generations, nationalities, and cultures, offering them all something they are looking for, whilst always maintaining Moncler's DNA.

Today, we are facing the era of digitalization, and I truly believe that Moncler Genius is bringing the company into the third phase of its development.

ER: What insights on consumers brought you to this? Why are collections put out so frequently? This is unique in luxury. Is there another sector that inspired you?

RR: What brought me to the "Genius idea" was observing the people in the streets and how the world is evolving. I increasingly got the impression that the rules of the game were changing, and that the diffusion of digital was influencing people's behaviors and desires.

In every sector, you can find companies that stand out for their character and uniqueness, that interpret the change of the wind better than others and are able to go beyond the pure concept of product as well as towards new experiences and contents.

ER: What are the constraints in terms of production and logistics, and is your staff under pressure? On the positive side, how is it energizing your team?

RR: Moncler Genius has been a challenge for the entire organization, particularly for operations and logistics. We are really happy with how everybody reacted. Over the past two years, internal changes have been not only constant but also exponential. The execution of the Moncler Genius project is quite complex as each collection needs to be delivered globally at a stated time, without any delay or mistake. All divisions need to work together, from design to communication, events, digital, and operations and logistics. This requires not only an efficient organization, but also highly integrated teams able to work cross function and cross divisions. This has translated also into a new leadership style, more cross functional, less hierarchical,

From Richard Quinn's Moncler Genius collection Fall/Winter 2019–20.

CREDIT: Courtesy of Moncler.

and with a shared approach based on empowerment. In general, all this would have not been possible without a lot of flexibility and agility and a culture of innovation in the company. The project has indeed created a great engagement internally and made our sense of belonging even stronger.

I judge the success of Genius collaborations mainly on their capacity to generate buzz around the brand and to create energy at all levels, both within the stores and the company.

ER: Are the clients recruited via Genius different? How has it fed the rest of your brand equity? How important is content or storytelling, and could you have done it differently?

RR: Some clients attracted by Moncler Genius are new to the brand, but some are existing Moncler customers that have become even more loyal. Our new challenge is to continue providing freshness to all these customers, while making the new ones "real Moncler clients."

When it comes to the importance of storytelling, monthly collections are not enough to make the magic happen. It's key to be able to build a real platform of unique and compelling contents around the collections. Indeed, content, storytelling, and engagement are crucial. Moncler Genius includes monthly editorial and communication activations, where virtual and real, online and offline, work in unison. Each collection is based on a dedicated 360-degree editorial plan that establishes an ongoing program of contents to reach a wide audience through all touch points (i.e., press, social media, in-store activations, pop-ups, e-tailers, dedicated events, etc.).

The project is still relatively young, only started in 2018, and we have so many things to learn, so many things that we can do better. We are clearly learning from the experience. I would not say that we have made big mistakes, but for sure, we can do some things differently and better.

ER: Genius helped you to move from functionality (buying a jacket) to an elevated experience (buying status and a dream). Is this different by age, gender, or nationality?

RR: The customers nowadays are looking more and more to live an experience than just buy a product. Younger generations see fashion trends as a way to express themselves and to feel part of a community. They are looking for the content generated by each brand, and they choose what to buy also based on this. It is increasingly crucial to communicate and share our values in every moment of the customer shopping experience and through all of our touch points.

ER: How dangerous is this, because you can't possibly accelerate from having something every month? Will other brands catch on, and when that happens, how do you ensure you keep the edge or gap ahead of others?

RR: I think that every brand has its own identity and must have its own tailor-made strategy. It is not only a matter of having monthly collections. What makes the difference is the experience that you build around it.

I cannot rule out a further evolution of the Moncler strategy in the future. Perhaps we could leverage Moncler Genius as our house of contents, which could be developed into new forms, maybe in a manner that we have not already figured out. I believe there is still a lot of potential to be explored in this project, and we can create one of the most modern companies in the luxury space.

ER: After such a transformation in the business model of luxury, what could be some next steps for your group? New projects in retail or distribution, mergers and acquisitions (M&A)—to apply best practice to other brands—or other areas?

RR: I still see Moncler as a start-up company. We still have so many things to do, so many projects to complete, so much more to come. When I bought the company in 2003, I saw it evolving and becoming something new every year. We still need to highly concentrate on Moncler and continue to develop new ideas.

Summary

Luxury buyers start young for many reasons, but the essential one is human nature and buying your place in society. Whether in China, the U.S., or emerging markets, the modal age of the population is much lower than in Japan or Europe. While the population of Asian youth will shrink in terms of proportion, the growth in absolute numbers will support the sector. In the West, youth demographics is increasingly diverse. The young generation of luxury buyers—including, most notably, people of color—around the world have transformed the luxury industry and should continue to do so, particularly in certain areas:

- CASUALIZATION: a more relaxed way of dressing up is not a fad, it is a generational shift.

- SOCIAL MEDIA: widespread information and the search for authenticity will put pressure on brands to have thoughtful, genuine messages.

- VALUES: With climate protests, ESG issues going mainstream, and a diverse generation that cares, brands need to behave and respect the planet as well as cultural differences and sensitivities. Younger generations are clearly purpose driven and expecting the companies they buy from to start "getting woke."

PART TWO

THE
SELLERS

— 4 —
SIZE MATTERS

*If I have seen further than others, it is by standing
on the shoulders of giants.*

ISAAC NEWTON

THIS MIGHT SOUND depressing, but I believe that, in the luxury sector, independent players are likely to disappear unless they can achieve scale. The fundamental reason for this is that the luxury sector is currently a recruitment more than a repeat purchase market: the majority of growth is driven by brands' capacity to recruit new consumers rather than their capacity to sell more to existing consumers. While many key companies in the food, cosmetics, or luggage sectors are being disrupted by new entrants, including digitally native vertical brands (DNVBs) and other entrepreneurs, the core of the luxury business is dominated by the bigger brands and the bigger groups, who are taking share in what remains, counterintuitively, a highly fragmented market. Obviously, for many companies, the existing customer segment will become an important driver eventually, but today, the sector is still relatively in its infancy; independent brands such as Moncler, as well as behemoths like Gucci, rely on newcomers to their brands for more than half of their sales.

Scaling up confers enormous benefits across many dimensions. The major players know this, and their pursuit of scale will drive them towards further growth, including M&A, which will ensure they continue to gain market share from independent players, with very few exceptions. While other groups will chase after them, major diversified players like LVMH will only increase their power in the luxury world.

VAST success

Size matters in luxury for four VAST reasons: voice, authority, synergies, and talent.

VOICE: HOW TO EMERGE FROM A CROWD
I lived in London twice, once as a twenty-year-old, single marketing executive on his first job and later in life as a father of three working for a bank. London is a proper cosmopolitan city with plenty of extroverts and a rare sense of freedom. One of the places I always thought was emblematic of London's spirit is Speakers' Corner in Hyde Park. This is not the only speakers' corner in the U.K. or globally, but the one in Hyde Park is the best known. The principle is simple: anyone who wishes to say something can turn up and speak. Karl Marx, Vladimir Lenin, and George Orwell have spoken there, but anyone can get up and exercise their freedom of speech. The catch? Well, unless you are funny, colorful, revolutionary, loud, or fascinating, it's unlikely many passersby will listen to you.

In the crowded luxury sector, having a voice is also difficult. Twenty years ago, potential consumers of handbags may have heard of Louis Vuitton and Gucci. Today, with access to social media, blogs and forums, Google, and Amazon, if you are in the market to purchase your first handbag, the possibilities will seem endless. Theoretically, you could choose between sixty premium handbag brands, but if you are buying one for the first time, you will be influenced by two simple realities. First, you are presumably purchasing a handbag to feel good about yourself and for others to know you have been successful. Will you be drawn to buy an unknown brand if you are seeking to fit in? That is unlikely. Second, you will be influenced by traditional advertising, the latest Oscars or Golden Globes celebration, the incredibly over-the-top runway show, the flashy and fun flagship, and of course social media like Instagram. With the means to use big brand ambassadors as well as legions of big and small influencers, Louis Vuitton and Gucci have 38 million and 40 million Instagram followers respectively, more than twenty times that of the independent Italian footwear and leather goods company Tod's. All of this influences what your girlfriends are buzzing about and inevitably brings you to consider very few brands: the ones that are dominating airwaves, making the most noise, and employing the latest genius designers. These will rarely be the independent underdogs— not because they lack talent, more because they lack means to make it known. With scale comes financial means, and that is a phenomenal voice amplifier.

Of course, consumers in the know will gravitate towards alternative, edgy brands, but the majority of consumers who are entering the sector will likely go to the established brands to tick the box in terms of fitting in. Purchasing a less well-known brand could run the risk of not maximizing the return (status, recognition) on their investment.

To keep to the handbag example, according to my estimates, in 2017, Louis Vuitton and Gucci were spending four to six times more on advertising than Ferragamo, a family-controlled, Florence-based brand known for leather goods and footwear. A year later, in 2018, those metrics had diverged even more. All three brands increased spending in 2018, but Gucci and Louis Vuitton increased spending by a respective fifteen and ten times more than Ferragamo. Their adspend ratio (advertising as a percentage of sales) remained stable when Ferragamo's adspend ratio rose slightly.

In July 2018, Ferragamo appointed a new CEO, a well-respected industry veteran with twenty years of experience at Gucci. A few months after her nomination, many changes had been implemented in terms of staff, product, merchandising, and retail. While on a trip to Milan, I visited the Ferragamo flagship on Via Montenapoleone, one of the most iconic luxury high streets in the world. I was thoroughly impressed by the visible changes at the brand: exciting new accessories, a refreshed layout, a new footwear collection, and more. But I had not seen much on social media or heard much about the Ferragamo transformation in the news, so that was not what prompted me to go and have a look. And it dawned on me that unfortunately for the brand, while it has gradually transformed itself and developed a more compelling set of products and an enticing store layout, it has limited means to make the world aware. Given the noise and spending of bigger brands, Ferragamo is unlikely to get the much-deserved attention it has theoretically earned.

Scale makes a big difference beyond pure advertising. It allows brands to generate publicity via lavish events or the hiring of superstar designers, which boosts a brand's PR clout. Christian Dior hosted an exuberant 2020 Cruise collection runway show in the sixteenth-century El Badi palace in Marrakech in April 2019. The extravaganza cost millions of euros and would have sunk the profitability of many independent rivals, but within LVMH accounts, it amounted to no more than a rounding error. With COVID-19, the gap of voice is likely to widen as bigger brands cut back on spending but still have phenomenal clout relative to smaller peers.

Designer power is not just about the products they design. Virgil Abloh, an American designer, artist, and DJ who turned forty in 2020, entered the fashion world in 2009 when he interned at Fendi (part of the LVMH group) with his friend and collaborator Kanye West. He worked with West on various projects before founding his own high-end streetwear brand, Off-White, in 2013. Louis Vuitton

CEO Michael Burke had been following Abloh's work since his time at Fendi and in 2018 offered him the role of men's ready-to-wear designer for Louis Vuitton. Today, Virgil Abloh is still approached by many brands for collaborations, notably Nike and IKEA. He is followed by more than 5 million Instagram accounts, making him part of a very limited number of key influential designers on social media alongside Donatella Versace (5.3 million followers), Olivier Rousteing (Balmain, 6 million), and Riccardo Tisci (Burberry, 2.5 million). Of course, these are not numbers as high as those of some of the celebrities now working in fashion (Victoria Beckham has 28 million followers) or fashion bloggers (Chiara Ferragni, who started The Blonde Salad blog, now has 20 million followers) or of course popular socialites, models, or celebrities (Kylie Jenner, Kendall Jenner, Jennifer Lopez, Beyoncé, and Selena Gomez all have more than 100 million followers each). However, some of the designers have a celebrity status and a tremendous influence on younger consumers and will prove to be difficult to hire unless you have substantial means.

AUTHORITY: BE THE DRIVER, NOT A PASSENGER
The scale advantage extends well beyond amassing Instagram followers. By virtue of their size and financial resources, big brands make bold decisions which could be catastrophic for some of the smaller brands. If you are part of a group or are a large independent brand and you don't like the way you are distributed, then change your distribution. Louis Vuitton, Christian Dior, Hermès, and Chanel do not participate in multi-brand e-commerce distribution. Why? Because they want to keep the control and the direct relationship with their end consumers without having to use an intermediary, who is at risk of disenfranchising that relationship. Bigger players have enough traffic on their own websites and on WeChat mini-programs in China for those channels to be sufficient and highly qualitative. Smaller players will likely need to go on third-party

platforms for traffic and conversion, taking on the risks linked to cutting the direct relationship with their end consumers and to a lower-quality representation of the brand.

Industry executives often mention the benefits of scale in the real estate balance of power as well. If the retail motto "location, location, location" is still relevant, then no doubt the bigger brands and groups have a key competitive advantage. In shopping malls or freestanding street locations, those brands will decide where they want to be. If they don't get satisfaction, they will just turn down the retail operators' offer. The big brands can pressure the operators to give them top locations and, in some instances, pay lower rent than most; big brands also enable the mall to gain credibility and traffic. Or they can walk without huge consequences.

When you have size and profits, and are usually family controlled, time is on your side. The longtime CEO of Louis Vuitton Yves Carcelle ran the brand from 1990 to 2012 and was known as a very big traveler. He would go to all the destinations he thought Louis Vuitton should have a presence in, refuse the subpar locations, and tell retail operators he had time. He once told me a story about Aruba, an island in the Dutch Caribbean, where he wanted the brand to be at the best possible location. It took close to ten years of holding out, but eventually, Louis Vuitton got the prime anchor location at the local Renaissance Mall in Oranjestad. If you are a small independent player trying to make a name for yourself, what authority do you have on influencing your location?

Authority and financial means can also lead to buying real estate if a location makes sense for the longer term. Hermès purchased its 65,000-square-foot flagship in Tokyo's fashionable Ginza area in 2001, later acquired four shops in Hong Kong in 2002 (all sold in 2018 for three-and-half times more), and also bought the Asprey building in London's New Bond Street in 2009. This last building is still occupied by the London jeweler and home goods manufacturer Asprey, so while the media thought Hermès was purchasing the building as a prelude to eventually purchasing Asprey, this has not occurred. It looks like Hermès just took a good opportunity on a prime location that isn't even used for its namesake brand. Talk about the luxury that scale provides!

This is why Apple, Louis Vuitton, and Gucci almost systematically have the best locations in shopping malls. This is also why some smaller brands within big groups manage to secure strong locations. For instance, Celine, a seventy-five-year-old ready-to-wear and leather luxury brand, part of the LVMH group since 1996, managed to hire star designer Hedi Slimane in 2018 and recently launched menswear. From a real estate perspective, both his fame and LVMH's heft have been instrumental in securing key locations.

Given that luxury remains a very fragmented market, the advertising and social media firepower of brands like Louis Vuitton or Gucci and their capacity to win the real estate battle within shopping malls and high streets are key differentiating factors relative to players with a fifth or a tenth of their sales. As Hong Kong demonstrations in the summer of 2019 started to hit inbound tourism flows from China and luxury sales in the city, Prada and Tod's looked to close stores. LVMH looked to negotiate rates and opportunistically capture better locations. The influence and the authority that scale gives is difficult to replace.

SYNERGIES: MANY PARTS MAKE A GREATER WHOLE

Scale can exponentially improve the effectiveness of data-driven efforts, provide a cushion for costly resets, and create a broader base of skill and innovation. Having several brands in the same group means you have a mirror. If one brand excels at a particular topic (digital, retail, training, CRM, etc.), others can learn from it. The ability to test tactics in smaller settings before deploying within the broader group can be powerful.

Recently, the luxury industry has talked a lot about analytics. Newly developed tech and online services can help small brands be disruptive in staples sectors such as cosmetics or beer, as these are businesses that are essentially wholesale driven, so volumes matter and structure costs can be light (no rent, no store staff). In the luxury sector, however, it seems that the tech revolution favors the large groups, which can invest in data analytics, artificial intelligence (AI), CRM systems, online concierge services, and more to attract new consumers and keep existing ones happy. Small independent companies do not have the customer base or the means to access data enabling them to service their clients flawlessly or anticipate their needs.

In early February 2020, Canada Goose, a listed company, issued a profit warning explaining that COVID-19 was to blame for earnings remaining flat in the fiscal year ending March 2020, while they had been previously predicted to grow at least 25%. Essentially, Chinese consumers had stopped buying products from one day to the next. But when I asked the management team what proportion of retail sales were accounted for by Chinese consumers in major markets for the brand in Canada and the U.S., they could only give me a rough guesstimate. It's not that the team was unwilling to give a more precise estimate; it's that they did not have the CRM system in place to actually quantify that information.

Multi-brand groups are better with data. Richemont's recent acquisition of online retailer YOOX NET-A-PORTER (YNAP) could trigger important changes within Richemont-run brands (Cartier and others), as an opportunity is now available to apply the digital and e-commerce expertise of YNAP across all the Richemont brands.

A concrete example of production synergies is LVMH's creation of Thélios in 2017. This entity was set up with eyewear specialist Marcolin in order to design, manufacture, and distribute eyewear for many of the LVMH brands, creating efficiencies that reduce costs and increase margins. LVMH competitor Kering had moved first by creating Kering Eyewear in 2014, which now produces eyewear for fifteen brands. Most of these are part of the group, such as Gucci,

Saint Laurent, and Alexander McQueen, but some outside partners like Cartier, Montblanc, and Courrèges are also included.

TALENT: THE BIGGEST GET THE BRIGHTEST

Finally, scale helps attract the best people. The diversity of products and positions found in a large brand or group means that if a specific brand employs exceptional managers, they may step up to run other brands in the portfolio. This abundance of opportunity gives larger groups or brands an advantage in terms of talent acquisition, retention, and promotion.

Think about career paths at Prada versus LVMH. Miuccia Prada is the head designer for the group, the founder and head of sister brand Miu Miu (named after her own nickname as a child), as well as the current creative inspiration for the eponymous Prada brand founded by her grandfather in 1913. Her husband, Patrizio Bertelli, is the CEO of the group, and their son Lorenzo Bertelli, known to the world as a World Rally Championship driver, was recently promoted within the group as head of marketing and communication. If you are high up within the Prada management structure, what are your chances of becoming the CEO some day? That's right: next to nothing. Of course, your chances of becoming LVMH's next CEO are similarly as slim, but if you are the number two at any LVMH brand and you are successful, chances are you will have a shot at becoming CEO of one of the group's seventy-six other brands.

Examples of great careers within the major groups abound. Anthony Ledru is undoubtedly one of the rising stars at LVMH. After more than ten years with Cartier in sales and retail operations in the U.S., Anthony became vice president of sales for jeweler Harry Winston and then senior VP for Tiffany's North American division. That's when LVMH made him an offer to run the Louis Vuitton brand in the U.S. After two years of a phenomenal track record there, Anthony became EVP of commercial activities for Louis Vuitton globally in Paris, essentially becoming the head of the international division for the largest luxury brand on the planet. Within Kering and more broadly in the sector, many look up to Marco Bizzarri, and not just because of his towering height, but more because he seems to have the Midas touch with luxury brands. Working within a diversified group has enabled him to go from running Stella McCartney in 2005 to Bottega Veneta in 2009 to powerhouse Gucci since early 2015.

Luxury's shark tank: M&A to continue to thrive

The luxury industry is dominated by families (such as those who control LVMH, Kering, Richemont, the Swatch Group, Hermès, and Chanel), and competitors to those are forced to think long term or they are likely to struggle to compete. Luxury companies that want the benefits of scale (and who wouldn't?) have a few routes to get there. They can chase growth by increasing sales of existing brands, develop new brands from scratch, or take the fastest route: M&A. The luxury sector has had a history filled with M&A ever since Louis Vuitton merged with Moët Hennessy in 1987, the latter having already been the result of the merger between champagne leader Moët & Chandon and cognac leader Hennessy back in 1971. This created the LVMH group, a group that has seventy-seven brands, made the largest deal ever in the sector recently (acquiring Tiffany for USD 16.2 billion in late 2019), and is by far the largest diversified group in luxury—but not the only one. The table on page 93 offers examples of recent M&A by LVMH and other groups in the luxury sector.

M&A feeds directly into scale, and so logically, the advantages I described above for scale will be boosted by new brands coming in to existing groups, particularly the advantages of synergy. M&A does not have to be only about brands. It can be about distribution, production sites, or acquiring a particular software, know-how, or technology. One of the consequences of COVID-19 is that some suppliers to luxury might find themselves in a financial predicament, and this could lead to them being integrated by the brands they

Recent M&A deals in luxury

Acquirer	Target	Date	Category	% Acquired	EV*	Sales	EV/sales
LVMH	Tiffany	2019	Jewelry	100	USD 16,200m	USD 4,424m	3.7×
LVMH	Bel-mond	2018	Hospitality	100	USD 3,200m	USD639m	5.6×
LVMH	Christian Dior	2017	Fashion	100	EUR 6,500m	EUR 2,130m	3.0×
LVMH	RIMOWA	2016	Luggage	80	EUR 640m	EUR400m	1.6×
Richemont	Buccellati	2019	Jewelry	100	EUR250m	EUR50m	5.0×
Richemont	Watchfinder	2018	Second-hand	100	EUR229m	EUR130m	1.8×
Richemont	YNAP	2018	Online	49	EUR 2,400m	EUR 2,300m	2.1×
Capri	Versace	2018	Fashion	100	USD 2,120m	USD 850m	2.5×
Capri	Jimmy Choo	2017	Footwear	100	USD 1,350m	USD 470m	2.9×
Tapestry	Kate Spade	2017	Fashion	100	USD 2,400m	USD 1,350m	1.8×

* Enterprise value, a measure of the company's total value including any debt or cash.

The largest sharks in the luxury tank continue to devour the competition.

SOURCES: Various company documents and press articles.

supply, in order to maintain jobs and know-how. Luxury seeks control, and that control enables pricing power. This implies that if a brand has the means to control its entire ecosystem, it should do so. For example, when I worked at Cartier more than fifteen years ago, about half of the jewelry production for the brand was outsourced. After several acquisitions, nowadays the vast majority is in-house, which has been helpful in terms of controlling the quality and increasing productivity. Importantly, it has also been a booster in terms of margin for the brand.

The benefits of scale are reason enough to believe M&A will continue to thrive in the sector and that most brands one way or another will be involved. But other factors support the prediction, which involve cash generation, hedging, and people.

Cash generation

Ten years ago, luxury brands relied on their capacity to open stores for sales growth. Nowadays, most of the bigger brands have the stores they need in the cities they need to have them in. While they might be extending or upgrading some locations, the capex-to-sales ratio has been coming down very quickly. The sector was highly profitable until the 2020 crisis hit, and in this absence of store capex pressure and with IT and digital investments remaining also under control, cash post-COVID-19 will be piling up so fast that many of the balance sheets in the sector might look under-leveraged (they won't have much debt). Families in the sector do not have a culture of giving back money to shareholders in the form of buybacks or special dividends. This contrasts with many non-family-held listed companies. Think Apple: the company has an amount of cash in excess of 10% of its market capitalization and has committed to give that cash all back to shareholders over time. Luxury groups at times talk about possibly returning some cash, and to be fair, LVMH and Kering have had small buyback programs, but more often they use cash at hand or some leverage to acquire new brands.

Hedging

A pretty simple reason to support M&A in the sector is the old adage of not keeping all of your eggs in the same basket. If your group relies on one brand for 80% or 100% of its profits, what happens if that brand falters? To use an investment analogy, equity investors should sleep better at night if they hold a portfolio of thirty stocks than if they have invested their earnings in a single one. So if you are a family managing assets for the long term, diversifying your luxury portfolio is just common sense.

Burberry is a mono-brand company listed on the London Stock Exchange. In 2017, the independent company welcomed its new CEO, who promptly made it clear that the financial metrics would go sideways for two years: the brand needed to be repositioned, meaning reinvesting, cleaning up the markets, and not expanding sales. The two years of stable margins that such a move entailed were only possible due to Burberry's size.

By contrast, RIMOWA, the luggage company, went through a big reset when LVMH took over in 2016. Margins approached zero, but given the scale of LVMH, this was not even visible at the group level. Also, as RIMOWA became part of a luxury empire, advertising costs were likely much lower as the brand benefited from LVMH rates. The brand has been incredibly visible for the three years following the acquisition, with a completely new retail footprint, many artistic collaborations, advertising galore, and an active Instagram feed, moving it from almost niche to almost unavoidable.

People

Generally speaking, companies purchase brands because they believe in the long-term growth prospects of the target (theoretically, smaller companies should grow at a faster pace than larger ones). Crucial to this is the buyer's belief in their capacity to do a better job than the current management team. In other words, managers will change following acquisitions. Within the LVMH group, fresh blood at Bulgari and RIMOWA following their acquisitions (in 2011 and 2016, respectively) enabled both brands to embrace a completely new growth trajectory.

But the flow of people can also go the other way. In late 2019, the press reported the rumor of a tie-up between Kering and Moncler, both of whose CEOs are interviewed in this book. On paper, the appeal to Kering would be access to the strong growth potential of Moncler, which can still increase its retail footprint (most developed luxury brands are already in all the important markets) and further diversify outside of outerwear. Another benefit, perhaps more important in my view, would be the value of having access to some of the key innovators in the industry, such as Remo Ruffini, Moncler's CEO, or Roberto Eggs, Moncler's chief marketing and operating officer.

And as mentioned above, the capacity to attract top talent will also come much more easily for groups that have different assets than for mono-brand companies, unless their culture and appeal are particularly strong like they are at independents Moncler, Hermès, and Chanel.

ALTHOUGH TIMING AND names are impossible to predict, much more transformation is likely for the sector from an M&A point of view. As some independent brands may feel some pressure from the macro environment, opportunities will arise. In 2020, as COVID-19 hit sales in the sector, it became clear that the larger groups weathered the storm better, while smaller independent companies were going through a much harder time. Of course, smaller family-controlled companies are not incentivized to sell out at a time when sales are collapsing and margins follow south—unless of course they are forced sellers (e.g., companies facing losses or struggling to finance their business), which is rare. However, when the situation stabilizes after this crisis, I believe that the bigger brands will benefit most from pent-up demand. Eventually, families are likely to come to the conclusion that scale is an issue and that they cannot thrive on their own. COVID-19 will be a consolidation accelerator. Grouping soft luxury companies is a rational move, given fashion trends can come and go and diversity is a hedge. Outside of soft luxury, grouping brands can work in segments that are predominantly wholesale driven (like fragrances and watches).

LVMH: And then there was one?

LVMH is already the largest luxury group in terms of sales, profit, and market capitalization but has often said it aims to expand market share in all of its markets, "increasing its global leadership position."[1] With size and diversity comes an element of visibility and lower volatility as assets that do poorly—of which LVMH has few—will be compensated by success stories, and parts of the portfolio appear staple like: Sephora, fragrances, wines and spirits, and, to a certain extent, Louis Vuitton. All the bigger groups in the industry (relative to independents) enjoy the advantages of scale, but the sheer size of the LVMH group means that gradually the dynamic could shift from "big versus small" to "LVMH versus the rest of the world." I believe the possibility is high that the group will become the proxy for the industry thanks to strong organic sales growth and acquisitions. If I continue to follow the luxury sector, I might have to publish a book in 2030 called *LVMH: A Luxury Supremacy.*

(As a side comment, you might be noticing that LVMH appears a lot in this book, but note that over time, both organic growth and M&A have made the group's market capitalization three times larger than that of any of its competitors'. So I am not giving LVMH preferential treatment but just reflecting its might.)

The group does not provide precise guidance to equity market observers, but LVMH clearly thinks long term. LVMH has done in luxury what Nike has done in sporting goods: it has invested massively in advertising means and in IT, supply chain, and real estate infrastructure to keep competition at bay. A recent illustration of this strategy was visible when the group reported H1 2019 results, during which sales beat estimates yet the margin missed expectations for the right reason—that is, because the group increased investments in an attempt to suffocate competition. Obviously, that is just my interpretation, not the way they communicated! Meanwhile, Christian Dior, one of the most visible brands of the LVMH stable, lost money in the U.S. and invested more in order to ensure its scale will be that much larger longer term, likely wanting to play catch up to Chanel in that market. According to my estimates, the Dior brand all in (with fragrance and cosmetics) will have generated close to EUR7bn (USD 7.5 billion) in sales in 2019. Given its proximity in positioning and attributes to Chanel (unlisted and independent), I would not be surprised if LVMH plans to grow the brand to a size comparable to Chanel, whose revenues exceeded EUR10bn (USD 10.7 billion) in 2019.

LVMH has a very strong history of deal-making and remains, for me, the default aggregator in the sector, with the balance sheet strength and cash to make major acquisitions. Selling to LVMH can appeal to other family-held businesses that seek long-term brand development. Imagine you are an independent luxury brand: in order to crystallize value, would you rather sell a stake to a private equity investor, who is likely to rough you up and list your brand on the equity markets with all their scrutiny and regulations, or sell to LVMH, who are the best in class at business but also think like a family, properly, for the long term?

In July 2019, Bernard Arnault, CEO of LVMH, became the second-wealthiest individual in the world. The first, Jeff Bezos, the founder and CEO of Amazon, once said: "There are two kinds of companies: those that work to charge more and those that work to charge less. We will be the second."[2] I think LVMH will continue to thrive by working relentlessly to charge *more*, to acquire and develop brands that consumers are so enthusiastic about that price is no object—or is even the appeal.

LVMH has many investment avenues to support future growth, but I see three main ones: skincare, hard luxury (watches and jewelry), and diversification outside luxury, notably into hospitality.

PREDICTION #6

Bernard Arnault, chairman and CEO of LVMH, will consistently top the list of the richest individuals in the world, ahead of Amazon's Bezos, as was already the case briefly in late 2019. His group will hold ninety to one hundred brands, up from seventy-seven at the time of writing.

Skincare

LVMH is underrepresented in skincare, with its only sizeable asset being Parfums Christian Dior. Its current portfolio is still very much skewed to the lower-growth, lower-margin fragrance category, reinforced by its purchase of a majority stake in Maison Francis Kurkdjian in early 2017. That add-on was part of an industry-wide buying frenzy of niche fragrance labels, following Estée Lauder's purchase of Le Labo, Frédéric Malle, and By Kilian, and L'Oréal's takeover of Atelier Cologne—but these are very small assets that will not move the needle. The success of LVMH's distribution arm Sephora supports the view that skincare is a promising subsector of consumption, bringing strong growth, loyalty, and higher margins. LVMH has grown organically in this sector by, for example, building FENTY, Rihanna's makeup brand, which generated the equivalent of EUR500m (USD550m) in its second year of existence and is part of the company's San Francisco–based Kendo incubator of beauty brands. However, unless you grow organically, acquisition multiples paid in makeup are exorbitant, as recent examples such as Estée Lauder's Too Faced acquisition show.

Hard luxury

Until it welcomed Tiffany into its stable after the acquisition was announced in November 2019, LVMH was tiny in this sector compared with Richemont, Swatch, and Rolex. Several theoretical arguments against such an approach had been made over time. Some observers cautioned that jewelry is a tough category due to high inventory commitments. Bulgari's success within LVMH, after the group acquired the brand in 2011, likely alleviated those concerns. The tie-up between Swatch and Tiffany for the production of Tiffany watches was an issue; that tie-up was dissolved in September 2011. Arnault may have had an issue with a jewelry brand that relies on more accessible silver products for more than 20% of its business, despite LVMH holding brands that sell champagne or fragrances at USD50 a pop. And LVMH may have been wary of acquiring U.S.-based assets in view of the patchy fortunes of Marc Jacobs (still a problematic asset within the group) and Donna Karan (sold by LVMH to G-III after twenty years of choppy ownership). However, after the success of FENTY and the opening of a third production site for Louis Vuitton in the U.S. in 2019 in Texas (larger than the first two in California), LVMH likely felt emboldened to take further initiatives in the U.S. Holding the distinct and complementary brands of Tiffany (New England rigor) and Bulgari (Roman exuberance) in the same portfolio makes a lot of sense.

Diversification

As a proxy for luxury, LVMH should aim to redefine luxury itself. The aspirations of wealthy American and Chinese consumers include travel, e-commerce, healthy living, and custom products (wine, art, etc.), so the possibilities are plentiful. Two recent LVMH purchases have expanded its footprint in luxury travel and hospitality: in 2016, it bought a majority stake in RIMOWA, the high-end German luggage brand, an ingenious way to capture consumer aspirations towards travel. Three years later, the group acquired Belmond, a high-end hospitality group owning the legendary Cipriani hotel in Venice and the Orient Express train service. In February 2020, LVMH named Andrea Guerra, a longtime CEO at eyewear giant Luxottica and one of the most respected executives in the consumer space, to run "LVMH Hospitality excellence." He became a member of the executive committee of the group in mid-March that year. Taking on board such a senior executive tells me the group should have many future projects in the hospitality area. In hindsight, acquiring a luggage brand and then a chain of high-end hotels in the time of COVID-19 may have been unfortunate timing. But unless you think travel is gone forever, which I don't, it is likely that these assets will see better days ahead.

Anyone wishing to understand the future of luxury should watch LVMH closely. What began as a partnership with Rihanna in makeup developed into the luxury fashion brand FENTY—undoubtedly unexpected, and a master stroke. When asked by a journalist if he thought Rihanna was the next Coco Chanel, LVMH's Bernard Arnault wittingly replied that for starters, "she's got a better voice." The group will have many more opportunities to think outside of the box, so expect the unexpected.

Is there space for an American LVMH?

The new kids on the luxury M&A block are <u>Tapestry</u>, the new name of the Coach group after it acquired American brands Kate Spade and Stuart Weitzman, and <u>Capri</u>, the new name of Michael Kors after it bought British brand Jimmy Choo and exuberant Italian brand Versace. The rationale for the Tapestry and Capri groups to attempt becoming "American LVMHs" (i.e., diversified luxury groups) is crystal clear to me: mono-brand companies, at least in soft luxury, are a risky investment because fashion comes and goes. In that context, diversity offers a natural hedge.

The fortunes of these two competing New York–based groups have been far from smooth sailing, though. I sought interviews with the CEOs of Tapestry and Capri, but the timing did not work out, so you'll have to settle for my analysis of these two groups in terms of their M&A strategies.

The management team at Tapestry had the ambition and the capacity to build a strong, diversified group to replicate the European groups' success in a more affordable brand positioning. Their acquisitions moved Tapestry swiftly from a mono-brand to democratic luxury American LVMH status. The advantage of that focus is that Tapestry can rely on greater synergies in terms of production and distribution. For example, traditional luxury players would not necessarily establish common production facilities and regional teams for multiple different brands, as Tapestry now does.

The problem with focusing on affordable luxury, though, is that it is a low-growth segment of the industry, at least in handbags, as I explain in chapter 6. Under the leadership of Victor Luis—long-term veteran within the Coach brand, group CEO, and architect of its multi-brand approach—Tapestry (Coach at the time) paid USD 2.6 billion for Kate Spade in 2017. Things did not go as planned, however, and the following years saw several disappointments linked to the integration of the brand and a dire share price performance. Victor left the group abruptly during the summer of 2019. Three months after his departure, Anna Bakst, CEO of the unsuccessful Kate Spade brand, also left the group as part of a major senior management overhaul. Another three months later, the CEO of Stuart Weitzman, Eraldo Poletto, was replaced, and in March 2020, the CEO of key brand Coach, Joshua Schulman, resigned, rounding out an incredible revolving door of senior executives. It was somewhat ironic that, having started his career at LVMH, and cognizant of the benefits of running a multi-brand group, Luis and his team were unsuccessful in executing what on paper was a fantastic strategic plan.

Following the acquisition of Jimmy Choo in 2017, Capri did not hide that this would not be the last deal, and the acquisition of Versace the next year was a lot more meaningful for the group. While Jimmy Choo's acquisition was more of a "plug and play" as the brand was solid but likely just needed some investment in stores and systems, Versace is a brand that needed much more thorough fixing, and the jury is still out on whether Capri management could prove to be stretched with such a turnaround project at hand. Given the price, the stakes are high. Unlike Tapestry, which made it clear they would focus on American affordable luxury, Capri is open to premium European brands, which do not necessarily have a similar price point or positioning to its central Kors brand. In terms of Versace, the price paid (USD 2.12 billion) implies a multiple on sales (2.5 times) that looks reasonable in light of the luxury sector's M&A history, while the multiple of EBITDA (earnings before interest, taxes, depreciation, and amortization), at 34 times, looks very high—though that is to be expected when the buyer comes from outside the usual European suspects. Indeed, when looking at premium European luxury brands, local European groups will have a sort of right of first refusal, as the ties between the families and the ecosystem are much tighter. In other words, if an interesting asset is up for sale in Europe, the likes of LVMH and Kering will take a look, and then if they do not bid or bid low, the asset may go at a higher price to a non-European bidder like Capri.

All told, Tapestry brought in brands that were not too pricey, but they are proving to be difficult to turn around. Capri brought in faster-growing brands but had to break the bank. There is no one clear winning strategy between the two, though Capri's management has been resilient while most of the Tapestry senior management has changed. The COVID-19 outbreak has caused both companies to suffer tremendously from their predominantly North American exposure because the U.S. shut stores in mid-March 2020.

Who else should you watch?

LVMH may be the dominant force in luxury, but there are several other groups and companies with the means to be involved in big

M&A shake-ups, and they should not be ignored. We can also expect luxury acquisitions from outside the sector, as private and overseas funding grow in importance.

Kering: The challenger

Having recently disposed of the majority stake it had in German sporting goods brand PUMA, Kering has successfully transformed itself from a diversified conglomerate dominated by retail assets, to a portfolio of strictly premium brands, with some of the most iconic companies in leather and accessories, directly competing with the likes of LVMH's Louis Vuitton and Dior. For many reasons, Kering could go back on the acquisition trail, but the most compelling of these is hedging. With the Gucci brand—which the group managed to control after a bitter fight with LVMH which ended with a sale on an unforgettable date (September 11, 2001)—doing very well recently and accounting for close to 80% of group profits, adding brands would help the group derisk its portfolio. Though the rumored tie-up with Moncler never materialized, many other options for the group have been mentioned over time in the press and could make sense: a merger with Richemont (see below), a purchase of Ferragamo, Valentino, or Prada, or more realistically in the short term, the development of a beauty business (most brands of Kering license this out to partners) or more assets in the eyewear segment.

Richemont: Absolute hard luxury

The Swiss-based group, chaired by South African entrepreneur Johann Rupert, has been active recently, taking in the stake it did not yet own in e-commerce operator YNAP, taking a 7.5% stake in duty-free operator Dufry, acquiring a secondhand watch retailer called Watchfinder & Co., and purchasing one of the rare independent jewelers, Milanese Buccellati, founded in 1919.

Richemont rightly considers its core competency to be hard luxury (watches and jewelry) and is very unlikely to venture outside of that area in terms of brands, in my view, and if it does, this would be risky. As Chairman Rupert prepares for the long term, further distribution integration (getting some skin in the game in e-commerce, alternative distribution, travel, etc.) might well continue.

The fact that both the Swatch Group and Richemont passed on acquiring Breitling, a solid family-controlled watch brand that was eventually sold to private equity firm CVC Capital Partners in April 2017, is telling. Given that Richemont was in the midst of a watch restructuring phase, purchasing Breitling would not have made sense, and the lack of interest in the asset was likely a warning for what sustainable growth may be in the watch category. I am not convinced there are many brands Richemont can look at—aside from the following four, which are interesting for scale and/or growth potential:

- Rolex, the iconic go-to luxury watch brand, notably for American consumers, which should continue to benefit from its scale and popularity with middle- and upper-class consumers

- Patek Philippe and Audemars Piguet, two ultra-high-end brands that should benefit from scarcity of supply, helping create healthy demand for them

- Chopard, a well-balanced watch and jewelry brand with powerful assets (e.g., a best-in-class watch manufacture, sponsorship of the Cannes Film Festival), whose growth should benefit from its jewelry exposure, a category which, as explained in chapter 1, will see growth as global female spending power grows

Swatch: The savior of Swiss-made watches

Swatch is unlikely to pay up for assets. The group, known for saving the mechanical Swiss watch industry, is likely to stick to what it knows. Separately, it has always been cautious in terms of the valuation multiples it pays for acquisitions, though overexposure to the watch category (slow growth) could perhaps lead the group to diversify more meaningfully into faster-growing categories such as jewelry. This was likely the intent of the 2013 acquisition of New York jeweler Harry Winston. Leaving aside small acquisitions linked to production or distribution, I do not see a big acquisition on the horizon for the group, given the disciplined nature of asset allocation.

Here is a look at what some of the other groups might do:

Tod's: Small diversified soft luxury

The small Italian multi-brand group has been rumored to be on the market, though Chairman Diego Della Valle has denied the speculation. LVMH has had a 3.5% stake since the initial public offering (IPO), and Tod's brands have been underperforming in the sector for a while. Selling the company would likely not be as easy as it sounds as all four brands have challenges:

- The core Tod's brand has potential to grow long term but lacks sufficient brand awareness and credibility in the U.S. and China. It is positioned between sneaker brands and higher-end luxury, to a certain extent stuck in the middle.

- Hogan is a younger, more affordable, more casual brand and similarly to Tod's, has not had the traction in China and the U.S. to make it a proper global concept.

- Roger Vivier is a niche fashion footwear brand that has thrived but has entered the same type of conundrum as we saw a few years back with Bottega Veneta (part of Kering): it relies on one product (the buckle shoe at Roger Vivier, the intrecciato leather products at Bottega Veneta), and it is in need of other pillars.

- Fay is an iconic outerwear brand with almost no sales or awareness outside of Italy.

Ferragamo: Florentine elegance

Ferragamo was in the press recently as a candidate for a sale or a delisting. Here again, the family has denied speculation. Also, for several reasons, a sale is unlikely to happen in the short term. First, the company picked former Gucci executive Micaela Le Divelec to be CEO in 2018 following the surprise departure of Eraldo Poletto. Changes linked to this appointment imply the family is not thinking of cashing out, because they are giving the new management team the chance to change the course of the brand, which cannot happen in just a year or two. Second, families move slowly. The structure of capital means many members of the family would need to be convinced for Ferragamo to sell. Third, the recent virus outbreak will make 2020 company metrics less attractive to buyers and so less likely that family members will get a good price, I believe. Finally, it is unlikely that family members will become forced sellers: beyond the leather goods and footwear brand, the family wealth includes land and buildings in Tuscany.

Prada: Milanese fashion forward

Prada has been acquisitive in the past, though assets like Helmut Lang and Jil Sander were not successful and were sold before the company became public in 2011. The Prada brand itself is going through a recovery phase, and focusing on anything else would not be reasonable for now. Yet given Prada's strong brand equity and potential, eventually expanding the portfolio or merging could make sense given what I mentioned on the importance of scale and how underdeveloped the brand is relative to Gucci and Louis Vuitton. Prada is an iconic fashion-forward brand with very strong equity, and the recent hiring of Raf Simons (formerly at Christian Dior and Calvin Klein) as co-creative director alongside Miuccia Prada will likely create some excitement in 2020 and beyond.

Moncler: Down with disruption

Investors have been wondering since long before the Kering rumor emerged if Moncler was an acquisition target. Another interesting angle would be to see the company itself acquire brands. For a few reasons, this could make sense:

- Moncler still has some white space to work with in terms of retail footprint, as the brand ended 2019 with slightly more than two hundred stores. While I think they might reach around three hundred eventually, this implies Moncler has only a few years of organic expansion left.

- Moncler has a surprisingly solid bench of managers for a mono-brand company, starting with CEO Remo Ruffini (see interview in chapter 3) as well as Roberto Eggs, chief marketing and operating officer, who, since joining from LVMH in 2015, has been instrumental in transitioning Moncler from a mid-sized to a large brand. The company has developed best practices (and frankly, disruptive business approaches, such as the Genius project, which the interview in chapter 3 focuses on), and its managers could well use those to develop other assets within an expanded portfolio.

- Moncler has the financial firepower to look at decently sized assets.

SMCP: Parisian chic

The owners of Sandro, Maje & Claudie Pierlot (SMCP) doubled sales between 2014 and 2018, reaching the EUR1bn (USD 1.07 billion) threshold. This put the group in a position to add to its portfolio, which it did in 2019 with the acquisition of De Fursac. CEO Daniel Lalonde, interviewed in chapter 6, had said earlier in the year: "For the first time, I can say that, if a brand corresponded to our company culture and an opportunity presented itself, we could indeed look into it seriously. We're ready. We've invested in our infrastructure, I think it's the right moment."[3] As SMCP develops into an affordable luxury aggregator of ready-to-wear, the company has many potential targets to look at.

Private equity and Chinese money

Diversified European luxury conglomerates get a sort of right of first refusal on deals simply because of their proximity to the majority of potential targets, which are Europe based. This does not mean they are the only buyers. Indeed, we are seeing a step-up in the consumer space by private equity and Chinese money:

- L Catterton—the result of the merger of L Capital and Catterton—remains dominant in the consumer space, with a portfolio of about one hundred investments ranging from affordable luxury (John Hardy, ba&sh, Genesis, Gentle Monster), to fitness and beauty (Peloton, Equinox, Bliss, Dr. Wu), to food (Cholula, Chopt, CÉ LA VI, Velvet Taco), and a whole lot more. Given that L Capital was founded as the private investment arm of LVMH's CEO Bernard Arnault, the assets are unlikely to be direct competitors of traditional luxury but will be relevant in terms of budget competition.

- A variety of other private equity firms have been active in the consumer space, such as Permira, Cerberus, The Carlyle Group, KKR, TPG, PAI, Apax Partners, General Atlantic, and NEO Investment Partners. And in May 2017, French private equity firm Eurazeo launched a new "brands" investment division, snapping up stakes in five consumer names in its first two years of operation.

- Separately, Chinese money has emerged with the diversification of Ruyi Group (a textiles company) into non-Chinese brands such as SMCP (French), Bally (Swiss), Aquascutum (British), and Renown (Japanese). The Fosun conglomerate has also been active, with investments in Club Med, Cirque du Soleil, and St. John, for example.

Summary

Scale in the luxury sector confers VAST advantages related to voice, authority, synergies, and talent, so it's no wonder the major players will strive to grow even bigger. M&A is a function of the benefits of scale and will be influenced by increased cash on hand, the importance of hedging, and personnel dynamics. All of this will ensure more consolidation. LVMH should remain the main luxury aggregator, but expect other groups to consolidate the industry as well.

PREDICTION #7

Very few luxury brands will remain independent, with the possible exceptions of Hermès, Chanel, and Rolex. Most of them will merge, go out of business, buy others, or be bought. Watch retailers will merge as volumes of watches sold remain under pressure and sales shift more to stores or websites operated directly by the brands.

— 5 —

BRICK
AND MORTAR
IS IMMORTAL

For last year's words belong to last year's language.
And next year's words await another voice.
And to make an end is to make a beginning.

T. S. ELIOT

M EDIA HAVE BEEN all over the concept of "retail apoc-
alypse" in the U.S. The decade-old trend saw over 9,000
stores closed in 2019, a 59% increase over the previous
year.¹ Some of this is a correction: gross leasing area (the amount of
floor space for commercial property) is way higher per capita in the
U.S. than anywhere else (e.g., about four to six times higher than
in Europe). Also, Amazon (and online sales generally) is undeniably
taking over. Indeed, Amazon's sales have gone from USD7bn in 2017
to USD280bn in 2019. Brick and mortar shut down in North America
in mid-March 2020 due to COVID-19, putting thousands of retail
staff out of work, and in May 2020, Neiman Marcus and JCPenney
were discussing bankruptcy, with others to follow. Even luxury sales
saw very strong growth in digital retail environments during the

crisis, making it seem as though the whole consumer world is going online.

This idea that the future of luxury is online has become so entrenched that many managers of luxury have been asking if it's true and inevitable. Well, as Yankees legend Yogi Berra said, "the future ain't what it used to be." I believe the future of luxury is very much in brick-and-mortar stores, not online, despite many consumers' having been forced to become more literate vis-à-vis online purchasing in 2020.

While the physical footprint for general retail could continue to shrink in the U.S., this is not necessarily true for luxury, which is not present in the vast majority of the mostly lower-tier malls that have shut across America. Luxury brands are not over-distributed in the American retail landscape. The ongoing restructuring is more a function of what Nike's management once referred to as "undifferentiated mediocre" retail. There are exceptions, but most luxury brands would not have been exposed to that type of distribution channel.

Amazon will ensure that commoditized products are easy to order via Alexa or automatic reordering of products: a Brita water filter is programmed to reorder its own filters, and Amazon can ship a fixed number of toilet paper rolls on a regular basis (Nespresso offers that service as well for your favorite caffeine shots). However, luxury brands and products are the exact opposite of what Amazon sells. Luxury is not a commodity, not needed, not repeatable, not an afterthought. Gaining time and getting a deal is essential for commodities. Spending time and money and feeling good about it is the principle of luxury. In other words, the polarization of consumption will mean commodities will be reordered automatically (and the brand is irrelevant as long as the product does the job). Luxury will remain a purchase with a purpose, a space where brands count—and will retain their pricing power.

I believe the 80/20 rule will continue over the next decade: the key consuming cohorts of luxury consumers (i.e., Asians, youth, and women) will contribute heavily to 80% of products being browsed online, while only 20% of luxury purchases should eventually occur online. Why? Stores are much better adapted to developing an emotional tie between the consumer and the brand. While storytelling remains a buzzword and a clear driver of sales, telling a story in a store (or, as happened during the COVID-19 shutdown in the U.S., salespeople going to wealthy individuals' homes to tell them about the latest and greatest collections) is easier than it is online (even if some believe that touching, smelling, sensing may well happen online in the not-too-distant future). Shopping is social. When consumers line up outside of Supreme or Apple or Nike, they are part of a communal experience. Shopping online is not remotely comparable. The exclusivity factor also plays a role. As a luxury veteran put it to me recently: "If it's luxury, it should be limited distribution. E-commerce is democratic, luxury is not."[2]

That said, the two worlds are not mutually exclusive. For a while now at Nike, you have been able to try on a pair of sneakers in a store and have them shipped to your home for no fee, which will avoid your having to carry the box around all day. Was that sale retail or digital? Similarly, at the peak of the pandemic in the U.S. in the spring of 2020, many watch and jewelry sales were done over the phone with sales associates calling their VIP clients. This blurring of traditional retail channels is the reason the term "omnichannel" is gradually becoming obsolete. Unfortunately, it is being replaced by the horrible word "phygital," meant to evoke a seamless and unified brand experience that offers the best of physical and digital platforms. You can also call it "harmonized retail," which sounds indeed more harmonious! As one news article put it, consumers don't really care about which channel they are shopping in, because they *are* the channel.[3] The issue with omni is that it implies being everything to everyone everywhere. Harmonized retail is seamless but catered, differentiated depending on various touch points, and recognizes shopping is a blur.

The irreplaceable value of the real-life experience will ensure the future of luxury includes a heavy reliance on physical stores. Online channels and DNVBs have a role to play, but luxury e-commerce has a cap and will not dominate. Brick and mortar will evolve in response to the rapidly changing retail ecosystem, though: travel retail stores (e.g., duty-free stores in airports) will boom as travel rebounds after the COVID-19 crisis, and luxury stores will adapt to better serve and connect to consumers. In ten years, more luxury stores will be unique, "third places" (not work, not home) that offer opportunities for learning and entertainment, in addition to selling watches and handbags.

Luxury online

E-commerce has a role in luxury, of course—and with the COVID-19 outbreak, even more consumers shifted their purchases online, the outbreak once again proving to be a trend accelerator. Brand web-sites (whether .com in the West or .cn in China) enable brands to showcase information about a broad range of products and allow consumers access to those products from nearly anywhere in the world. This is convenient for wealthy consumers who know what they want and might be living in a "third-tier" city in China or, say, Seattle in the U.S. Most brands will also work with multi-brand online platforms such as, in the West, YNAP, MATCHESFASHION, ASOS, Zalando, and Farfetch.

Farfetch and Gucci announced with much fanfare in the spring of 2017 that they were launching a service in ten cities around the world that would deliver a selection of Gucci items from "store to door" in ninety minutes. Amazon and food delivery services have accustomed consumers to expect quick delivery, and that is difficult for brands to keep up with. But do these services really correspond to a true need? Do you need that handbag in the next hour? I am not so sure. There are considerations beyond convenience. If you want a custom experience, custom service, product personalization, and a unique memory of how exciting it was to wear your product for the first time, e-commerce has limitations.

E-commerce is even more popular in China, which has the largest and fastest-growing online market. Initially, a lot of hope was pinned on up-and-coming diversified luxury platforms in China, such as Luxury Pavilion (operated under Alibaba's Tmall) and VIPLUX and Toplife (JD.com). But luxury brands grew wary and focused more on their own websites, or on WeChat mini-programs, which can be used as pop-ups for particular events or launches. One of the most successful fashion and luxury platforms in China is user driven: Xiaohongshu (Little Red Book) is a social shopping app created in 2013 and has over 300 million registered users, mostly women born after 1990. It encourages a safe space for like-minded consumers to write reviews, share their shopping experiences, and purchase products. The most popular category on the app is beauty and cosmetics.

Recent changes in the Chinese landscape will likely see more Chinese luxury consumers move online. In 2019, Farfetch (an inventory-less online distributor) and JD.com (Jingdong, China's second-largest B2C retailer, with more than 300 million users and owner of a stake in Farfetch) announced plans to build the "Premier luxury gateway to China," according to their press release.[4] Through this expanded partnership, Farfetch offers the full suite of its technology and logistics platform to brands wanting to reach luxury consumers in China, which should account for significant growth in the luxury industry. Late in 2019, Alibaba's joint venture with Richemont for the development of NET-A-PORTER and MR PORTER in China finally launched, with 130 initial brands.

Despite this growth, some of the bigger iconic brands in the industry who have scale and are obsessed about controlling the relationship to the end consumer are not on any of those platforms, and I doubt they ever will be. These are Louis Vuitton, Dior, Hermès, and

Chanel. If I had to guess, many brands will aspire to be as clean and retail heavy as those eventually, so I believe the end game is for more brands to gradually move away from multi-brand platforms. All told, if you are selling sporting goods, cosmetics, or affordable luxury, online sales might be the future. If you are a premium European luxury brand and sales online are more than 20% of your business, something has gone wrong.

PREDICTION #8

Nike will generate more than 50% of its sales online, mostly via directly operated apps and its own websites. The rest of its business will occur mostly via its own full-price stores and outlets. Brick-and-mortar wholesale partners will contribute less than 25% of group sales.

DNVBs

A new phenomenon has made a lot of noise recently: DNVBs or digitally native vertical brands, in other words brands born online. The success of some of these start-ups—such as Bonobos in menswear, Allbirds in footwear, Warby Parker in eyewear, Away in luggage, Casper in mattresses, Glossier in beauty, and Dollar Shave Club and quip in personal care—has reinforced the view some have that luxury will be big online. For a list of some of the most successful American DNVBs in recent years, including the companies mentioned above, see the table on page 118. The direct-to-consumer approach, whether it is online or in stores, is not specific to luxury or DNVBs. Brands like Nike or Apple can significantly gain either financially or emotionally by cutting out the intermediary for a direct relationship to the consumer. And by selling online only, companies ensure a limited cost base and the creation of proprietary data.

DNVBS

Digitally native vertical brands: A DNVB is a brand born online and which controls its own sales. Many have emerged over the last few years, and they have been seen as threats to traditional brands, though not luxury brands, in my view. Most DNVBs, as we will see in this book, end up opening physical stores eventually and even sometimes wholesale distribution. The latter means that the direct relationship with the consumer gets lost.

Most DNVBs are really more premium rather than luxury in terms of positioning. Nevertheless, they share many attributes with luxury players. DNVBs are the opposite of Amazon in that they carry few yet high-quality, selected, curated products, and the approach is not price driven. Away has only four sizes of hardcase luggage, four frames you might say, which come in different colors. Like for luxury brands, DNVBs have no promotions, discounts, and outlets. (Actually, some luxury brands have outlets, but I would argue they shouldn't!) Unlike luxury brands, however, who centrally control their content, DNVBs have been working with a lot of user-generated content to influence other consumers.

I believe that counterintuitively, the future of DNVBs is not fully online either, despite their having been born there. DNVBs have limitations. As the cost of acquiring clients goes up, these companies, in my view, have a quasi-obligation to start a retail footprint. There is no easy substitute to direct, controlled human communication that avoids an intermediary and gives you data. Indeed, a retail presence enables brands to keep control of pricing and selection of merchandise as well as have complete oversight of the way products are experienced.

Examples of DNVBS

COMPANY	CATEGORY	FOUNDED
Bonobos	Apparel	2007
Warby Parker	Eyewear	2010
Everlane	Clothing	2010
Dollar Shave Club	Personal care	2011
Harry's	Personal care	2012
Mejuri	Jewelry	2012
quip	Personal care	2014
Allbirds	Footwear	2014
Casper	Mattresses	2014
Brooklinen	Bedding	2014
Glossier	Beauty	2014
Away	Travel	2015

Some of the most successful American DNVBs in recent years.
SOURCE: Erwan Rambourg.

Travel retail's bright future

Though local consumption is bound to become dominant in luxury, travel retail still has a great role to play. Airports and downtown duty-free stores may be the next frontier for luxury brands, even though writing this in the spring of 2020, when all planes are grounded, feels awkward. In my opinion, travel retail will prove to be a much more interesting growth engine for luxury's future than online. And it could be quite profitable as well. Not only do the sales densities tend to be three times higher in airports than in a downtown boutique, they should be one of the fastest-growing channels for luxury brands, as it is more convenient to purchase goods at the last minute that are already exempt from taxes rather than to carry them around with you for the entire duration of a trip. Leading luxury brands opened thirty-three new airport stores between 2016 and 2018, even while expansion slowed elsewhere.[5]

Duty-free outlets top the list of preferred points of sale for wealthy Chinese consumers when overseas, per McKinsey.[6] With spending at home becoming a growing trend in mainland China, this preference for duty-free should continue as China is counting on domestic duty-free stores to keep luxury spenders at home, lift local consumption, and spur domestic tourism. China's southernmost province, Hainan, has four offshore duty-free shops, two of which opened in January 2019. Beginning December 1, 2018, it relaxed duty-free shopping restrictions, to allow travelers and locals to buy duty-free products worth up to RMB30,000 (USD4,228).

As travel retail becomes a big growth driver for the luxury industry, Louis Vuitton is again using its leverage as an anchor tenant to negotiate the best locations and the best rents. In London's Heathrow Terminal 5, Louis Vuitton doesn't have one of those narrow stores in a corridor; they have a proper flagship. In the Hong Kong airport, the biggest destination for Chinese travelers by far, Louis Vuitton is only one of two brands (with Chanel) to have been allocated what the airport authority has called a duplex icon store, by far the biggest and best location, meant to open by late 2020.[7] With COVID-19-related delays, this could be early 2021, in my view. This follows openings of Louis Vuitton megastores in the new Istanbul Grand Airport in late 2018, which is likely to accommodate up to 200 million passengers a year by 2028, and in the spectacular futuristic Beijing Daxing International Airport. This airport was opened in late 2019 and is known as "the starfish" for the shape of its terminal, which was designed by Zaha Hadid Architects and is the largest single-structure terminal on the planet.

ANCHOR TENANT OR ANCHOR STORE

An expression to describe the key brand (or brands) that will generate the most excitement, traffic, and differentiation for a shopping mall. These are the brands that a mall cannot do without. Typically, for a premium mall, these would be an Apple store and/or a Louis Vuitton flagship.

SUPER Stores

One commentator has talked about the potential for stores to become places for "story doing" beyond just "story telling." "Retail prophet" Doug Stephens (another author with Figure 1 Publishing) has a very interesting view on how physical stores could continue to be as relevant as ever. Many of these insights can be adapted to the world of luxury.

Stephens argues that physical stores should aspire to delivering an experience that is "S.U.P.E.R.":[8]

SURPRISING A store that would produce a "my gosh, I have never seen this before" reaction. Some commentators have focused on the awkward-sounding concept of "retail-tainment." Above all, shopping needs to have some fun embedded, so give me something I don't expect, and trust me, I'll be back for more. The Gucci store on Wooster Street in SoHo, New York, or the Saint Laurent Rive Droite store in Paris are good examples of this.

UNIQUE This is highly relevant for luxury, as was evident five or six years ago when brands such as Louis Vuitton moved from a cookie-cutter approach ("this concept works in this location; I'll roll it out globally") to one that emphasizes the specificities of a neighborhood, with custom artwork and exclusive location-specific products. It is great to be surprised, but if I see the same "surprise" from a brand in each location, I won't be impressed.

PERSONALIZED Luxury has to work with mass customization. In other words, items are produced in tens of thousands of units if not more, but they need to appear to be specifically catered to you, not your neighbor. This has led, for instance, to the successful development of Mon Monogram at Louis Vuitton (personalize your bag with your initials and colorful stripes) and Nike By You, Nike's webpage where you can personalize footwear and apparel in endless ways. Coach gives consumers the possibility to fully create their pair of sneakers and offers the Coach Create counter to customize bags and accessories.

E NGAGING Ensure the store is not just about product displays, but that space is allocated to other experiences. In luxury, this can mean themes, complimentary services, or event space for particular collaborations.

R EPEATABLE This points to the ability of brands to execute a store concept differently over and over again. An exhibition might be a good idea as long as it can travel. A pop-up store could have limitations because it's not obvious that it can be replicated with the same design attributes in different countries and, at the end of the day, can appear to be a costly venture.

Another strong insight from Doug Stephens is the concept that physical stores are now the most manageable media channel for a brand. Media started with the agora, drifted to print media, then radio, TV, and finally digital. But as returns on digital investments are dwindling fast, he argues that the physical store is becoming the key for a brand's communication.[9] Contrary to the idea that stores are about to lose relevance forever, he argues that the store can become a powerful medium for a brand. This reinforces the view that stores are paramount in luxury.

In this view, analysts like me and retail commentators generally may have been focusing on the wrong metric to judge retail efficiency: same-store sales growth, which is too short term. Considering physical stores are a form of media, Stephens believes that they should be allocated net promoter scores (NPS), a calculation of the difference between promoters (potential consumers having a positive impression of the brand) and detractors (potential consumers having a negative impression of the brand).[10]

NPS measurements present some limitations, though, because different measurements gather feedback in different ways. Resorting to surveys can generate quite a bit of irritation from consumers—I am not sure luxury stores will place smiley feedback buttons at the exit—and generate results from a limited number of people, who may not be representative. Still, the brand equity enhancement of accumulated positive impressions should indeed count more to assess the value of a store than a quarter's like-for-like growth.

In my job—and in many jobs in the luxury and fashion industries, I suspect—I often have friends or colleagues who are based in Europe or in Asia ask me what stores they should visit in Hudson Yards, the latest (and only?) contemporary shopping mall in New York City; in the Meatpacking District, once a cutthroat neighborhood which became edgy and then packed, pun intended, with local and foreign shoppers; or in downtown Manhattan. What tourists like to visit in terms of New York retail is also likely what stands out and is worthy of a story without being gimmicky. Retail has a great role to play in luxury, and I would agree that stores that fulfill their function should develop an important media role for brand promotion.

The luxury store of the future

I am not going to pretend I have the solution for all brands on how they should think about their brick-and-mortar footprint in the future—far from it. But the essential idea for me is that if you focus on making the consumer feel great and remember their time in the store, rather than just on selling them a product, you will be off to a great start. With that in mind, here are four ways to think about the future of physical space in luxury.

Uniqueness
To Doug Stephens's point, brands should ensure their stores are not "copy and pastes" of one another. Every store will have to convey its

own personality, specific product assortment, decor, art pieces, and animations—all elements that cannot be visible anywhere else. If you are going to a friend's country house, wouldn't you be spooked if it were exactly the same as their downtown apartment or his seaside shack? You can have consistency in messaging, color coding, and the overall look and feel but make every physical place unique.

A *third place*

Make people stick around. Make the store their "third place": not work, not home, but somewhere to socialize and chill out. A friend of mine recently told me he went to Gucci on Wooster Street in Manhattan just to browse, with no intention of buying anything. After a chat with a sales associate about the weather, politics, and sports, she asked him, "Hey, would you like a smoothie?" That did it. He found the place so friendly and exciting that he is now hooked: he goes there regularly to have a chat and also purchases stuff on occasion. Just having a place to relax goes a long way. In my recent visit to Burberry's SoHo store in Manhattan, I was looking around and was offered a coffee and a glass of water. Instantly, that makes you feel more welcome and chattier. It makes you more likely to have positive associations with the brand and ultimately to buy products there.

The coffee shop, one of the friendliest places to get together, has actually become a feature in many retail projects associated with brands. L'Occitane en Provence, a natural cosmetics brand, started having coffee shops above its stores in some of its Japanese locations a while ago and then ran with that for, among others, its Macau and Paris flagships. Bulgari opened a chocolate shop on top of its Tokyo Ginza building. Ralph Lauren has a bar in Manhattan and more recently opened a coffee shop adjacent to its Club Monaco brand store. The latest PUMA flagship in Manhattan also serves Birch Coffee (a local New York coffee roaster) and, of course, Barnes & Noble has locations to sip a cup if ever you want to buy and read this book there.

Coffee shops are a good opportunity for consumers to mingle and spend more time. But if you want to relax and feel good, maybe a cocktail bar works better at alleviating you from a few extra dollars. This is likely what the owners of Watches of Switzerland, a large British watch retailer, were thinking as they started to roll out stores in the U.S., a country well known for its cocktail culture. In its first three American stores, this multi-brand watch store has a fully loaded bar. So if you want to think about buying that Rolex or Panerai watch, this might just put you in the right spirit for it. And if you don't buy, you'll have fond memories of the place and will think of it first for your next purchase.

Education

Learning, as we will see in chapter 8, is a great hook. With social media, blogs, and forums, consumers at times know as much if not more about a brand than does the sales associate. But what about learning something you can't pick up on the Internet? Visit the ATELIER BEAUTÉ CHANEL in New York, put your bag and anything distracting you have in a Chanel locker at the entrance, and you will be ready to go on a tour that you will unlikely forget anytime soon. You can learn a new skincare routine, see how to use foundation, and go on an emotional journey by blind testing scents to discover what fragrances you love and what exceptional raw materials were sourced in manufacturing them. Apple developed the Genius Bar for consumers to learn about hardware and software and exchange views with other users. Apple also has larger stores, so-called Town Squares, with boardrooms for local businesses to meet and many services you would not find in a regular Apple store. In 2012, Van Cleef & Arpels created L'École, a school of jewelry arts, for consumers to learn about gemology, jewelry-making techniques, and the history of jewelry and precious stones. Will this translate immediately into sales? Unlikely. But it will position the brand as the go-to icon in the art of high-end jewelry for sure.

Entertainment

The latest PUMA flagship in New York is a great example of how to make a store entertaining, and a testament to the fact that retail is far from dead. Using some of its brand ambassadors, the brand enables you to experience some fun in the store. For example, you can race down the streets of New York like PUMA ambassador Lewis Hamilton in a professional F1 racing simulator that uses a giant screen to replicate the moves from the road. You can dribble, shoot, and play around with a soccer ball in a cube while being coached by French star Antoine Griezmann or Belgian striker Romelu Lukaku. The store has mirrors that enable you to see what a jersey in another color than the one you are trying on might look like.

PREDICTION #9

When walking into your favorite store, you will be able to choose whether you want to use the iris scanner at the door. The scanner will call your favorite sales associate and download on their smartphone all the details of your previous transactions, favorite colors, key dates, and other information and tell the associate what products they should be showing you today. Already, at Sephora, you can choose between a red basket if you need help ("I would like to be assisted") or a black one if you want to be let alone ("I would like to shop on my own"). This is just a slightly more contemporary version of that. Welcome to the future of luxury!

ONE EXAMPLE OF a place trying to pitch itself as the store of the future is Nordstrom's first women's store, which started welcoming shoppers in New York in October 2019. The opening ticked many boxes. First, it is unique in its layout, services, and space. There are "make it personal" booths to customize products, and shoe repair, denim alteration, and more to make sure you get the right fit. Second, the store is designed for you to stick around, with a "shoe bar" serving cocktails, seating everywhere, a stylist lounge, restaurants, and on every floor, a place to charge your phone so you can browse happily without being stressed that you will run out of juice. The store might be a bit light on the learning and entertainment front, though some add-ons like a children's shoe conveyor belt are fun. The real issue for me is more that a department store is not necessarily adapted to expressing different brand territories fully, and that is a limitation.

INTERVIEW: On the future of luxury brand distribution

Private equity has to look at the industry with a different approach to the family-controlled groups in the sector. Here to give her view on issues linked to brands and distribution is Katie Harris Storer, vice president of consumer and retail at the private equity firm The Carlyle Group.[11]

ERWAN RAMBOURG: How do you go about selecting the brands you want to invest in? What is the process?

KATIE HARRIS STORER: We look for brands that have staying power and a unique differentiation in the market. The formula sounds simple, but the execution is far from it. Oftentimes, identifying a brand with clear longevity is product driven. Is it selling a product that is meeting a distinct customer need? And then we layer on top the ability to drive customer loyalty both on an absolute basis and a relative basis (relative to the brand's peer set). And we're specifically looking for spikes in areas that drive both functional and emotional loyalty ideally. We assess brands along those lines in a number of ways including focus groups, consumer surveys, and expert interviews.

ER: How can independent brands compete against the multi-brand groups in the sector?

KHS: Clarity of mission and brand vision again sounds simple, but it is the single most important way independents can stand out. This is the consistent thread in a world where brands can show up across multiple channels and have thousands of potential touch points with customers.

ER: What are your thoughts on digitally native vertical brands (DNVBs) in terms of competitive advantages and limitations?

KHS: These brands have the advantage of being small and nimble and are tailor-made to meet consumer demands. Newer DNVBs have the ability to test and learn faster and more cheaply, and they have more data to inform product and operation decisions. The ability to read and react at a faster pace is critical in adapting to both the pace of change in consumer behavior but also new points of connection, or importantly, points of sales, emerging every day.

Sustainability is an important purchase consideration, for both Millennials and particularly for Gen Z, and DNVBs are able to build their supply chain around the need to reduce their environmental impact and enhance transparency. Larger, established companies instead must invest millions in an effort to adapt. The same theory applies for technology systems, brand messaging, and store foot-prints: it's much more difficult to steer a large ship on a different direction than to move a small speedboat. Big brands are not set up for the type of bold approach that we've seen smaller players take.

ER: Describe the evolutions you have seen in terms of distribution of premium brands with the arrival of younger consumers and what you think key challenges and opportunities are to correctly service that younger generation.

KHS: Gen Z customers, unlike any other generation before them, were born in a mobile world. There is not the "surprise and delight" impact of showing up in multiple channels. Gen Z instead have the expectation that they can shop for a brand whenever and wherever they want to. They are essentially channel agnostic but value experiences and expect all touch points to deliver the goods. Channels are now way more diverse, from online and in store, to social and pop-ups.

So the challenge for brands is to show up everywhere consistently (consistency in message, pricing, product availability) or to have a tailored strategy by channel. The latter is more difficult to manage than traditional ways of selling. And the opportunity is that, in showing up everywhere consistently, brands are amassing large amounts of data on their consumer and the consumer's shopping patterns along the way, which in turn influences strategy, brand positioning, and growth opportunities.

ER: If you were to help entrepreneurs set up a brand from scratch, what advice would you give them?

KHS: In building a business, be flexible, hire good talent, and maintain consistency of brand across selling channels. But I haven't been in entrepreneurs' shoes, so I don't want to imply that it's straightforward. From my shoes, I recognize that founders and leaders spend more time fundraising and less time on the business than they'd like. Sometimes, that's inevitable, but I would say, where possible, try to align your investor base with your strategy. It takes time to build brands—some investors are patient, others less so. Some will focus on top-line growth above all else to gain scale and win in the market. Others will encourage an earlier focus on profitability. Some will have experience investing in brands and will know what makes them unique; others will not. There is no clear right or wrong. It's oftentimes sector or company specific, but keep in mind who is on your board and in your capital structure and try to create alignment that will support the growth of your brand in healthy ways. It's also important to supplement your team with investors and board members who bring capabilities that are complementary to your own.

ER: How do you think about the different e-commerce options in terms of potential risk and reward?

KHS: There are challenges and opportunities with each channel. I believe that mobile is critical (transactional) and outpacing other channels, web is important (educational), and stores supplement all of this to enhance the consumer experience. There is a natural evolution that has developed over time with many DNVBs.

First, you start online: you test and learn, build up a set of data that helps inform your strategy, and learn about your customer and how to enhance long-term value. Then, you open selective retail locations, which lowers customer acquisition costs, drives organic traffic, and allows customers to engage with and experience the brand in different ways.

Finally, you can selectively move into wholesale, and that will drive increased revenue but with two important caveats: you lose some brand control and visibility into the sell-through, and you don't tap into customer data.

Wholesale can be additive, but there is some risk in believing that wholesale is a requisite next pillar of growth, or in allowing wholesale to become too large in terms of total sales, if it does not fit your brand and your objectives. Over time, I think the drivers of growth won't be as clearly segmented by channel because the lines are being blurred.

Summary

While the consumer world is going online, e-commerce will have some limitations as a contributor to luxury brand sales, almost by definition. Separately, many luxury brands might aspire eventually to control their distribution as strictly as Louis Vuitton does. DNVBS control their sales and data, and that is what makes their business models similar to luxury, but most will also have to diversify out of just relying on online sales.

PREDICTION #10

Luxury will be one of the few sectors to prioritize brick and mortar and physical interaction over online sales. For most luxury brands, a maximum of 20% of sales (versus Nike's more than 50%) will be generated online over the next decade. Most luxury brands will distance themselves from online wholesale, after having broadly eliminated their exposure to brick-and-mortar wholesale. And while luxury brands' own websites will give access to their products online, they should be used essentially for storytelling rather than selling purposes.

Brick and mortar is still the future for luxury, and in that context, I see greater potential long term for growth in travel retail concepts than online. Of course, the stores of tomorrow will not be comparable to the ones you are experiencing today, and as long as your main target is not just to sell, you should do well as a brand by offering consumers a unique experience and a place to spend time and socialize, learn, and be entertained. NPS should be the measure of success of a retail location, more so than like-for-like growth, the traditional and likely soon-to-be obsolete manner of measuring retail performance.

PART THREE

THE
FUTURE

– 6 –

DEMOCRATIC
LUXURY

It is expensive to be cheap.

PROVERB

IN THEORY, GIVEN the robustness of the U.S. economy in the ten years following the global financial crisis of 2008-09 and with the Chinese middle class flourishing, affordable luxury should be in the midst of very strong growth. Consumers have become increasingly able to indulge and work their way up the luxury pyramid (see page 135).

In practice, the growth of affordable luxury companies has lagged behind that of their higher-end peers. There are exceptions: growth has been strong in affordable jewelry (think Danish brand Pandora) and ready to wear, including SMCP (whose CEO is interviewed at the end of this chapter). However, leather goods and accessories brands, such as Coach, Michael Kors, Kate Spade, and Tory Burch, have struggled significantly.

This is likely because this is the most important category in the industry: the product is visible, used frequently, and meant to make a point. In other words, it is the one for which brand power counts the most.

AFFORDABLE LUXURY

Also described as "accessible luxury," "democratic luxury," or "masstige." For soft luxury brands, this includes the two biggest American companies: Coach and Michael Kors. By extension, affordable luxury is a term used for high-end cosmetics or premium wines and spirits.

PREDICTION #11

Given the complexity of managing a low-growth business in affordable luxury handbags, I expect ownership of Michael Kors, Coach, Tory Burch, and/or Furla will have changed in ten years.

The growing potential

Let's look at the opportunity. The affordable luxury segment should be driven by value-for-money American consumers and aspirational Chinese consumers who are just entering the sector. The U.S. is the land of the deal. It is the country that invented Walmart, Amazon, eBay, refillable Coke, couponing, all-you-can-eat menus, outlet malls, the doggie bag, buy one get one free, and more. So presumably, affordable luxury should resonate well there. In the decade between 2000 and 2010, the U.S. saw a rise of the affluent, with more people becoming wealthier and the middle class getting more money to spend. Indeed, analysis by the Pew Research Center suggests that relative to middle-class income in Western European countries, middle-class income in the U.S. is higher, making it one of the wealthiest middle classes in the world and with significant spending power.[1] In 2019, consumer confidence was very high, and the unemployment rate in the U.S. at the lowest it's been in fifty years. It appeared

Luxury leather goods pyramid

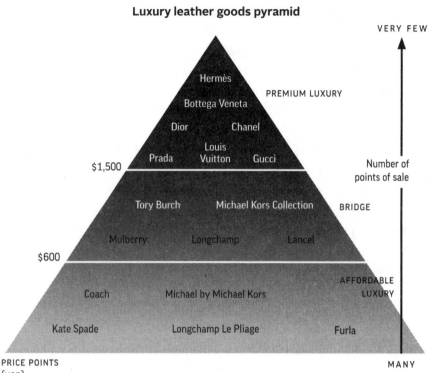

American brands dominate the accessible and bridge sectors of the leather goods pyramid, and these have a far greater North American retail presence— but the peak belongs to the more exclusive European brands.

SOURCE: Erwan Rambourg.

then that consumers in the U.S. had every reason to be excited about the economy and to go shopping. Obviously employment numbers changed dramatically in 2020, and the recent period has not been easy to navigate.

In 2015, China's middle class accounted for 57% of the economy, and it should amount to as much as 75% by 2030 according to *The Economist*.[2] It could grow at a much faster rate of 6% annually or more according to Brookings,[3] and in 2019, Chinese consumer confidence was the highest it has been since 2000. Because Chinese consumers are more connected and knowledgeable and e-commerce in China has been tied to promotions, it would also be natural to believe that affordable luxury would do well with Chinese consumers.

Separately, if looking at the leather goods pyramid of brands, space seems to be available for consumers to logically trade up, with affordable luxury brands building a bridge to aspirational luxury. Many brands stand at the bottom and at the top, leaving a relatively untapped market in between. This is what is often referred to as "white space." Few affordable luxury brands have been able to penetrate this white space. Coach developed a 1941 collection a few years back, and Longchamp is looking to move away from its entry-price-point, best-selling foldable bag (known as Le Pliage) by developing higher-end leather-based products. Otherwise, there are few key players and a lot of potential, especially given the expanding global middle class.

All of these factors together should, in theory, create a profitable opportunity for brands to be successful here. The reality, though, is that Coach has seen a pedestrian rate of sales growth over the past years, while Michael Kors has actually seen declining sales. So, what has gone wrong? A few things.

The disappointing results

First, it is a classic case of buy less, buy better. When consumers decide to spend money on a handbag, they prefer to allocate more money to a premium product, thus leaving affordable brands behind and boosting higher-end peers. The phenomenon is not limited to bags. In beer and spirits, CGA, a U.K.-based market research firm, notes that in 2019 in both the U.K. and the U.S., "rather than buying high volumes of lower priced beer, consumers are opting for lower volumes of quality beer" such as craft or imported beers.[4] In many categories, consumers are switching to more expensive,

Selected brands' retail footprint in North America as of November 2019

BRAND	NUMBER OF STORES IN NORTH AMERICA
Coach	391
Michael Kors	371
Louis Vuitton	105
Gucci	94
Hermès	41

SOURCES: Company data and websites.

higher-quality products, and to a certain extent, "buy less, buy better" attitudes could be reinforced in a post-COVID-19 consumer world. Similarly, in the U.S., super-premium volumes have increased the most in 2018 and 2019, when the lowest-priced spirits actually saw decreasing volumes. Consumers desire quality and are willing to trade up for a superior product. This trend helps explain why comparatively affordable brands like Coach and Michael Kors are seeing limited growth, but premium brands like Gucci or Louis Vuitton have managed to see growth in double digits for ten quarters in a row from mid-2017 to late 2019.

Compounding the problem for the likes of Coach and Michael Kors is that traditional luxury players have invested in the white space between affordable and aspirational luxury. Indeed, Louis Vuitton, Gucci, Prada, and smaller European luxury brands driven by streetwear (e.g., Balenciaga) have revamped their access price points, which is resonating well with consumers and hence capping the growth of affordable luxury competitors. Recently, in 2018-19, logo-driven products have had a comeback, and it seems up-and-coming consumers would rather wait to buy a European brand with higher prestige than purchase lower-end, usually American, alternatives. The Europeans are filling the white space with a bridge to their own higher-end products.

Second, not being truly global could be an issue. As the Internet becomes accessible in every corner of the globe and travel costs fall, consumers become more global. They incrementally study abroad, vacation around the world, and consume media—whether traditional mass media or social media influencer—from all over the world. They want to buy brands that are as global as they are, or as they aspire to be. Brands that are not recognized globally do not carry the same status and desirability. This can affect demand, particularly for those that are heavily exposed to one particular region—for example Coach and Michael Kors, which have most of their sales in the U.S. As the table on page 137 shows, these two brands have far more stores in North America than do some of the biggest higher-end luxury brands.

Third, brand equity itself could be affected by the ubiquity of brands or by a strong outlet presence that makes it difficult for the brands to gain prestige. Brands are competing for prestige and appeal, for the luxury status that allows them to charge luxury prices. When brands are associated in consumers' minds with outlets and promotions, they begin to feel accessible and cheap and lose their brand equity. Walking the line between visibility and exclusivity can be difficult. Be too exclusive, and you run the risk of leaving money on the table and alienating potential customers. Be too visible, and your higher-end consumers who are willing to pay more for your product will look for more exclusive brands. The cleanout and restructuring of the brand that is required to restore it to its former glory can be painful, especially if your customer base resists the price increases necessary to become more exclusive.

UBIQUITY

The state of being everywhere at once (or perceived to be). A real risk in luxury, as ubiquity is not compatible with exclusivity, a key appeal for many consumers.

Having long relied on outlets and promotions, notably in North America, some affordable luxury brands are now trying to restructure and regain the prestige that allows them to command luxury prices with limited promotions. This was true of Coach a few years back and Michael Kors more recently and is true of Kate Spade now. Many of the brands in this space appear to be over-distributed, and the heightened visibility makes them ubiquitous. In luxury, ubiquity doesn't get you anything; the illusions of scarcity and exclusivity do.

Lastly, given the issue of lower brand equity, newly developed secondhand concepts in luxury are eroding the value proposition of Coach and Michael Kors. You can visit a luxury secondhand store such as The RealReal, which has a buzzing location in downtown Manhattan, and buy a secondhand Burberry, Prada, or Celine bag at the price of a new Coach bag. That is an attractive proposition, especially as you will value the creativity of the premium European brands more. In a visit to a Michael Kors flagship store recently, I walked the floor with a sales associate who was telling me "this is our take on the so-and-so Prada bag, this is our version of the Vuitton whatever carry-on" and so forth to the point where I had to ask her what was developed from scratch for the brand itself. Sure, imitation is the sincerest form of flattery, but imitation doesn't buy loyalty. If you can get the original secondhand at the same price, why bother purchasing the affordable luxury equivalent?

HANDBAGS AND ACCESSORIES are a very tough market for affordable luxury brands, given the status-seeking of the buyer, the crowded nature of the sector, and the reality that consumers will want to trade up to stronger brand equity propositions. Jewelry and ready-to-wear affordable brands have much more potential for growth.

In affordable jewelry, there are in my mind only two global, relevant brands: Swarovski, which is owned and run by the eponymous family in Switzerland, and Pandora, which is a Danish listed company.

They both have had issues. Pandora has experienced a lot of management instability and has suffered from "charms fatigue": charms were its bread and butter for ages, many copycats followed suit, and it did not diversify quickly enough. While sales expanded more than sixfold between 2009 and 2016, these issues have meant that the business has pretty much stalled since. It is difficult to have an informed view on Swarovski, because figures are scarce given it is a private company, but I have thought for a while now that the brand and its retail could be better run.

PREDICTION #12

Leaving aside Swarovski and Pandora, no other affordable jewelry brand has been successful on a global basis. This is clearly a gap, in my view, and I expect new entrants will revolutionize the branded market for affordable jewelry over the next decade.

INTERVIEW: On prospects for growth of affordable luxury

In ready to wear, the market is highly fragmented and opportunities abound, but Daniel Lalonde, the CEO of SMCP (Sandro, Maje & Claudie Pierlot), which includes De Fursac, can explain that to you better than I ever could.[5]

ERWAN RAMBOURG: Explain how you built a group that sells ready to wear that is neither premium luxury (like Gucci) nor fast-moving consumer goods (like Zara) but somewhere in the middle. What is the value proposition of your brands?

DANIEL LALONDE: Accessible luxury is today a big market with sales of EUR127bn [USD140bn] in 2018 with two main categories:

ready to wear (52%) and accessories (48%). Affordable luxury has grown very quickly over the past years, benefiting from the permanent rise of the middle-class consumer and their new consumption habits (fewer logos, more frequent changes, temporality, and increased newness), especially Millennials. This has become particularly relevant with the strong rise of luxury prices over the past years, as indeed this has widened the gap between accessible luxury and luxury.

Our group, SMCP, blends the codes between fast fashion and luxury, taking the best of each. With luxury, we share the same creative process, high-end image, prestigious locations, and personalized service. With fast fashion, we share a fast and agile product cycle, creation within a frame, newness all the time, and a scalable retail model.

Our model leverages different new consumer trends and needs which are reshaping the market:

- See now, buy now, wear now: consumers will not wait six months after the Fashion week to buy!

- Mixing and matching: very popular among Millennials, the mix-and-match trend is also affecting the increasingly sophisticated Chinese consumer; and with the urban middle-class expansion in China, our segment is likely to see even higher rates of growth in the future.

- Increased sensitivity to cost per wear: for example, a luxury dress costing EUR3,000 [USD3,235] worn three times versus one of our Maje dresses costing EUR300 [USD323] worn ten times. This applies particularly to ready to wear, less to leather goods.

- Newness, all the time!

- The rise of social media is also playing well for us, fostering see now buy now and mix and matches through influencers that we leverage all the time.

- In this context, our value proposition is very clear: on-trend and high-quality products at affordable prices for three distinct brands with their own DNA and codes.

ER: Growth seems to be hard to come by in affordable leather goods, but for ready to wear, the segment seems more fragmented and prone to consolidation. Why do you think this is the case?

DL: There are fewer players in accessible luxury for leather goods. Luxury companies are dominating the accessories category (the main part of their business), and as a result, competition is strongest in this segment as affordable luxury competes directly against luxury players in leather goods (more than in ready to wear). Besides, luxury is a very concentrated market with a few big players owning most of the brands (e.g., LVMH, Kering), while accessible luxury is much more fragmented with few global players (SMCP being one of them) and many regional players.

The leather goods category is driven by different consumer behaviors:

- The category responds to demand for status-enhancing products.

- Prior to purchasing a bag, women (and men) do an extensive amount of research for weeks or months (on websites, in retail stores, and via social media).

- A woman considers the purchase to be an investment in her style and personality, regardless of the price point, and she does not want to make a wrong choice. Just like buying a car, it's a very personal choice.

- Finally, cost per wear is important in leather goods as the consumer will wear it many times (unlike for ready to wear).

Accessible luxury in ready to wear is poised for consolidation for the following reasons:

- There are several regional players, and few of them benefit from a global desirability like we do

- Few of them rely on a strong platform to scale the business across the world

- We are well positioned to play an important role in the consolidation (along with a few others)

ER: What is your competitive landscape, and why are there few global alternatives to your brands?

DL: Our competitive landscape is made up of players in accessories (such as Coach and Michael Kors) and in ready to wear with few global players like us. Our main competitors, to name a few, are mostly regional players such as The Kooples, Zadig & Voltaire, and Sézane in France; Reformation in the U.S.; Acne Studios, Hugo Boss, REDValentino, and Ted Baker in Europe; the U.S. brand Theory and the Italian brands TWIN-SET and MAX&CO., which are quite visible in China; Kate Spade; Coach; and Michael Kors.

The reason there are few alternatives to our brands is a matter of products and DNA fitting to a global approach. Few brands benefit from a global desirability; this is really a matter of creative design and position. To be global and have a strong presence in the key regions of the world requires a global mindset, brands that are desirable, and financial resources to fund stores, digital platforms, and infrastructure. Few today have all these ingredients, but that will change.

ER: How difficult is the creative process? What are the key constraints of your business model?

DL: The creative process relates mainly to product design and image. The first need is for clarity of the brand name and positioning. That is where it started. Second, a talented team, which is inspired by current trends (globally) and new ideas. Also, we have a pure retail profile, which is the best model to control pricing, image, and stock.

In our creative process, there is less fashion risk. We do not create the trend; we are inspired by the trends and have "on-trend products." Our risk is diversified among three brands, four regions, and twenty-four mini-collections. Furthermore, we have a very smooth process as we have adopted a rational approach: the three brands follow the same successful recipe/method to build a collection. Our main challenges are to permanently remain "on-trend," to maintain our global desirability, to manage the right balance between quality and speed, and to continuously improve our agility. We are also investing a lot in our store network, our first brand development tool. We thus need more scale before increasing our marketing spends in order to continue to increase our brand awareness, which is still relatively low, despite great likeability scores in each market. In the meantime, we are a growth company, and we need permanently to fuel future growth; managing pace of growth is a real challenge every day!

ER: As collections evolve quickly, how do you manage obsolete inventories, discounts, and outlets, and is this an issue is terms of brand equity and pricing power?

DL: We have very few obsolete inventories and a high sell-through in store of 75%. We do not produce for outlets, and purposely we have a very limited footprint in outlets (offline and online) to manage and preserve our brand equity. We use our own outlets to liquidate the old season, and sometimes, we can have some punctual liquidation operations through some other platforms like VIP.com. In terms of the discount rate, the objective is to sell more at full price, and this is a day-to-day battle.

ER: Last year, you announced the acquisition of a French menswear brand, De Fursac. How will you transform that asset, and what do you think about M&A in your space on a five-year timeline?

DL: After ten years of successful organic growth developing a robust platform, SMCP was ready for an acquisition. SMCP accelerates its strategic roadmap by reinforcing one of its key pillars of growth: menswear, one of the most attractive segments in ready to wear, with EUR22bn [USD24bn] in sales and likely a compound annual growth rate (CAGR) of 4.4% in sales between 2018 and 2022.

De Fursac is a French leader in men's accessible luxury. With this acquisition, SMCP expands its menswear brands portfolio by entering a new segment in menswear which offers a lot of white space: modern tailoring, mixing the codes between tailoring and the casual style.

By leveraging SMCP's international and digital expertise, De Fursac will accelerate its growth trajectory:

- SMCP will support De Fursac in its geographical expansion internationally, particularly in Europe (Germany, U.K., Spain, Netherlands) and greater China.

- SMCP will leverage its strong networks, including department stores and knowledge, in these regions: SMCP targets more than 30% of international sales exposure for the brand over the midterm.

- The Group also plans to accompany De Fursac in its digital journey, targeting more than 10% of sales to be online over the midterm.

- Finally, SMCP will continue to support the development of De Fursac's accessories offer and its casual offer, building on its current success. We are convinced that De Fursac has the potential to reach its first EUR100m [USD107m] in sales in the midterm. Our common values, vision, and business model will significantly ease the integration and expansion of De Fursac.

Regarding M&A, the objective is to continue to develop our existing brands and to deliver against our roadmap—that is, developing our four growth levers and grasping all international expansion opportunities through store expansion. On top of that, in the long run we could consider another acquisition as our ambition is to become a global leader in accessible luxury. For now, we will remain focused on the integration and development of De Fursac.

Summary

In theory, affordable luxury should have great growth potential as brands in the sector tap into a quick development in middle-class clienteles. In practice, at least for the key handbag and accessories segment, growth is likely to be difficult for reasons linked to

- Consumers' adoption of a buy less, buy better approach
- The lack of a global presence for brands in the affordable handbag space
- The presence of outlets, which can threaten brand equity
- The threat of secondhand purchases

Outside of core leather handbags, though, a lot of growth potential remains in affordable jewelry and ready to wear as long as execution is rigorous.

— 7 —

THE LUXURY
OF HEALTH

Our bodies are our gardens, to the which our wills are gardeners.
WILLIAM SHAKESPEARE, *Othello*, ACT I, SCENE III

THE SCALE OF the global environmental crisis that has inten-
sified in recent years has made it clear that breathing fresh air,
drinking clean water, and eating healthy food are luxuries in
themselves. The majority of humanity already lacks access to these
three basic necessities.

Much of the West is, so far, insulated from these problems, but in
China, where the economy has seen a tremendous expansion since
the early 1980s, soil contamination and water and air pollution
are pervasive. Sometimes, the problem is spectacularly visible: in
March 2013, a total of 16,000 dead hogs were pulled from the
Huangpu River near Shanghai. A local official said there was evidence that the hogs carried porcine circovirus, which caused a
public outcry, the river being the main source of drinking water for
the city.[1] When I lived in Hong Kong from 2011 to 2016, it felt like
every conversation with Chinese contacts or consumers revolved
around stress linked to pollution (notably air pollution driven by
coal burning). The government in China has reacted assertively, and

in the first four years of the Xi Jinping administration, between 2013 and 2016, particle pollution dropped on average by nearly a third in sixty-two cities monitored by the World Health Organization, with particles in Beijing down 36% and sulfur dioxide down 70%.[2] In China, it is now common to hear that "health is wealth."

The UN believes around 700 million people currently suffer from water scarcity, and that 58% of the global population currently lack access to safely managed drinking water services. Water stress is not going away either; an estimated 1.8 billion people are likely to be suffering from water scarcity by 2025, and almost half of the world's population will be living in areas of high water stress by 2030.[3]

Pollution issues are also on the minds of American consumers, with the recent Flint water contamination issue seeing a lot of attention. After the Michigan city switched over its source of drinking water in 2014, 100,000 residents were exposed to lead contamination. Flint dwellers still do not have access to clean water today. And while European and Chinese administrations have taken effective measures to curb pollution, the U.S. administration has relaxed policies that were putting pressure on the coal and fossil fuel industries. At the time of writing, nearly half of the political appointees to the Environmental Protection Agency (EPA) have experience in heavily polluting industries regulated by the EPA, and the current administration has rolled back fifty-eight environmental rules, with another thirty-seven in progress, an approach that according to one report "could significantly increase greenhouse gas emissions and lead to thousands of extra deaths from poor air quality every year."[4]

So before the self-rewards of elevated experiences and exceptional products, a healthy environment seems to be a pragmatic, basic need, one that would be at the base of the hierarchy of needs as defined by Abraham Maslow (see page 149). Younger generations are especially eager to secure a healthy environment; they are deeply concerned and active on this issue, and it informs their spending habits. For luxury, this translates into growth for higher-end

Maslow's hierarchy of needs

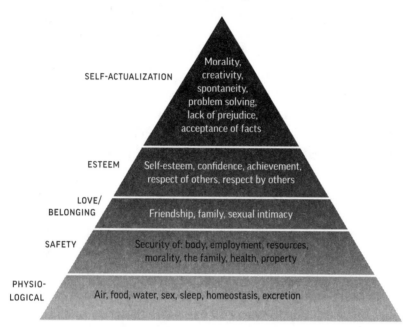

Psychologist Abraham Maslow's theory of a hierarchy of needs proposes that fundamental needs (at the base of the pyramid) must be fulfilled to move on to higher motivations. These basic needs of food and water are increasingly under threat in the era of climate change.

SOURCE: A. H. Maslow, "A Theory of Human Motivation," *Psychological Review* 50, no. 4 (1943): 370–96.

products related to diet, exercise and sports, sleep, and mindfulness. Every crisis has at least one silver lining. As COVID-19 spread around the world in 2020 and highlighted the unpreparedness of political administrations and insufficiencies of health infrastructure and medical supplies, consumers around the world likely came to think long and hard about their priorities in life; eating healthy food, exercising, and making sure their immune system was well supported were likely part of that reflection.

The holy trinity of health

The world has come a long way since Jane Fonda made aerobics a popular discipline in the early 1980s. With the clear shift in cultural values, many consumers say they want to live healthier lives. Your country may not be able to provide the ultimate conditions to achieve that, but you can seek balance on your own. Gym subscriptions are on the rise as large numbers of people around the world start to exercise more and eat more healthily. Data from Nielsen suggests that more than 70% of people are changing their habits in an effort to improve their health, with Asia and North America standing out.[5] The share of adults worldwide who smoke cigarettes has been falling for some time (see the table below); while all generations are quitting, the sharpest falls are within the youngest cohorts, and as this age group becomes a bigger share of the population, aggregate smoking activity should fall even more quickly than it already is. In the U.K., the under-twenty-fours and twenty-five-to-forty-four-year-old group have seen the biggest drop in the share of the population that regularly drink alcohol, and the share who drink excessively has also fallen by far the most within these age groups.

Global prevalence of tobacco smoking

YEAR	TOTAL PREVALENCE (%)	MALE PREVALENCE (%)	FEMALE PREVALENCE (%)
2000	26.0	43.0	10.9
2005	24.3	39.6	9.0
2010	22.1	36.6	7.5
2015	20.2	34.1	6.4
2020*	18.7	31.9	5.4
2025*	17.3	30.0	4.7

*PROJECTED

The World Health Organization projects that worldwide, smoking rates in 2025 will have decreased by about 35% from 2000 levels.

SOURCE: Adapted from WHO *Global Report on Trends in Prevalence of Tobacco Smoking 2000–2025* (Geneva: WHO, 2018).

"Wellth" is a term coined by John Gerzema—a best-selling author, social scientist, and CEO of the Harris Poll—to describe how well-off consumers view their health and wellness as the next step up in terms of self-realization. Consumers around the world who have financial means have spent a lot of time and money trying to master the holy trinity of health: a good diet, some exercise, and, more rarely, sleep.

Diet: Knowledge is power

It is difficult, given the flood of information and sources, to actually figure out what is good for you. One of the fundamental approaches in embarking on a healthy diet is actually similar to consumption in luxury: less is more; buy fewer items but better ones. Sugar, fat, and salt are recurrently named as the cause of many health issues, not just obesity rates, which have been going up steadily in the U.S. and China. With the advent of agricultural factory production (Ever read about poultry produced in the U.S.? Don't look it up if you intend to sleep tonight!) and other forms of intensive farming, consumers have grown weary of processed foods whose taste barely resembles real food. There has been a swift development of alternatives featuring superfoods (kale, avocado, chia seeds, flax, quinoa, goji berries, and more), juice bars, and full-on fasting or diet programs.

One very successful book came out more than ten years ago and is simply called *Clean.* It started off as the explanation by cardiologist Alejandro Junger of how a good diet could prevent most of the health issues humans face in life, and it has now grown into a proper business with more books, food supplements, a USD475 twenty-one-day program, and coaches ready to answer any question online or on the phone. The principle is quite simple: in as little as three weeks, the diet can make you feel reset, incredibly healthier, and, in a word, clean. This is just part of what is now a multi-billion-dollar industry fed by celebrity endorsements, luxury grocery stores such as Whole Foods, and legions of social media influencers.

PREDICTION #13

With some of the best management teams in the consumer space, great storytelling, emotional relationships with consumers, and some of the most inspiring brand ambassadors out there, Nike, adidas, and PUMA will be three of the fastest-growing consumer goods companies over the next decade in terms of sales.

Exercise: A cross-generational aspiration

While viewership of sports around the world is very high—enough to justify airline carrier Emirates paying USD80m for the Real Madrid soccer sponsorship or LeBron James signing a billion-dollar lifetime deal with Nike—the widespread practice of sports and exercise is still developing. Some forms of exercise are quite affordable (anyone with a pair of sneakers can go jogging), but premium and luxury exercise activities have risen in popularity. Witness the success of Peloton Interactive, the makers of stationary bikes enabling you to participate in spinning classes from your home, a NASDAQ-listed company since September 2019 and one that should almost certainly emerge from the COVID-19 crisis much stronger. And for those willing to leave their house, the Equinox Group, founded on New York's Upper West Side thirty years ago, has emerged as a go-to fitness and lifestyle company operating gyms and hotels under the group name as well as the incrementally ubiquitous Pure Yoga or SoulCycle studios.

Exercise has been gaining ground in China in recent years. For example, in 2011 there were 22 marathons or related events (road races with more than eight hundred participants or cross-country races with more than three hundred). This number skyrocketed to 328 in only five years, and from 2016 to 2018 nearly quintupled to 1,581 events.[6] Part of this development is linked to consumers getting geared up and getting fit on their own. But the administration in

China has also been instrumental by making the practice of sports compulsory at school, investing heavily in infrastructure, and securing the 2022 Winter Olympics for Beijing. This last involved further investments and could enhance the chances for the country to eventually organize the FIFA World Cup by 2050.

Of course, all of this generates opportunities to buy the apparel and accessories to accompany exercise. Purchasing sportswear that you believe makes you look good and feels comfortable is another way to fit in to society and develop confidence. Similar to luxury, sportswear is really about how the product makes you feel.

Sleep: An elusive luxury

You hear many wealthy consumers bragging about the amount of Pilates or yoga they practice, the fact that they managed to have a "dry January" after having drunk a bit too much during the December holidays, or how they feel great after having embarked on a high-fat, low-carb keto diet. But have you ever heard someone brag about how much sleep they have had lately and how that has made them feel alive? I haven't. Usually, it is the opposite. Professional success matters, and many people are active on social media and want to be seen as multitasking, energetic, driven human beings. I've heard more people bragging about how little sleep they were having as a consequence of leading such an exhilarating life. Obviously, that is a bit of an issue given that sleep is one essential part of the trinity of health, alongside nutrition and exercise.

Sleeping may not be fashionable yet, but the international success of the recent book *Why We Sleep: Unlocking the Power of Sleep and Dreams,* by sleep specialist Matthew Walker, and the quick development of sleep studios, suggest that is changing. Whether it is the Dreamery in New York set up by mattress company Casper, where a forty-five-minute nap will set you back USD25 (includes beverages, PJs, and a private space for resting), or ZZZen trucks in France, inspired by food trucks and brought to you by the inventors of the Parisian nap bar, consumers are willing to pay to recharge during stressful weekdays.

Mindfulness and "being whole"

"Anima sana in corpore sano," the adaptation of the Latin expression "mens sana in corpore sano," led to the acronym of Japanese sporting goods brand ASICS. It literally means "a sound mind in a sound body." It is similar idea to the ancient Greek idea of paideia: the education of the ideal member of society, which combined the study of music, poetry, liberal arts, and sciences with the practice of gymnastics and wrestling. In modern society, we talk about the importance of work-life balance and the need for mindfulness. As country singer Dolly Parton has said: "Don't get so busy making a living that you forget to make a life."[7]

One example of the development of mindfulness, alongside the health trinity of diet, exercise, and sleep, has been the spread of yoga and meditation to Western societies, which has generated premium products and experiences that consumers are happy to spend money on.

lululemon, a Canadian brand founded in 1998 as a purveyor of upmarket yoga gear, has gradually transformed into a premium holistic-living brand. lululemon prides itself on having brought the culture of yoga out of the ashram and into the mainstream, or as some employees say, bringing sweat to the world. Because yoga is more than a physical practice, lululemon sees itself as helping consumers unlock their full potential for their body, mind, and spirit—and brand managers at lululemon see yoga as enabling the brand to stay close to the current cultural pulse of consumers. Unlike Nike, lululemon has never relied on big sponsorship deals with brand ambassadors to tell its story; it has been more about relationships and community-building. The brand doubled sales between 2015 and 2020, with yoga participants in the U.S. doubling in the same time frame to reach around 55 million. During the COVID-19 shutdown, free online yoga classes were, not surprisingly, the craze, with some instructors getting millions of views.

Beyond yoga, consumers have developed an interest in meditation, including the kind that can be monetized. Ten years ago, a former Buddhist monk founded Headspace, a meditation app which now counts more than 60 million downloads and over 2 million paid subscribers as of early 2020. The app helps you breathe, address anxiety, sleep, be more productive, and exercise; helps your kids calm down; and does a lot more. Here again, it is no surprise that at the apex of the COVID-19 crisis in the state of New York, Governor Andrew Cuomo and Headspace partnered to provide free guided meditations and workouts for stressed-out New Yorkers, a smart investment for the long term. Calm is a similar app with a similar number of subscribers and was valued at USD1bn in early 2019, having quadrupled its sales the year before. It is a star-studded platform employing tennis great John McEnroe and Hollywood darling Matthew McConaughey, who will tell bedtime stories to ensure you get your Zzz's (and I can confirm that it works). The success of these apps is a sign that consumers are ready to pay for mindfulness.

PREDICTION #14

Apple will be known as a health-monitoring, visual entertainment (notably, movies and gaming), and banking corporation (and more), with iPhone sales accounting for less than a third of its business, down from more than 60% in 2018.

Since 2019, more Apple watches have been sold globally each year than Swiss-made watches, and while the latter serve no function apart from social status enhancement, the former have an endless number of functions beyond just the ones linked to your iPhone. Many of these other functions are health related, including an ECG app, health-rate notifications, a fall detection system that links up with emergency services, and medical ID. It may have come as a surprise when in early 2019, Apple CEO Tim Cook said that the brand's "biggest contribution to mankind … will be about health,"[8] but that is now becoming a reality and will likely grow over time.

INTERVIEW: On growth in the sporting goods industry

One brand that spans health and lifestyle is PUMA, which has seen strong growth over the past four years. (For an example of PUMA's slick styling, see the photo on page 160.) Here to talk about its prospects for the sporting goods industry and how it relates to luxury is PUMA CEO Bjørn Gulden.[9]

ERWAN RAMBOURG: The PUMA brand started building awareness in the late forties around soccer boots, but it is now a broader global sports lifestyle company. Explain how that came about and how sport informs style and vice versa.

BJÖRN GULDEN: PUMA was founded in 1948 by Rudolf Dassler, who had run a shoe company with his brother Adolf [the founder of adidas] before they went their separate ways after [the Second World War]. They had experimented with football boots and added studs and spikes to improve the performance on the pitch. That is how the sports industry was born. It wasn't until the late 1980s that sports as an activity grew significantly, and consumers started to wear running shoes to simply walk around. I worked at adidas at the time, and clearly, this move to lifestyle was not born in marketing departments: the consumer made it happen. Another example is apparel, which up until the 1970s none of the brands made. Consumers started wearing products made for sports on the street. Demand then increased substantially, as sportswear was used for different purposes. PUMA took this even one step further, as it became the first brand which dared to talk about fashion. In the late 1990s, it created the fashion side of sports with a Jil Sander collaboration.

If you look at the footwear market, it is only the sporting goods industry that really invests in R&D. An important reason for consumers to wear the products is comfort. In terms of performance-driven sales, it is fair to say that Western markets are stable, while there is growth in places such as China and India, where consumers are increasingly starting to take up sports. Outside of performance, fashion is growing with the younger generation, comfort with older people. If you look at the branded side, the longevity and credibility of Nike, adidas, and PUMA are deeply rooted. If you look into other categories, such as denim for instance, brands come and go. The sporting goods sector is much more consistent.

ER: How is your positioning a key competitive advantage relative to the bigger brands such as Nike and adidas? Presumably, scale counts, but do you see some advantages in being a smaller competitor?

BG: You need to be relevant whatever you do as a consumer brand. Our design approach is quite simple: we make "cool stuff that works." Performance is a given in our industry; fashion comes on top. From a marketing point of view, we have to be honest. We invest in credible people and influencers who are relevant for our young target audience. I have also realized that being relatively small can make you quicker, and social media works well for relevant brands—quite the opposite to the slow agencies we used to work with twenty years ago. Our idea is to develop good products, work with relevant partners, and have a good balance between globally and locally relevant influencers. We are definitely fast when it comes to consumers, but we are also quick to respond to retailers. We want to be a dependable,

relatable, and pleasant partner and not have a confrontational attitude. It's part of the culture we've developed for years, and we also
continue this approach with our new management team.

ER: Many investors and journalists are concerned that casualization,
the sneakers and sports lifestyle, may be a fad. Why do you believe
that is not the case? How do you track sports participation and viewership, and how can you help increase both?

BG: If it's a fad, it's the biggest one that has ever existed! You need to
look at this industry as more than performance or fashion; there is a
lot in the middle. Participation in sports is growing, and there is still
potential in that area in China and India. Popular sports like running,
basketball, and football are not necessarily growing much in terms
of participation, but going to the gym, practicing yoga, and working
out to live a healthier lifestyle is a large, worldwide trend. There are
other segments that are emerging including e-sports and gaming.
As they are relevant for our consumers, they are also relevant for us.
This will require us to look beyond the traditional sports arenas and
develop special products. We do not see big alternatives to casualization, as there is limited innovation in plain brown and black shoes.

In the U.S., we are getting close to four pairs of running shoes per
person. That is clearly a level of penetration not seen anywhere else,
be it Europe or Asia, so there is still a lot of potential growth ahead.
Skechers has turned from a brown shoe to a sports company. The
hype surrounding sneakers by Gucci and Balenciaga might come
and go, but sporting goods companies will continue to dominate
and drive the market.

ER: Is your positioning resonating better with specific nationalities,
age groups, or genders? Where do you see the most potential for
growth for the PUMA brand and your industry more generally? How
young is your consumer today on average?

BG: PUMA resonates well around the world. In some instances, for historical reasons, we may even be well ahead of others, like in India, but overall, consumers of all nationalities like us. Relative to others, the brand has had a bigger fan base among female consumers as the fashion side got traction earlier and competitors may not have focused as much on women as we have. With men, we may have lagged behind slightly, especially in the U.S., as we were not present in basketball, a male-driven subsegment, for a long time. Today, the brand targets both genders equally.

By region, we are growing faster in Asia than in the U.S. or Europe. The market in Europe is more saturated, while in Asia the middle class is expanding. In the U.S., our penetration is smaller, and we should be able to grow faster than the market. However, we are not there yet. Our target consumer is very young, but you could also argue that age is just a number as our products span across generations.

ER: How do you choose brand ambassadors or collaborations to fit in with your message (e.g., Selena Gomez, Rihanna, Antoine Griezmann, Cara Delevingne, Liu Wen)? Explain the rationale to have asked Jay-Z to become the creative director of your basketball business. How do you limit cost inflation here if at all possible?

BG: You need to have a certain visibility in order to build credibility over time, so sports marketing is important. Our sponsoring includes soccer players, teams, federations, track and field athletes, as well as NBA players. The advantage of not being the biggest is that we have more quality time for the athletes we sign. On the influencer side, it's the same thing. Being small and having a flatter hierarchy means that many musicians and entertainers prefer working with us. We have a different attitude: they can all get hold of me when they want to. In terms of costs, the logic is for marketing to account for 11.0% to 11.5% of sales, and we think we can manage that over time.

In soccer, there was a huge inflation of costs for sponsoring three years ago; now, it has calmed down. We are adding fewer ambassadors, but we are doing more with them. As part of our culture, we understand that we can't deal with everything at a distance and have empowered our local teams, given them leeway. Global celebrities give status; local celebrities give you the conversion that is needed. Working with Jay-Z enables us to connect to an urban lifestyle, a culture, where he can influence what the kids want and also the people around him. In basketball, for example, what happens off the court is just as important as what happens on it. What do the celebrities who visit a game wear? Music is also very important. There are different lenses of culture through which we approach the game.

As health becomes increasingly important to consumers, sporting goods leaders like PUMA should see sustained growth. CREDIT: Courtesy of PUMA.

ER: What is your view on luxury brands such as Louis Vuitton, Moncler, Prada, and Gucci developing sneaker ranges? Is this a threat or an opportunity to make the category more premium? Is there any overlap between what luxury brands offer and what you are selling? Is there a lack of barriers to entry in this field?

BG: The manufacturing process in our industry is quite complex, which is a barrier to entry. Producing a shoe that looks good and is technically efficient is not that easy. I don't think sneaker ranges in luxury brands are that big. Gucci developed classics, where barriers to entry are not high, because the construction of the shoe is basic. Luxury brands have lifted price points, which means our products look compelling from a value perspective. Frankly, there is not much overlap with luxury. Creatively, the Triple S shoe from Balenciaga helped to create a new trend, what industry executives called the "ugly shoe" or "dad shoe." It was one of the rare instances of a design that was not created from sports. In that instance, I think the luxury side helped to create a trend that inspired the entire industry.

ER: What is the role of your owned and operated stores and e-commerce versus a legacy of wholesale partners? It seems the entire industry is moving towards more direct-to-consumer sales. What are the pros and cons?

BG: We still have room to grow in all channels. Our DTC (direct-to-consumer) channel is around 24% of our sales and will move towards 30% in the midterm, driven by a combination of full-price stores, outlets, and e-commerce. Growth will not be linear, as the various markets are very different. In India, there is no structured retail, some European markets still have important brick-and-mortar footprints, and outlets are important in the U.S. We also still have quite a bit of room to grow in wholesale, and brick and mortar is very relevant as the culture of lifestyle is still to shop around in stores.

ER: Are your consumers putting pressure on your industry in terms of sustainability/recyclability of products, and how can you address these requests? Are you expecting important changes in your supply chain infrastructure in the coming years?

BG: Our industry has improved a lot in terms of working conditions and health and safety compared with thirty years ago. Most brands have a very ethical supply chain, and wages have improved. The industry has come a long way. In terms of products, the consumer has not been ready to pay more for a sustainable product until now. Ten years ago, PUMA produced very sustainable products, but consumers and retailers didn't really care, probably because sustainability on its own is not enough. That is changing; now, consumers, especially the younger generation, are increasingly looking for sustainable products. As an industry, we need to adapt, and there can be a premium on sustainability. Sustainability is a key value at PUMA, and we aim to get better in environmental, health and safety, human rights, and governance matters within PUMA and our supply chain. The new generation is more conscious about what to do than my generation was, and that is good, if it helps to take care of the planet and of the people living on it.

ER: What makes you optimistic about your industry long term? What are your main concerns?

BG: I am very optimistic about the sector and would recommend it to any of my kids. It is a global sector; it's got growth and it is fun to work in. My concern right now is the reality that there is a lot of noise in the world, trade wars, tensions between countries, and Brexit. Such uncertainties are not very helpful when making investments and supply chain decisions. Again, being small with a flat organization helps us to be quicker on our toes.

Summary

Health is a major concern for many consumers, and they are ready to invest in order to live healthier lives. Spending on the so-called trinity of health (diet, exercise, sleep), as well as on mindfulness products, could divert from spending on traditional luxury products—especially given the greater overlap today between brands and experiences that make you feel healthy and luxury propositions. If anything, the COVID-19 outbreak in 2020 will accelerate consumers' greater focus on health and wellness.

— 8 —

THE "PREMIUMIZATION" OF EVERYTHING

You only live once, but if you do it right, once is enough.

MAE WEST

CONSUMER BEHAVIORS OF indulgence and choice are permeating every subsection of the marketplace. "Premiumization," the process whereby previously mundane products or services are elevated to luxury goods, is affecting daily consumer products like coffee, and an illusion of scarcity is being cultivated in the hospitality trade, with, for example, the emergence of Soho House. These everyday lifestyle choices are gradually growing to become a substitute for classic luxury products. In autos, consumer electronics, beer, wine, cupcakes, ice cream, and now cannabis, wherever you look, there will always be a premium product that consumers will be willing to pay top dollar for, so they can brag about it to their friends and coworkers or simply enjoy the special treat for themselves. It's no longer enough to wear a few luxury products—as premiumization takes hold, luxury is what you do, every day. Filling every niche of your life with custom experiences, from the way you navigate the city, to what you spend your leisure time on, to how you decorate your walls, is the ultimate luxury.

We saw in the first two parts of this book that a) the consumer is changing, with women, Asians, and youth greatly influencing the luxury sector, and b) the companies and distribution are changing. Therefore, I believe the definition of luxury itself will evolve, and this will lead to the fast development of new segments.

PREDICTION #15

In the next decade, travel, hospitality, cannabis, fine food, e-sports, and e-learning will be the fastest-growing luxury segments.

PREMIUMIZATION

Term coined by the spirits industry to describe the process of trading up, whether driven by pure price increases or favorable mix impacts (i.e., consumers drinking higher-end spirits). By extension, this is the tendency consumers have to "buy less, buy better" in many consumer subsegments.

Starbucks Reserve: From commodity to luxury

Starbucks was started in Seattle in 1971 and now operates more than 31,000 locations globally. Sales in 2019 topped USD26bn, and the operating margins were luxury-like. After all, as some cynics would put it, the company is just selling water with a little something in it for USD4 a pop.

Starbucks was the catalyst of coffee's "second wave." The first wave was essentially the democratization of coffee starting in the 1800s, a move to mass consumption and mass production of coffee with the emergence of "ready for the pot," vacuum packaging, instant coffee, and U.S. brands such as Folgers and Maxwell House. The industry's second wave was above all a reaction to the poor taste marketed by the first wave. Coffee became an experience with consumer interest in roasting and in knowing the origin of coffee beans. The second wave addressed a more sophisticated consumer who started to look for specialty coffees and learned about espressos versus lattes and drip coffee. Howard Schultz, the longtime CEO of Starbucks (and, briefly, an independent U.S. presidential candidate), did not found the business but bought it in its early stages and transformed it, inspired by his experiences as a coffee machinery salesman in Italy in the 1980s. His idea was to make the Italian experience accessible to the world.

A third wave has emerged recently, which is made up of coffee shops who roast their own coffee and are seen as specialty shops, looking at coffee beans like wine lovers look at grape varieties. In the U.S., three major players from the third wave are Intelligentsia from Chicago, Stumptown Coffee Roasters from Portland, Oregon (both of which were acquired by Peet's Coffee in 2015), and Counter Culture Coffee from North Carolina. There have been others, such as Blue Bottle Coffee, which was sold to Nestlé in 2017.

In 2014, Starbucks spent about USD20m on opening its first Reserve coffee roastery in the company's birthplace, Seattle. In late 2019, the company opened its sixth roastery and biggest store globally (35,000 square feet) in Chicago on Michigan Avenue—where all the luxury brand flagships are situated—after having rolled the concept out in Shanghai, Tokyo, New York, and, of all places, Milan. Living in New York, I can clearly see that the Starbucks roastery in the edgy Meatpacking District has become a destination location. Its neighbors include the Hermès flagship that opened in 2018, a Soho House club next door, and the rooftop bar and restaurant at Restoration Hardware, a few blocks away from the Whitney Museum's new location. Like Apple's Town Square stores, the roastery takes the principle of the third place, not the home nor the workplace but a sort of real-life Facebook and LinkedIn (themselves virtual coffee shops) where people come to meet others, and elevates it to a destination-worthy experience. It's not just about coffee being roasted on the premises and cold brew and different types of coffees poured. The space is beautiful. The roastery offers lovely Italian food to try out, with Starbucks partnering with Milanese brand Princi. There is even a sixty-foot-long cocktail bar on a mezzanine floor called ARRIVIAMO, which translates into "we are coming" but given the premium experience feels more like "we have arrived," to me! For tourists, both domestic and foreign, a big merchandising section of the store enables you to tell friends and family "been there, done that," and selfies abound.

At first look, the Starbucks Reserve initiative seemed to be a way to go after the third-wave competitors. In reality, I believe that given the potential commoditization risk of the brand linked to having 31,000 retail units, it was above all a means for Starbucks to not be seen as substitutable by lower-end operators. Even if the coffee quality is maintained, a very high number of stores can trigger a loss of exclusivity and aspirational value, and the brand could come across as less aspirational. Separately, in the U.S. market, high-traffic fast food chains such as Dunkin' Donuts and McDonald's have improved their coffee quality and gone to great lengths to make it known to the public. To Starbucks, it is important that these chains are not seen as substitutes. The brand needs to maintain an image a good notch above them. It is possible that by opening too many stores, Starbucks jeopardized the initial emotional connection with its consumer, and so opening roasteries that offer an exceptional experience is a way to find the essence of the brand again.

To a certain extent, roasteries are a means to have a flagship retail landmark like all the big brands, luxury or otherwise. The high quality of the coffee there should not be lost on consumers, but the stores play a more meaningful role in addressing the dichotomy inherent in Starbucks given the size of the company. Many of its stores will probably become MOP (mobile order and pay) with limited, if any, human interaction. This, alongside drive-throughs, will imply a very profitable business model but one which is too low on human inter-action, which is at the core of the third place concept. The group likely needs to balance metrics and image. Roasteries can reignite a passion for coffee, inspired by a European way of life—the space provides soft seating, inviting people to stick around, exactly like in Italy—and give consumers a sense of community.

Roasteries are not really about competing with the third wave—Starbucks is not exactly a small independent brand—but more about reaffirming a connection to the consumers and leading the coffee world into the future with quality, sustainability, and the support of local communities. They are the maximum expression of the brand, and they are unlikely to have ambitions of profitability, because their role focuses more on PR and the overall brand perception.

Soho House: A club for socialites

While Starbucks has convinced me to pay USD5 for a Caramel Frap-puccino, Soho House has been able to extract thousands of dollars a head for access to what cynics might call a well-appointed gym and bar. I was willing to pay, but they were not willing to have me. Finance executives are not what the club wants; membership is only allowed for creative types that are selected by a committee. I could say, like Groucho Marx, that "I refuse to join any club that would have me as a member," but here, I just don't even have the option.

Membership clubs are a long-standing British tradition. Some of these remain very old school, with men-only clubs in London where you can drink with fellow male members, smoke a cigar, have dinner, and, if need be, sleep over for the night. In London, I know many British friends and colleagues who live in the countryside on farms and commute to work, some of them arguing that London's city center is really for foreigners to live in, not proper English gentlemen. And when they are planning for a night out in London, they will stay over at their club. When I was based in Hong Kong, I had many friends and business contacts who were members of the local clubs, and I had the opportunity to join one myself. The club was more about the outdoors, meals with family and friends, tennis, squash, bowling, and swimming: the epitome of an antiquated expat life, with a nice balance between local Hong Kongese members and a mix of American, British, other Asian, and continental European nationals. These clubs have dress codes, a certain notion of etiquette, staff in uniforms, several restaurants, wine sales, and a distinctively old-school feel to them.

The surprising element is that most clubs in London (e.g., Arts Club, Home House) or in Hong Kong (e.g., Ladies' Recreation Club, Royal Hong Kong Yacht Club, Hong Kong Country Club) are one of a kind. Despite some of these businesses being over 150 years old, none has seen the opportunity to develop several locations to leverage membership and really develop synergies based on an expansive brand. And none has targeted the younger generation by shifting the focus from ostentatious displays of wealth and privilege to building a place for bohemian-like creative professionals to form a "community of like-minded individuals," as Soho House founder Nick Jones puts it.[1]

The old-school club model has changed recently with the creation of Soho House, a membership club founded in London in 1995 by this genius British entrepreneur. Soho House is now almost a mini-empire with twenty-seven locations. Some of the recurring features are in-house locations of the club-owned Italian chain Cecconi's, gyms, screening rooms, a natural cosmetics brand called Cowshed, special events, rooftop pools and bars, and designer hotel rooms. Compared with the traditional London or Hong Kong club, Soho Houses are younger, hipper, and meant for individuals in the "creative industries" (if you are, like me, in finance or in a

legal profession, forget it). They also have stunning locations in up-
and-coming neighborhoods (for instance, the Meatpacking District,
Ludlow Street, and DUMBO in New York, and White City and the
original Soho Dean Street location in London), often with equally
stunning views. What helps to make the crowd young and lively is
the fact that youngsters (twenty-seven years old and younger) pay
their membership at half price, and the club is used more for social
and cultural connections than for nine-to-five work activities. For
work, the company has ramped up a few Soho Works locations, an
upscale version of WeWork. The company had 10,000 members in
2017; now, they have ten times more and annual memberships are
either local (USD2,200 before tax and a one-time registration fee if
you're in New York) or global ("every house" membership goes for
USD3,400) if you want to be accessing the entire network as you
travel. The genius of the model is that it aggregates leisure spending
that would otherwise be spread across various recreational facilities, bars and restaurants, and other entertainment venues in one
place, and then multiplies it through marketing and the conscious
creation of exclusivity.

What is the relationship between Soho House and luxury?
Well, like Hermès, Soho House has waiting lists, with about 30,000
people hoping to get in as of early 2020. The desire is so high that
some members are part of "cities without a house," meaning they
are members of the club despite living in a city where the club has
no premises. That helps the company gauge where they should be
opening next. This is how the Hong Kong club opened in September
2019. Soho House has pricing power, which it has used: membership
fees do go up regularly, and the membership was not particularly
cheap to start. During the global financial crisis in 2008, membership attrition remained very low, however, as the lifestyle component
of Soho House meant that high-end consumers may have cut back
on such indulgences as restaurants, movies, nightclubs, and gym

memberships and actually increased their usage of Soho House, which offers all of that and more.

Finally, like luxury goods, at Soho House, it is not the facts of what your membership buys you that matter, but how it makes you feel and the bragging rights associated with it. As the *Financial Times* noted in June 2018: "Technology has not eliminated a millennial desire for community experience."[2] Soho House very much epitomizes that.

Cannabis: Substitute for luxury?

Why spend time on cannabis in a book focusing on the future of luxury? Because younger, wealthy consumers are being drawn to experiences linked to the world of cannabis, which are seen as a substitute for luxury products.

In Canada, use of cannabis for medicinal purposes has been legal since 2001. But what really triggered growth in and attention to the industry was the long-awaited federal Cannabis Act, which was passed in October 2018, making Canada the second nation, after Uruguay, to legalize the cultivation, possession, sale, and consumption of cannabis for recreational purposes. That same year, the country of Georgia also legalized recreational cannabis, though only for possession and consumption, not cultivation and sale; South Africa legalized recreational cannabis for cultivation, possession, and consumption, but not sale; and Mexico's Supreme Court upheld an earlier ruling that made cannabis prohibition unconstitutional. The following year, Canada made edible cannabis, cannabis extracts, and cannabis topicals legal.

Two-thirds of Americans (67%) are in favor of legalization, according to a Pew Research Center poll from September 2019, with attitudes very closely correlated to age (76% of Millennials are in favor).[3] Usually, states in the U.S. allow consumers to carry up to an ounce of cannabis (2.5 ounces in some states) provided they are twenty-one or older, but legislation about growing plants for your own consumption differs from state to state. At the time of writing, eleven states have legalized cannabis for recreational use and thirty-three states for medical purposes; cannabis is also legal for recreational and medical uses in Washington, D.C. In November 2019, the House Judiciary Committee approved a bill that legalizes cannabis federally in the U.S., but this bill needs to go through the House and the Senate. Given the divide on the topic along party lines (broadly, Democrats are more in favor of legalization than are Republicans), it is unlikely the bill will be adopted before 2021. All in, recreational cannabis remains illegal in most countries around the world, but in the U.S. states in which it has been legalized, it appears to be another sector for discretionary luxury spending.

Tilray, a Canadian company, became the first cannabis producer to complete an IPO in June 2018. The three founders of cannabis investment fund Privateer Holdings, which had a majority stake in Tilray, became billionaires. Shortly after, in August 2018, Constellation Brands—a large producer of spirits and beer, and owners of Svedka vodka, Robert Mondavi wine, and beers such as Corona, Modelo, and Pacifico brands—invested USD4bn to take a stake in another large Canadian cannabis company called Canopy Growth. At the time of acquisition, research firm Euromonitor estimated that the American market for legal cannabis would triple between 2015 and 2020 to reach a value of up to USD16bn.[4] Recently, many cannabis conferences have been set up, as the sector benefits from more infrastructure and means and becomes an asset class in itself. The stock market now lists dozens of cannabis-related companies and even several ETFs (exchange-traded funds), such as Alternative Harvest, for investors who want to have exposure to the sector without taking company-specific risks.

Here are examples of some brands involved in cannabis that have pitched themselves as premium products:

- Beboe was created more than five years ago and was likely the first luxury cannabis brand to gain significant media attention. The concept was born from the unlikely pairing of a fashion executive (Clement Kwan, previously with YOOX and D&G) and a celebrity tattoo artist (Scott Campbell). The company was sold to Green Thumb Industries, one of the largest listed companies in the sector, in February 2019.

- dosist launched in 2016 and offers precise "doses" (via vape pen or dissolvable tablet) in six different ratios of THC to CBD (the two main active ingredients in cannabis), depending on what consumers are after. The brand opened its first retail store on Abbot Kinney Boulevard in Los Angeles, facing a MedMen location (the largest cannabis retailer in the U.S.), and competing for space with premium fashion and leisure brands, coffee shops, and ice cream parlors.

- Ignite, founded by an Instagram sensation, pitches itself as the reference for premium CBD-based products. Hemp-derived CBD is legal at the federal level in the U.S. The fact that all products from Ignite are CBD based ensures they are easier to sell nationwide.

- Astleys of London is a lifestyle brand, an iconic pipe purveyor based in Jermyn Street in London that was revived and given a facelift to adapt to cannabis development. Cannabis is illegal in the U.K., but the brand is selling hardware, not cannabis itself.

- In March 2019, Barneys, the famous high-end Manhattan department store that has since gone bankrupt, opened a luxury cannabis lifestyle shop in its Beverly Hills flagship. Elsewhere in Los Angeles, multi-brand resellers have opened. Similarly, Higher Standards, a shop that opened in the Chelsea Market in New York, has another flagship in Atlanta and "shop in shops" in Los Angeles and Santa Ana, California.

The shift from private (in-home, hidden) consumption to social consumption is bringing in new lifestyle trends like event dinners, cannabis tours in Colorado, and cannabis-friendly boutique hotels in states in which cannabis is legal. Similar to the higher-quality wines and brown spirits (whiskey, cognac) industry, the cannabis industry is now offering more elevated experiences, including vaping lounges, tastings, and dinner pairings as well as cask-aged cannabis oil. The similarities with traditional luxury products will likely increase over time, as cannabis competes for retail space and management talent while taking wallet share from the traditional luxury segments.

The luxury of time and custom experiences

In 1998, Renault, the French car giant, ran an ad campaign for its Espace SUV range that included the line "Et si le vrai luxe, c'était l'Espace" ("and what if real luxury were to have space"). I would argue that in the current fast-paced world, the real luxury is time: having time off, having time to think, to breathe, to meditate, to disconnect from the news flow. Certain consumers are ready to pay for time. Think about the TSA prechecks in U.S. airports that enable you to avoid queuing, which cost USD85 and last five years. Think about Uber or Via or whatever other ride-hailing company you use to not have to wait around trying to find a cab. And what about all those apps on your smartphone to see what restaurants are around you, locate where your family members are, and tell you the weather forecast? Siri or Alexa will help you call a friend without having to look up their number, learn about an artist without typing their name, hear a two-minute news blurb when you want to, and learn the recipe of your wife's favorite cocktail—all just by asking. And with time on your hands, you can spend it (and some money) on entertainment: shows, NBA games, streaming, gaming, Netflix, Apple TV, or whatever tickles your fancy. Is this a substitute to luxury? Well, in as much as you are spending money on it and it makes you feel good, definitely. During the peak of the COVID-19 pandemic, many consumers had extra free time. Hopefully they made the most of it. Those who went on virtual gallery tours or watched opera or became yoga experts might remember the lockdown as a period when finally they did more of what they like or even discovered new passions in life.

In 2019, I started taking wine-tasting lessons for fun in the evening and got my WSET (Wine & Spirit Education Trust) Level 2 Award and went on to take Level 3 in January 2020. It cost me more than a Burberry trench coat, but a) I learned a lot about winemaking, b) I am incredibly proud of having been able to learn and get a diploma at my old age, and c) if I wanted to, I could brag about it at dinner parties, not just in this book! Is that a substitute to a luxury product? Absolutely! Interestingly, for Level 2, most students were people who worked in the wine industry (e.g., liquor store staff members, bed and breakfast managers, barmaids, hotel employees), but for Level 3, which is tougher and costlier, about half of the students were older, wealthier, and not working in the wine industry but just taking the course for fun.

Another example of premium leisure activity is MasterClass, an American online education platform founded in 2014, with personalities sharing knowledge about their respective fields via interview sessions. Learn how to cook with celebrity chefs Gordon Ramsay or Thomas Keller. Learn creative writing with Margaret Atwood (author of the best-seller *The Handmaid's Tale*) or with Malcolm Gladwell. Learn filmmaking with Martin Scorsese, photography with Annie Leibovitz, business leadership with Starbucks' Howard Schultz, and the list goes on. This is the crème de la crème, a proper luxury twist on learning from the best.

The next generation could well spend a lot of time (and money) in the world of AI and dreams. In the 1960s, legendary sci-fi author Philip K. Dick wrote a story called "We Can Remember It for You Wholesale," which was adapted for the 1990 movie *Total Recall*. In it, Arnold Schwarzenegger's character is a client of Rekall, a company that provides memory implants of vacations. Things get out of control when he can't discern dream from reality and eventually realizes that he is a secret agent. The possibility of buying dreams, virtual vacations, or memories of experiences is one that will be worth paying for, and you won't need be a secret agent to participate! Today, products such as the Oculus Quest, whose founding company belongs to Facebook, are starting to show the way to what virtual reality (VR) entertainment can start to look like. The product, essentially a sophisticated VR headset retailing for a luxury-like price of USD499, launched in late 2019 with more than fifty games. Since its launch, it has been very successful and was at times sold out in some stores ahead of the holiday season. This is likely just the beginning of the popularity of AI products.

PREDICTION #16

Louis Vuitton, still one of the largest and most influential brands in luxury, will diversify into travel in a big way, not just selling luggage and city guides, like it does today, but also selling VR packages for consumers to discover the world in style without leaving their living room.

INTERVIEW: On the role of art as the ultimate custom luxury good

The difficulty in luxury is to be able to give the appearance of scarcity. The most effective brands manage to create the illusion through shrewd marketing, but nothing can replace the allure of a unique product, whether it is an exceptional experience (think omotenashi, the Japanese art of hospitality) or an exceptional object (think contemporary art). It is difficult for luxury to replicate those types of products, given the business model relies on at least a degree of replicability. Maybe the best the sector can do is be inspired by them. I believe luxury has a lot to learn from the world of art. Here is an interview on that topic with Francis Belin, president of Asia Pacific at Christie's.[5] (For details about auction revenues broken down by auction house and bidders' nationality, see the tables on page 178.)

ERWAN RAMBOURG: Given your background in luxury and retail, do you see a potential for luxury brands to learn from auction houses, and in turn, what can auction houses learn from the luxury world?

FRANCIS BELIN: Luxury has had a fascination for art for a long time, and you have seen evidence of that with brands like Cartier and Louis Vuitton having their own art foundations as well as collaborations with artists on the design of products. Luxury has wanted to get closer to art as a means to mitigate a blunt reality which is that luxury items are mass produced with industrial processes and brands sell very few unique objects. The luxury sector remains a big machine that feeds many products into many channels and with an acceleration of the product cycle can get inspiration from the unicity that art has. Luxury needs marketing, advertising, packaging, PR, and more. Art needs nothing.

Art is all about the object, nothing else, and you need to do very little around that object. You can explain it, you can put it in context, show why it is important, but at the end of the day, it should be self-sufficient, and the market will decide what will stick and have value and what will disappear. You don't need much fluff around it. I believe luxury needs art, but a work of art needs no one. Art specialists who sell exceptional pieces might even think that they are not serving a client or an auction house; they are serving art itself. Obviously, given the price tags, you will have speculation here and there, but the essence of our business is laser focused on unique objects. Art has traveled early on. Artists have looked for inspiration from other cultures and by doing so have become the first properly cosmopolitan influencers. Collectors tell a story, connect an object, help it make sense, but again, the object should be able to live by itself.

One difficulty in the auction ecosystem is that business is focused on finding the objects to sell; that is the priority and that makes the model quite short term and ad hoc in nature. What luxury can bring to art in terms of the business model is a more long-term, strategic

Top art auction houses by auction turnover (2019)

	AUCTION HOUSES	AUCTION REVENUE ($)	SOLD LOTS
1	Christie's	3,647,885,000	15,320
2	Sotheby's	3,589,239,300	14,134
3	Poly Auction	617,015,000	4,575
4	China Guardian	587,802,200	8,659
5	Phillips	583,821,200	4,613

Christie's, the leading house by both turnover and lots sold, closed five transactions above $50 million in 2019, but half its transactions were below $20,000.

SOURCE: Adapted from "The Art Market in 2019: Global Assessment," Artprice.com, n.d., https://www.artprice.com/artprice-reports/the-art-market-in-2019.

Art sales at auction by country (2019)

	AUCTION REVENUE ($)	SOLD LOTS	BEST RESULT ($)
United States	4,613,929,700	99,095	110,747,000
China	4,101,689,400	66,106	38,850,000
United Kingdom	2,175,511,300	70,319	49,561,790
France	826,633,100	82,016	26,777,270
Germany	268,010,300	45,741	3,535,930

The U.S. led the art world in sales and lots sold in 2019. Claude Monet's *Meules* (1890) sold for $110 million at Sotheby's New York in May, the highest price paid in the world for the year, and a record for any Impressionist work.

SOURCE: Adapted from "The Art Market in 2019: Global Assessment," Artprice.com, n.d., https://www.artprice.com/artprice-reports/the-art-market-in-2019.

way of thinking. Besides, by nature art is more object centric than client centric, and that is also an area where luxury models can help.

ER: Explain the consumer psychology when buying an art piece. Some prices may seem irrational, and at the same time, there is a resell market. Explain how that tension works.

FB: The unique character of a piece of art will lead to the way it is being valued. While the brain is usually rational, there are many elements of context which can lead to prices being disconnected from the original asking price. A consumer can become obsessed with an art piece as he falls in love with the aesthetics, or it has a meaning for his descendants, or it fits well within a thoroughly curated collection of his, or he can see it fit well in his living room with another piece, or any other element influencing judgment. The money you are ready to spend is a very personal decision. There is no universal pricing, as price will be linked to the emotions the object generates. Of course, you have reference points, a history of past transactions, and so on, but it is fundamentally about a person's unique rationale and in some instances fear of losing out. Record auction prices can even occur with a handful of bidders competing fiercely. Those left have very specific personal reasons [why] they want to acquire the piece.

ER: Luxury consumers who enter the luxury pyramid tend to want products and brands that enable them to fit in. By essence, art pieces are unique. How have auction house clients evolved recently in terms of gender, age, and nationality, and who do you expect your core consumer to be in the next few years?

FB: Essentially, auction house activity is correlated to the creation of wealth, and this points to emerging markets in general and China in particular. In some of the established wealthy markets like Europe and Japan, we are now seeing more sellers than buyers. New money means a younger buyer as millionaires in Asia are much younger than in the West. What we are seeing is an evolution in terms of what Chinese consumers are purchasing as they grow bolder and have an increased knowledge within the art world. Logically, you start with what is closer to home. Chinese collectors would typically be starting with classic Chinese art and notably, ink wash paintings. They could then evolve towards Western art and notably, Impressionism. The bolder collector or the ones from a second or third generation of wealth, having lived abroad, might venture in post-war art. Asian buyers are dominant in Asian art, but they are now becoming more meaningful in Western art sales as well. Art is becoming more sensational, with galleries and fairs that are really more about a social outing than necessarily about the core: unique objects.

ER: How do you think about the potential for growth at Christie's, and is growth essentially linked to supply (getting new mandates) or demand (wealth creation)? Why do you feel Christie's is well placed?

FB: There is more and more demand and notably, for the old masters as well as post-war. The issue is really supply, and while the emergence of a greater number of museums is culturally a great thing, it also puts incremental constraints on the supply side of the equation. Indeed, by nature, museums rarely resell art. Everyone is after exceptional objects, and prices are rising, especially on the higher end. Contemporary art is different, as you will find many living artists, some of whom produce a lot of pieces. This has led to the development of galleries as well as international art fairs.

We are appealing for many collectors, given our 150 years of experience in the art world and our means to authenticate, research, and price art appropriately. Collectors also know that if they come to us, it is likely the objects they purchase will hold a resell value. We also certify provenance of objects and can act as an advisor on how to protect and enhance an existing collection.

Summary

Everything can be premiumized, from coffee to clubs, cannabis to entertainment. The issue the traditional luxury brands will face is that the next generation of consumers will be diverting their spending away from plain vanilla product categories like watches or handbags to free up spending on products or experiences that they will perceive as being edgier or more in line with their values. For the time being, the luxury sector is still in a recruitment phase and will be resistant to these changes as long as that remains the case. As traditional luxury evolves to become a repeat purchase business, however, the threat from alternative spending patterns will rise.

– 9 –
TRAVEL—
AND ARRIVE

If you think adventure is dangerous, try routine—it's lethal.
PAULO COELHO

I MET ONE OF the cofounders and CEO of luggage and accessories brand Away two years ago, and when I asked her if there were any business models in branded goods that she admired, she instantly replied "LVMH," and this did not come as a surprise. Away's mission is quite simply to become the biggest travel brand in the world. It sounds incredibly naive or arrogant for a brand that's been around since 2016, but when I spoke to Steph Korey, she was dead serious about it. The quick pitch Away gives is that they produce TUMI-like suitcases at Samsonite-like prices, sell directly via their website, and thus cut out the distributor. Having owned an Away suitcase for a while myself, I have to say that the luggage offers value for the money, while the feature I prefer by far is the rechargeable battery pack, which comes in handy all the time if you are a big traveler. I lost the battery in early 2020 and went to the downtown store in New York, where they gave me a new one free, no questions asked. Away started online and later opened a showroom in downtown Manhattan with a cafe which became a permanent store, the one I went to for the battery. At the time of writing, the brand has ten stores, and the company likely has a lot more in the pipeline (COVID-19 permitting), given Away's willingness to quickly expand the brand in Europe and Asia.

What is the relationship between travel and luxury? If you return home to Shanghai from a trip to Florence with some souvenirs, nice pics on your smartphone, the latest bag from Gucci, and a pair of Ferragamo sneakers, you'll have a lot to tell your friends. Now imagine purchasing Gucci and Ferragamo on Nanjing Road. That's a lot easier, but you'll have to accept that bragging rights will have vanished somewhat.

Travel has a certain snobbism. Similar to the purchase of luxury products, it tells your friends and colleagues that you are in the know and experienced. This is not a new notion. My father worked at the UN as a diplomat for decades and spent most of his life traveling to Africa for work. He once received a letter from an admirer calling him the "James Bond of public administration." This became a favorite family story to tell as he couldn't help himself from crying with laughter at the absolute contrast between the burden of long flights, busy airports, jet lag, bad food, and dull hotel rooms that his professional trips entailed, and the flawed perception that these may have been thrilling adventures.

PREDICTION #17

Wealthy consumers will favor boutique hotels over hotel chains. The latter, while having the incentive of loyalty programs, will suffer from a feeling of "copy and paste" and lack of authenticity.

From the 1930s in France when the Popular Front government invented paid holidays, to the development of mass tourism in the

1960s, to the much more recent boom of outbound Chinese travel, vacations are seen as a luxury because they imply you have the money to spend and the time to be away.

In late 2018, the International Air Transport Association (IATA) projected that passenger numbers would double by 2037, reaching 8.2 billion and generating 100 million jobs. The impressive numbers—which represent a CAGR of 3.5%—will be the result of "an increasing shift Eastwards in the center of gravity of the industry," with over half of the growth expected to come from the Asia Pacific region.[1] China alone is forecast to triple its number of passengers, adding 1 billion passengers for a total of 1.6 billion by 2037, and displacing the U.S. as the largest aviation market in the mid-2020s.

Emerging countries now have a large number of young consumers who are ready and able to spend much more on travel. A study by the Visa Travel Insights team finds that income, not age, is the main determinant of international travel, and as many emerging market consumers become able to afford to travel, tourism numbers should continue to spike.[2]

The IATA also presented a bear-case scenario coined the "reverse globalization," where protectionism would hit and the CAGR would drop to "only" 2.4%, and a bull-case scenario called "maximum liberalization," in which the CAGR would hit 5.5%. Whatever the scenario, the travel industry will clearly enjoy good growth and a related boost in infrastructure and jobs. The 2020 pandemic may change *how* people travel, but the severe decline in the *volume* of travel in 2020 due to COVID-19 should be seen as a one-off.

Chinese travel: The key for luxury

In 2018, for the first time, Estée Lauder made more money in airports than in shopping malls.[3] The reason? Traveling Chinese citizens. And while I have explained in chapter 2 that Chinese consumers would be incrementally purchasing a lot more luxury at home than abroad, this does not mean that the travel retail market will stop growing. Far from it. The passport penetration rate continues to grow very quickly in China. It is likely still less than 15%, up from 4% in 2014. (It was close to 45% in the U.S. in 2019.)[4] Before the COVID-19 outbreak, most countries were making it easier for Chinese travelers to visit. In fact, the number of countries that do not require a visa for Chinese visitors reached an all-time high of seventy-four in 2019. A combination of continuous wealth creation and consumer confidence should continue to fuel that growth. For a list of the ten largest air passenger markets (current and projected), see the graph below.

The ten largest air passenger markets, 2017–37

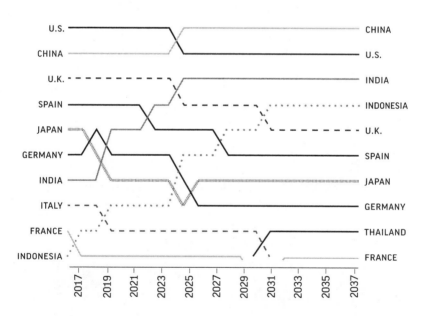

The International Air Transport Association (IATA) predicts that in the mid-2020s, China will overtake the U.S. as the world's largest source of air travelers (ranked by passenger numbers to, from, and within each country).

SOURCE: Adapted from IATA, "IATA Forecast Predicts 8.2 Billion Air Travelers in 2037," press release no. 62, October 24, 2018, https://www.iata.org/en/pressroom/pr/2018-10-24-02/.

As I discussed in chapter 2, even if the proportion that outbound travel accounts for gradually declines to less than 50% of total Chinese luxury spending, that would still represent in excess of 20% of global luxury spending today. Sales to Chinese travelers will still be key not just to the turnover of the brands today but also in shaping the perception for tomorrow.

Mainland Chinese visitors have, for now, traveled mostly closer to home, but this might gradually change. Here are the prospects for nearby destinations:

- **Hong Kong** has long been the key destination for mainland Chinese, who only need a permit to go there. It is close, shopping and accommodation infrastructure is very good, and it is a duty-free area. Two infrastructure projects in the Greater Bay Area, the Hong Kong–Zhuhai–Macau Bridge and the Guangzhou–Shenzhen–Hong Kong Express Rail Link, both opened in late 2018 and could act as catalysts for further growth. The issue recently is that a combination of protests in 2019–20, the COVID-19 outbreak, and unfavorable currency (strong HKD to the RMB) have led to a sharp deceleration

Value of Hong Kong personal luxury goods market (EUR billions)

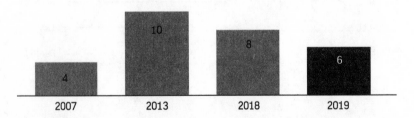

2007	2013	2018	2019
4	10	8	6

Luxury sales in Hong Kong enjoyed a 15% compound annual growth rate from 2007 to 2013, but were already depressed by protests before the COVID-19 outbreak. Look for most of this market to return to mainland China.

SOURCE: Adapted from Claudia D'Arpizio et al., "Eight Themes That Are Rewriting the Future of Luxury Goods," Bain and Company, February 5, 2020, https://www.bain.com/insights/eight-themes-that-are-rewriting-the-future-of-luxury-goods/.

of inbound flows from mainland China. Already, before the virus hit, Chinese tourists were fearful about security issues and had more options for traveling. This has been an issue for luxury because Hong Kong has long been the most profitable region for brands in the sector, with mainland Chinese accounting for 60% to 80% of Hong Kong sales for most brands. The graph on page 186 shows the value of Hong Kong as a luxury market over the last thirteen years.

- **Macau**, as part of greater China, has been the second-most-visited destination by mainlanders. Tourism flows support the substantial gaming industry and luxury purchases.

Mainlanders have started to discover many options outside of greater China:

- **Japan** is seen as very fashionable and offers a lot more diversity than Hong Kong and Macau, which are essentially luxury Meccas. Japan has different food and culture, skiing, temples, and much more and has made great strides at adapting its hospitality infrastructure and relaxing visa rules for Chinese travelers. Overseas tourist arrivals to Japan crossed the 30 million mark in 2018, way above the administration's goals, with Chinese tourists representing close to a third. Japan was targeting 40 million visitors in 2020 as Tokyo planned to host the Summer Olympics, but those got postponed by a year because of the COVID-19 crisis.

- Visitation to **Thailand** has been choppy. In 2016, the Thai administration banned "zero-dollar tours," free tours during which tour operators forced tourists to go to certain malls as a way to recoup their investment. A boat accident involving Chinese tourists in July 2018 was off-putting and was followed by a dengue outbreak in September 2018. However, in November 2018, a gigantic luxury mall,

ICONSIAM, opened south of the river in Bangkok, and the next year, Thailand waived visa on arrival fees. In other words, everything is being done to motivate Chinese to come and spend.

- **Singapore** is a traditional destination for medical tourism but also luxury, though there is a certain level of luxury mall saturation there. Competition has been creeping up from other destinations over time, with neighbors Malaysia, Vietnam, and Thailand taking share.

- **Taiwan** suffered from a tense relationship and limited inbound flows from the mainland after the election of Tsai Ing-wen (from the Democratic Progressive Party) as president in 2016, but tourism has picked up since.

- Similarly, in **South Korea**, the mainland Chinese tourism flow has rebounded after some years of tension linked to South Korea's decision to install a U.S.-designed anti-missile system (THAAD).

Outside of neighboring Asian countries, wealthy Chinese consumers have also been going to Australia, where they spent more in 2019 than tourists from the U.S., Japan, New Zealand, and the U.K. combined. European destinations accounted for a bit more than 10% of Chinese tourism in 2019, making it the second-most-popular continent for travelers after Asia. But here again, currency fluctuations (such as a more appealing GBP after the Brexit vote in June 2016) and security issues (such as the yellow vests movement in France, which started in October 2018) can play both ways. Finally, inbound Chinese flows into the U.S. have been dragged down by currency fluctuations, trade tensions, and like everywhere else in 2020, the impacts of COVID-19, but this slowdown is not one I would imagine will be structural.

Global travel: Promising but with one big environmental caveat

In short, I do not subscribe to the idea that the spread of the virus which shut down travel globally in 2020 will keep travel trends under pressure for a prolonged period. Globally, tourism is bound to continue being pushed by three big socioeconomic factors:

1. The cost of flying has collapsed due to the arrival of low-cost carriers, better price transparency, and deregulation. The arrival of Airbnb and similar apartment rental services has pulled down accommodation costs in many cities, with hotels having to compete on price.

2. Consumers have greater awareness of where to go as the Internet, travel blogs, and Instagram have allowed previously obscure destinations to emerge, and social media has created a culture in which travels are documented like never before. According to recent research by Expedia, "The biggest priority for young people travelling abroad is how Instagrammable their destination is."[5]

3. More safety supports more travel. While it may not feel like it, many parts of the world have become far more accessible to tourists over the past decade or so due to more stable political environments and the end of conflicts. To take one example, Croatia, at war from 1991 to 1995, is now one of Europe's tourism hot spots.

The quick development of tourism has come with some concerns, notably around overcrowding and pollution. The popularity of certain destinations is bound to become both off-putting and environmentally hazardous. The EU has 105 areas where "tourism exceeds physical, ecological, social, economic, psychological, and/ or political capacity thresholds."[6] Dubrovnik, Croatia, had to limit the number of cruise ships stopping there following the enthusiastic reaction to *Game of Thrones*, which was partly filmed there. Issues are not limited to Europe. The beautiful island of Boracay was shut down by the Filipino administration for six months in 2018 to undergo rehabilitation after problems with sewage dumped into the sea and buildings constructed too close to the shore. That same year, Thailand closed Ko Phi Phi's Maya Bay due to overcrowding and damage to the coral reef. As Yogi Berra would have said: "No one goes there nowadays. It's too crowded."

And of course, getting to your destination poses its own environmental issues. In aviation, the dependence on kerosene is difficult to limit given the growth of tourism. Airlines are improving the fuel efficiency of aircrafts through aerodynamic gains and the use of lighter composites, but traffic is increasing more than enough to offset those measures, with aircraft emissions predicted to at least triple by 2050.[7] From a policy perspective, multiple governments have pushed the EU to introduce new aviation taxation or kerosene taxation.

The world's largest cruise companies have scrubbers on the majority of their ships, but these rely on technology that essentially turns air pollution into water pollution. Cruise ships are meant to eliminate this in a regulated manner, but many discharge pollutants into the oceans. Regulations have developed to either monitor, fine, or impose other changes on the industry to keep pollution at bay.

PREDICTION #18

The combination of eco-friendly attitudes and COVID-19 impacts will mean that cruises and commercial flights will be transformed; flygskam, or flight shaming, might become more than just an obscure Swedish concept; and fast rail and self-driving electric vehicles will become preferred means of transportation.

As I detail more thoroughly in chapter 10, concerns around environmental issues have clearly increased, notably with the younger generation. This could span trying to limit your footprint by driving less, buying carbon credits to offset your flights (and to address flight shaming in some countries), and overall developing a greater conscience of what your movements imply for the planet.

INTERVIEW: On the future of travel and luggage

Who's better to talk about travel than the leader of the luggage industry? The Samsonite brand was born in 1910 and has been transformed into a multi-brand group over time, remaining by far the leader in selling product related to travel. (For a photo of one of Samsonite's innovative products, made from recycled materials, see page 194.) Here to share his insights is Kyle Gendreau, CEO of Samsonite.[8]

ERWAN RAMBOURG: When you think about the future of travel globally, what are key supporting factors and limitations? What makes you confident about the long-term potential for travel? What indicators do you track?

KYLE GENDREAU: From a generational perspective, there are two important supports at each end of the spectrum. First, every next generation wants to travel, looking to accumulate experiences rather than material possessions. Second, Baby Boomers support the travel industry. People are living longer and retiring with some wealth to allow them to see the world. In terms of forward indicators, we might be looking at air travel metrics in the short term, and international arrivals have been up mid-single digits year after year for some time now. Longer term, we look at indicators such as aircraft orders, new airport developments, and hotel chains' forward views on growth. All of these indicators are pointing in a very positive direction. A significant development recently has been the reality that travel has become cheaper for every new generation and as a consequence, access to travel increases. We are also seeing a step change in access in some developing markets, notably China, India, and Indonesia, where travel is blossoming. These are exciting times for the citizens of these countries.

In terms of headwinds, we are seeing some noise around the environmental impacts of travel which puts travel in the wrong light, and we believe there are other ways to limit travel's impact.

ER: How have international travelers evolved in terms of age, gender, or nationality, and does it influence the way you design and price your luggage products?

KG: From an age perspective, we are seeing a good mix between Millennials and young families on one side and a generation of retirees on the other. Similarly, while Asian travelers are gaining in terms of influence, this remains a truly global industry. From a gender perspective, it is true that the luggage market had been more masculine focused for a long time, so there is a lot of opportunity to work with catering to female consumers in travel but also with business bags and backpacks, for instance. The power of having a true multi-brand portfolio is that we can cater to very different needs. We can address family-focused, value-conscious consumers with our American Tourister brand, more experienced and premium consumers with Samsonite, and self-made, selective business and new luxury travelers with TUMI.

We deliver across all price points and have relevant products for all consumer needs, so we are clearly away from a "one size fits all" approach.

ER: What are your key competitive advantages within the luggage industry, and are you seeing threats from new entrants?

KG: In 2020, we are celebrating 110 years of expertise as leaders in innovation and technology in the sector, developing the next generation of products: more durable and lighter luggage. Consumers have considered us to be fully trustworthy, with global warranties on our products. Scale is a key competitive advantage not just relative to peers but more as there are efficiencies in what we do, and we can deliver on all price points thanks to our infrastructure. Our decentralized strategy enables us to be nimble in offering very country-specific products. In other words, we are operating the business in a very local manner but with the advantages of a substantial global scale. That scale means we can invest in logistics and R&D like no other player within a highly fragmented industry. It also means we can stay the course and keep true to a DNA centered on true innovation and a wide spectrum of products to meet different consumer needs. We have a genuine history of developing truly next-generation products. Our top three brands, Samsonite, TUMI, and American Tourister, have a global footprint with strong local managers, whilst our competitors are very local.

The next exciting focus for us is sustainability. We are working on how we can offer more sustainable attributes to all our products for all our consumers. As the industry's leader, we will lead the charge on this very important development. Not all consumers are looking for sustainability, but we need to be able to deliver on what should become a prerequisite eventually: that the majority of materials used for all luggage, not just a few ranges, are recycled. The more we can incorporate sustainable materials, the larger the positive impact we can have on the environment.

ER: How do you project distribution to evolve for your products between your own retail, wholesale partners, and online sales?

KG: When we IPO-ed, direct-to-consumer sales were around 22% of our sales. The TUMI acquisition brought that to around 30%. Our

Marketing for Samsonite's Eco Collection highlights the sustainability aspects of the new line. CREDIT: Courtesy of Samsonite.

current direct-to-consumer sales represent a mid-thirties percentage of total sales, with brick and mortar around 25% and online about 10%. Over the next four to five years, I see this increasing to above 40% of total sales, as notably online sales contribute much more to our P&L. For TUMI, retail makes sense because with premium offerings, product proliferation is more limited as you want to have the same representation in all markets. To be fair, the move from wholesale to retail and brick and mortar to online is not specific to luggage. We have seen that shift occur with consumers across different segments of consumption, and we are simply looking to anticipate those changes. We are notably hyper-focused on e-commerce because we see that consumers are as well. Given our capacity to differentiate and engineer products for different needs, we can be relevant on a very wide spectrum of channels, unlike most of our competitors. We can sell on Amazon, at Macy's, on our own website, anywhere really. We will end up being a lot more direct-to-consumer driven because that is where the world is going.

ER: What is the life expectancy of a piece of luggage, and how much do you rely on existing consumers versus new consumers for growth?

KG: Our sales growth is a combination of newcomers and repeat purchasers. American Tourister is capturing many new entrants, younger families, while Samsonite benefits from both consumers trading up as well as repeat consumers. On life expectancy, it is difficult to assess, but changes in regulation have been helpful in pushing lightweight luggage—a shift we have led thanks to innovation with the Samsonite Cosmolite range, launched more than ten years ago, and iterations of that range, as well as new initiatives like the Magnum range, launched in 2019. The trend towards products that are just as strong and durable but lighter is likely to continue. As a general rule, we feel carry-on luggage is likely used three to five years while checked-in luggage will have a longer life-span of five to seven years. Over time, we have grown our non-travel bags business to over 40%, and this has a much lower replacement cycle.

ER: Are consumers brand conscious or brand agnostic in luggage?

KG: Except at the very entry level (i.e., below USD60), they are brand conscious, absolutely. Consumers want peace of mind and security, especially if they are frequent travelers, and brands will give you trust in the way products have been manufactured. With that trust in brands come high expectations on quality and the global warranty on the items purchased. For TUMI, the brand is very strong and impactful; it is an image enhancer that consumers are proud to carry with them. In many ways, these are trophy products.

Summary

Travel trends are well supported by wealth creation and will be a positive factor for luxury demand ahead as with travel come bragging rights. In that context, the COVID-19-induced stay-at-home reality of 2020 should not be a great influence in the long term even if consumers will be intent on keeping safe. Structural factors will enable travel to thrive, notably the lower costs, greater awareness of destinations, and increased safety of the world. As with luxury demand overall, the continued emergence of a wealthy Chinese consumer will dominate travel trends and the associated spending for the next ten years. This consumer will change destinations depending on foreign exchange moves, political and security concerns, and fashion trends.

One big concern, however, remains: travel comes with high greenhouse gas emissions, and as we will see in the next chapter, being environmentally friendly will be increasingly important to the up-and-coming luxury consumers.

— 10 —

DISRUPTING
LUXURY
THE DECADE AHEAD

The snake which cannot cast its skin has to die.

FRIEDRICH NIETZSCHE

I AM SKEPTICAL OF those who say technology will disrupt luxury. The reason is pretty simple: you buy luxury goods (unlike an iPhone) not for technical attributes but because they make you feel good. If the product has some technical elements that help you feel even better, that's fine, and if technology means the product is presented to you in a more entertaining fashion (3D rendering online, fun VR presentation), all the better. But luxury goods will not be made obsolete by technology anytime soon. Luxury is in essence unneeded, a "nice to have," never an absolute necessity. And it is this "cherry on the cake," "why not spoil myself" attribute that makes the temptation so difficult to resist—and so enduring.

So what risks do luxury brands face, apart from not having sufficient scale to fight against the larger competitors? The biggest risks—and, for those with the foresight to anticipate and adjust ahead of time, the biggest opportunities—concern the raw materials of luxury products, and the obligations brands will increasingly have to better explain where and how their products are manufactured.

Consumers concerned about ethical and environmentally friendly products are prompting sweeping changes in many industries, especially food. As they become aware of the significant environmental impacts of meat and dairy consumption, an increasing number of consumers are becoming vegan or vegetarian. The food and agricultural production industry is responsible for around 25% of all global emissions, and the livestock sector accounts for two-thirds of that number, according to the UN Food and Agriculture Organization.[1] The meat industry uses vast amounts of energy, water, and resources and is a contributing factor to high deforestation rates around the world: in the Amazon basin, cattle ranching is responsible for 80% of forest clearing, and worldwide, meat production is responsible for nearly 60% of total biodiversity loss thus far.[2] The UN estimates that a global switch to low meat or completely meatless diets by 2050 would reduce the monetary costs of climate change mitigation by between 70% and more than 80%.[3]

Issues with meat and dairy go beyond the environmental. Overconsumption of red meat or processed meat is linked to heart issues and heightened cholesterol levels. Animal welfare concerns are a factor, too: 70 billion farm animals are reared for food every year, and in the U.S., 99% are reared on factory farms. As I mentioned before, anyone who has seen a video or two of how a factory farm operates might grow uneasy about buying meat or poultry in the U.S.

The cumulative effect of all this is a shift towards plant-based food. In the U.S., the growth of plant-based food sales was ten times that of all food sales growth in 2018, according to Nielsen.[4] Parliaments in Denmark, Germany, and Sweden have already discussed the introduction of a meat tax, similar to taxes on alcohol and tobacco, which would encourage an even wider demographic to switch away from meat consumption.

Youth protest climate change in Maastricht, Netherlands, May 11, 2019.
CREDIT: Vincent M.A. Janssen.

It's not a good time to be in the meat business—but it's a fantastic time to be in the vegetarian food business. On May 2, 2019, the entire floor at my office stopped to watch the stock market launch of Beyond Meat. The company began in 2009 but was mostly unknown until its plant-based burgers, hotdogs, and other meat substitutes developed a reputation for being virtually indistinguishable from real meat, to the extent that non-vegetarians are the bulk of Beyond Meat's customers, constituting as many as 93% according to one study.[5] The stock was first pitched at a range of USD21 to USD23 a share but started the trading session at twice that (USD46) and hit an intraday high of USD73, basically tripling its value. It tripled again during the summer of 2019, with a high close to USD240. In other words, the stock grew tenfold in a matter of weeks and was the best-performing IPO in nearly two decades. Beyond Meat continues to do well, and vegetarian products are also catching on in Europe, proving that changing social attitudes can mean big business.

WHAT WILL BE the Beyond Meat of the luxury industry? Environmental and ethical concerns will affect the fast fashion industry, leading to the growth of sustainable garments. Fur and exotic skins will no longer be used, and mined diamonds will likely lose out to lab-grown diamonds selling at a fifth of the price. In certain categories, the next generation will seek to lessen their carbon footprint by renting rather than buying goods, a move that goes way beyond luxury and apparel, as has been experienced by the automobile industry, for instance. And finally, an increasingly environmentally conscious society will look to local consumption to help make an impact.

One of many COVID-19 memes that floated around on social media during 2020 was the idea that "climate change needs to hire coronavirus's publicist." One of the silver linings of the crisis is that it will undoubtedly make consumers think differently about how and where products they consume are made and whether they can trust the brands that manufacture them. Climate change and other environmental concerns have been a bit of an afterthought for years. COVID-19 may act as a wake-up call.

PREDICTION #19

The majority of suitcases and athletic shoes from top brands will be made out of recycled and/or recyclable material. Meanwhile, most handbags will still be made from real leather, but fur will be banned in many countries as substitutes take over (despite not being earth friendly, because they are made with plastic derivatives).

Fast fashion: Take the money and run

When the *New York Times* reviewed Dana Thomas's book *Fashionopolis: The Price of Fast Fashion and the Future of Clothes*, the headline didn't mince words: "fast fashion is destroying the planet."[6] While the tone might seem extreme, the underlying reality is that working conditions in the garment industry are often deplorable, and the textile industry is amongst the most polluting. The majority of fabric fibers are synthetics derived from fossil fuels, and 85% of clothing in the U.S. ends up in landfills and will not decay. A bleak documentary called *The True Cost*, which was screened at the 2015 Cannes Film Festival, focused on working conditions following the 2013 Rana Plaza tragedy, when a textile factory in Bangladesh collapsed, killing more than 1,000 garment employees. While the documentary focuses on the implications of global capitalism, it also served as an eye-opener to many who did not have in mind how noxious the fashion industry truly is. In her book, Thomas makes the case that despite incidents like Rana Plaza, consumers are still addicted to fast fashion: it is cheap, easy to wear, and fashionable for the season.

Some high-street fashion retailers restock their clothing lines up to twenty-four times per year, spoiling consumers for choice and tempting them into frequent purchases. These clothes wear out faster, as they are not designed to last, and end up being worn only a few times during a season, before being discarded. A recent McKinsey report shows that relative to fifteen years ago, the average consumer purchases 60% more clothes and keeps the clothing for half as long.[7]

The fashion industry is responsible for 20% of wastewater. Dyeing is a big issue, but even the production of cotton requires enormous amounts of water: between 10,000 and 20,000 liters for a kilo (i.e., just enough for a pair of jeans and a shirt). With fashion accounting for 10% of global greenhouse gas emissions (more than aviation and shipping combined) and environmental issues getting more coverage, sustainable brands have become more popular with Millennials and Gen Z consumers.

Some brands have recently been in the spotlight for approaching production in earth-friendly manners. Reformation is a sustainable, vertically integrated women's clothing brand born in downtown

Los Angeles. It prides itself on using sustainable raw materials in its design, mostly what it calls A and B materials. Respectively, these stand for "Allstars," natural fibers that are rapidly renewable and plant based and have a potential for circularity, and "Better than most," fibers that are almost all natural or recycled. The goal is for A and B fibers to account for 75% of the goods. The motto of the company is droll and simple to remember: "Being naked is the #1 most sustainable option. We're #2." Allbirds is another brand that has been very visible and commercially successful at selling footwear products made from eucalyptus tree fiber, merino wool, and foam derived from sugar cane. The brand is known by consumers for comfort but also made the news because it has made a lot of its production open source. Veja, a French company producing sneakers in Brazil, is another example of a footwear brand that keeps transparency and fair-trade issues as priorities.

Fake fur, real benefits

Many luxury brands have stopped working with animal fur, notably Gucci, Chanel, Versace, Michael Kors, and, recently, Prada. And in 2019, California became the first state to ban the sale of animal fur products. To be fair, very few luxury brands still carry fur products. Some organizations such as PETA (People for the Ethical Treatment of Animals) have been highly vocal and efficient at raising the awareness of some dubious production methods. At the time of writing, one well-known holdout is Fendi, which started as a fur and leather shop in Rome nearly a century ago in 1925.

In 2017, Gustave Maisonrouge and Chloé Mendel launched Maison Atia with the idea of becoming the first luxury faux-fur brand, and many brands are competing now for that space. My understanding is that there is no substitute for natural fur in terms of keeping warm, but it seems the faux furs are now coming close. The other caveat is that faux-fur coats usually are manufactured with synthetic fibers such as modacrylic, which at the end of the day is a plastic derivative. In other words, you are saving animals but theoretically not saving the planet by switching to faux fur, and articles have questioned the rationale of doing that. What the faux-fur industry responds, rightly so, is that luxury fur or faux fur should be an exceptional product, and you should buy one that you will keep forever so you will not end up polluting the planet anytime soon.

Diamonds aren't forever?

Ironically, diamonds are a notoriously opaque industry. In 2012, Graff, a very high-end jewelry brand, meant to file an IPO. While I was working on the deal (which eventually got pulled), I traveled to South Africa and Botswana, where my contacts in the trade recommended I read a 943-page book published in 2007 called *From Mine to Mistress* to understand the fundamentals of the industry. The book helped me understand the ins and outs of the supply and demand of a secretive trade, but it is now likely that a new book on the diamond industry is needed and Paul Zimnisky of Diamond Analytics could well be its author. Zimnisky is a former investor who specialized in metals and mining and now works with investors, private equity firms, and brands alike through his own diamond consultancy firm. From my conversations with Zimnisky, I have learned about two realities and counterintuitive consequences. First, the price of mined diamonds has come down dramatically since the 2011 peak but should be well supported ahead. Second, the artificial or lab-grown diamonds that have appeared on the jewelry scene could well prove to be disruptive to parts of the industry.

Oddly enough, despite the advent of lab-made diamonds, the prices of traditional diamonds are likely to go up. This seems indeed to not make sense, but there are good reasons for it. Because demand was high and supply low, the 2011 price peak spurred investment in mines, culminating in the opening of three new mines recently: the

Renard mine in Quebec, Canada, in 2014; the GK (Gahcho Kué) mine in Canada's Northwest Territories in late 2016; and the Liqhobong mine in Lesotho that same year. These projects came right after a 2014-15 slowdown in China, which was triggered by the anti-graft campaign from the Xi Jinping administration. Because the average price of a one-carat diamond has come down 25% since 2011, Zimnisky believes that some mining operations will inevitably have to close.

Diamonds can be extracted from the earth in other ways. One development has been to search the ocean floor off the coast of Namibia, literally vacuuming the sediments with diamond mining boats. This has generated both environmental questions and insufficient volumes to change the reality of scarcity for the diamond industry. Besides, while the U.S. accounts for roughly 50% of the market, demand in China and India could prove to support the industry in the long run. And while lab-made diamonds could be a threat, I believe the current small size of that market and differences in usage might not impair natural-mined diamond prices just yet. Finally, demand should provide long-term support for higher prices: while the number of weddings wanes, gifting and self-purchasing are rising, with each representing a third of jewelry diamond usage.

While natural diamonds take millions of years to form and vast resources to extract from the earth, manufactured diamonds can be produced in a lab in a matter of weeks. Historically, these synthetic diamonds were created for industrial purposes in the 1950s (General Electric discovered the HPHT, high-pressure high-temperature, process in late 1954) for applications in high tech, optics, laser, healthcare, and quantum computing. Today, these remain the key products for which they are used, much more than jewelry. Notably, De Beers, a de facto monopoly in the diamond industry up until twenty years ago, launched its own lab-grown company called Lightbox in September 2018. Today, Lightbox has the capacity to produce up to 500,000 synthetic carats in its Oregon-based facility. Separately, many Chinese and Indian operators have ramped up production, and more than 90% of the diamonds produced for industrial and abrasive applications come from China. For those used for the jewelry trade, the origins are a bit more diverse, though China leads there as well.

While about 150 million carats of natural diamonds are mined every year, today more than 12 billion carats of lab-grown diamonds are being fabricated, close to one hundred times more. And prices have fallen dramatically: the cost of lab-grown diamonds was virtually on par with mined diamonds six years ago and is now nearing a tenth of the price. At the time of writing, lab-grown diamonds represent less than 3% of graded diamonds in the world, according to Paul Zimnisky, and he believes by 2035 they will represent around 5% of sales of graded diamonds, arguing the market will be worth north of USD5bn by 2023 and three times that (i.e., USD15bn) by 2035.[8]

Research from MVI Marketing indicates the percentage of consumers willing to buy an engagement ring with lab-grown diamonds rose from 55% in 2016 to 70% in 2018.[9] Aside from ESG concerns, younger consumers are keen to understand the pricing of their products, and traceability of man-made diamonds is much easier. As one investor in a diamond lab put it: "When you go to a jewelry store, 32 people on average have touched the diamond before it reaches you, and those people are not traceable. In the case of lab-grown diamonds, they go straight from the factory to the jeweler."[10]

While many luxury jewelers are understandably a bit nervous to see lab-grown diamonds become a common sight, they will likely not completely displace the high-end market, for several reasons:

- First, cost deflation is a huge issue: if you purchase a USD20,000 ring with a lab-grown diamond and the lab-grown industry proves to be a race to the bottom in terms of prices, how will you feel about that same ring being worth half the price the following year?

- Second, flawless has no charm: Your knowing that all-natural diamonds are one of a kind while fabricated diamonds are flawless is not great from a marketing point of view. Presumably, you would like your stone to be unique.

- Finally, environmental and social issues are not as simple as you would imagine. An American lab-grown diamond producer called Diamond Foundry got a lot of press coverage because its diamonds are made 100% in the U.S., it claims to be ethical and carbon neutral (but the only way it manages that is by purchasing solar credits), and it counts actor Leonardo DiCaprio as an investor; as well as being an active environmentalist, he starred in *Blood Diamond*, the 2006 film that shed some light on the disturbing history of mines in Africa. The reality, however, is that Diamond Foundry produces about only 100,000 carats a year. The biggest producers of lab-grown diamonds are in India (producing more than ten times more) and use electricity which is subsidized by the administration and often derived from coal mines, increasing greenhouse gas emissions.

Sure, lab-made diamonds don't lead to deforestation or soil erosion and are unlikely to come from countries that are in conflict zones, but they aren't exactly earth friendly either. Also, traditional mining often supports entire communities: for instance, the diamond trade accounts for around 30% of the GDP of Botswana, employing more than 30,000 people. In that region, known as "the diamond route," De Beers is rehabilitating and conserving six hectares of land for every hectare it mines. It is also looking to use kimberlite rock to absorb carbon dioxide, pushing the counterintuitive idea that its actions could actually prove carbon positive. In other words, the debate around lab-grown diamonds being more eco-friendly is not clear-cut.

So, what is the end game? The jewelry sector will have to wait until prices of lab-grown diamonds stabilize. When that happens, I think the brands will split into three categories:

1. Luxury brands are likely to stick to mined diamonds because of consumers' perception of uniqueness and belief that the product will hold its value. I think the real differentiator for the luxury brands will be in trust and notably, traceability of stones, an area in which Tiffany clearly has an edge. In 2018, the brand announced it would start to share the provenance of all newly sourced, individually registered diamonds it sells as part of its Diamond Source Initiative. Lab-grown diamonds could be used by luxury brands for watches or the smaller stones in rings for which the main diamond is mined, but I do not believe top brands will stop using mined diamonds soon. The idea of proposing to your girlfriend with a lab-grown Cartier diamond as a sign of enduring love sounds kind of awkward and, to be blunt, unromantic.

2. "Bridge" brands or costume jewelry, such as Swarovski, Pandora, or APM Monaco, will likely use lab-grown diamonds and other artificial stones such as rubies, emeralds, and sapphires to increase their value-for-money propositions. These brands cater to a consumer more driven by fun, colorful, interchangeable products. In June 2018, actress Penélope Cruz launched the first sustainable jewelry range at Swarovski, a capsule collection of thirteen pieces with a claim on using "responsibly sourced materials," including fair-trade gold and "created" diamonds and gemstones such as rubies and sapphires. JCPenney and Macy's started their own bridal collections with lab-grown diamonds for the 2018 Christmas season, and many department stores and other jewelry resellers will likely adopt the trend. Signet, one of the world's largest retailers of jewelry and owner of Kay Jewelers and Zales, sells synthetic sapphires and rubies, but for some reason, only carries mined diamonds, not artificial substitutes. I trust this could change eventually.

3. Finally, we will likely see the emergence of new brands, pure plays offering lab-grown diamond products at the low and high end. In

May 2018, a new brand called Courbet was set up at Place Vendôme, the birthplace of all Parisian luxury jewelers. It is run by a manager formerly at Richemont (owner of Cartier and Van Cleef & Arpels). While the product range looks good, it is relatively classic in design and close to the traditional jewelry brands, which is almost a pity: if a brand is starting from scratch with a new product, it might as well adopt completely new codes. Lark & Berry was launched the same month with a design self-described as "conversational, modern, and offbeat," and another lab-grown diamond brand appeared in late 2018 called Kimai. Expect many others to appear shortly.

I am convinced traditional and lab-grown diamonds might be able to coexist and thrive in jewelry, offering consumers completely different reasons to buy. A bigger threat for traditionally mined diamonds is the cultural shift: there is a perception that diamond engagement rings are a somewhat sexist and outdated tradition. The industry long relied on the incredible marketing and PR firepower of De Beers to create and keep that market afloat, but the monopoly gradually got dismantled in the early 2000s with Russian, Canadian, and Australian mines starting to step in. Consumers my age are likely still purchasing diamonds with that De Beers legacy and motto in mind ("A diamond is forever"), but those in their twenties have likely never heard about it. As explained in the first chapter of this book, however, there should be many other avenues to growth for the jewelry industry outside of engagements.

PREDICTION #20

Cartier, Tiffany, and Bulgari will be using mostly lab-grown diamonds for their watches and jewelry, though center stones on the higher-end jewelry pieces will still be from mined diamonds.

Rental and secondhand goods:
The circular luxury economy

An attractive alternative to purchasing fast fashion brands is purchasing higher-end, more sophisticated products secondhand. The latter contributes to a circular economy that ultimately produces less waste (see page 210). Recently, I worked with a consumer-insights agency to survey high-end consumers on their willingness to purchase secondhand luxury products. A negligible percentage of Chinese buyers were open to the idea, while in the U.S., over 20% of respondents said they would consider it.

In 2011, e-commerce entrepreneur Julie Wainwright founded The RealReal. The company, listed as of June 2019, employs experts to authenticate secondhand luxury products that are sold on consignment. It also operates two brick-and-mortar stores, one in New York and another in Los Angeles, and is the U.S. poster child for the principle of "re-commerce" of luxury. Rebag is a New York–based website that launched in 2014 as a platform to buy and sell designer handbags; now, they too have brick-and-mortar stores. And in a somewhat extreme take on secondhand, there is a burgeoning market for used makeup among Millennial consumers in Japan, with brands like Chanel active on resale sites.

Many other companies are starting up on the principle of secondhand ownership, taking a sort of vintage approach to luxury. Vestiaire Collective is ten years old and has 8 million members, who buy and sell authenticated luxury fashion items; similar companies include Material World, thredUP, Poshmark, and Depop. In hard luxury, Watchfinder & Co. was founded in 2002 as an online secondhand watch retailer and was purchased by the Richemont group in 2018. In ten years, the resale market is likely, in my view, to surpass that of fast fashion in value.

Rent the Runway represents a similar ethos, though with a very different business model. Launched in 2009 as a pure e-commerce concept, it now has a handful of brick-and-mortar locations in the

The advent of circular luxury

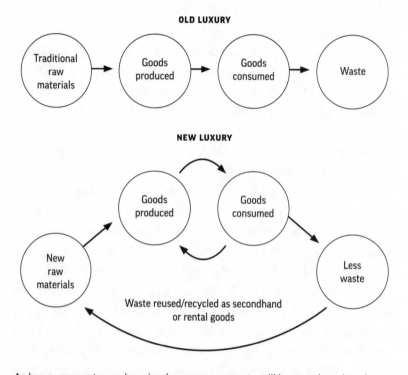

As luxury moves towards a circular economy, waste will be greatly reduced.
SOURCE: Erwan Rambourg.

U.S. The principle is for consumers to be able to rent designer clothing for a four-day or an eight-day period at 10% of the retail price of the piece, dry cleaning included. So that exceptional dress you wanted to buy for an event, you can access for a tenth of the price, and people won't say, "oh, I've seen her wearing that already."

Speaking of which, Kate Middleton, the Duchess of Cambridge, has been known (and appreciated by some fans) for wearing the same outfit several times. This has been seen as a sign that royals can also be down to earth and have timeless taste. More importantly, it sends a message that preventing waste is a good thing.

As the younger generation moves away from ownership and looks to accumulate experiences rather than things, these concepts will likely gain traction over time. Notably, most of these initiatives are based in Western countries. This does not mean they have limited potential globally; it is simply a sign that for the time being, Asian luxury consumers are more into purchasing the latest and greatest and are maybe less value-for-money driven than Western clienteles.

Global citizens, local consumers

The "think global, buy local" approach to sustainability has been growing in popularity for several years now. More consumers are becoming "locavores"—that is, they prefer locally grown products that support their local community or ecosystem. This is highly visible in food. In 2007, two Canadian citizens recounted their experience of restricting their diet to local foods in *The 100-Mile Diet: A Year of Local Eating*. In Italy, zero km food (0 km food) is a concept that developed to describe food that is not processed, has not traveled far, and has not been stored. Not only does this not generate much pollution, but it is also a guarantee of quality and freshness.

PREDICTION #21

With Louis Vuitton now producing in the U.S. for the U.S., with sites in California and in Texas, being a locavore will extend into wanting to buy other products that are manufactured closer to home. Supply chains in luxury will shift a lot closer to their end markets: "made in Italy" or "made in France" will gradually shift to "made in a production site near you." For watches, "made in Switzerland" will persist, but fewer clients will buy those watches.

In March 2020, as most restaurants and stores in Manhattan were closing following the COVID-19 outbreak, I went to the fresh, local market on the Upper West Side. It was surprisingly busy, given emphasis on social distancing at that time. Why? Simple: consumers wanted to buy products they could trust and that were sourced very close to where they got sold. One of the silver linings of the virus, aside from lower pollution globally (as production, transportation, and general activity waned), is that consumers were incentivized to pay much more attention to what they bought, and to how and where items have been produced.

Beyond food, some brands in fashion also point to local production, such as the 100% made in France underwear brand Le Slip Français or Scottish scarves from Green Thomas made in Glasgow. Cynics might say Louis Vuitton opened a production site in Texas in 2019 to please the U.S. administration by creating American jobs, but the move could also let consumers be proud of purchasing a product that has not traveled the world to get to them.

AS DISRUPTION SEEPS into the industry, the better brands and groups will accept that they have to change, or lose relevance. They will be compelled to disrupt themselves. They should also have an interest in staying on top of new technologies that can be game changing (e.g., blockchain technology to monitor authentic products) and of start-ups that they can learn from. Kering has been involved with sustainability founders, and LVMH has also invested in an accelerator program to ensure they can help develop and capture the benefits of new trends.

INTERVIEW: On the importance of sustainability in luxury

To talk about disruption in the luxury space, sustainability, and challenges the sector is facing, I have interviewed two influential professionals in the field, Marie-Claire Daveu from Kering and Miroslava Duma from Future Tech Lab. Alongside other leaders such as Stella McCartney and Ellen MacArthur, both Daveu and Duma have influenced much of the thinking on sustainability and the circular economy of luxury. First up is Marie-Claire Daveu, the chief sustainability officer and head of institutional affairs for Kering."

ERWAN RAMBOURG: Your career brought you from the French Ministry for Ecology and Sustainable Development to running sustainability at Kering. What were the first few steps you took to make Kering such a voice for sustainability in the luxury sector, and what level of support did you find when you joined the group?

MARIE-CLAIRE DAVEU: A key reason for me to join the group was the profound personal commitment of group CEO François-Henri Pinault [who wrote the foreword to this book] to sustainability issues. Way before the group built its reputation for being a strong corporate citizen, sustainability was at the core of the vision and strategy at the group level. From early on, bonuses have been correlated to results on sustainability metrics for brand CEOs and other key managers, and we have implemented sustainability reviews and a series of performance indicators enabling us to track performance on these matters.

Our idea has always been to involve others as well, as we consider that for all to make progress, it is key to open-source many of our achievements. In 2015, we open-sourced our group environmental profit and loss (EP&L) results and methodology. In 2018, we did the same for our raw materials standards. In 2019, we shared our approach on animal welfare, and as we think about the future, sharing our initiatives with the broader community makes sense.

Sustainability is at the heart of our internal governance, and the corporate level is a sparring partner with the brands. After some initiatives taken between 2013 and 2016, we decided in 2017 to accelerate the change, with a new chapter linked to the development of a 2025 strategy shared with the brands and all of their partners around a broad environmental, social, and innovation agenda. The idea is to have measurable results with a strict calendar and internal as well as external transparency so if execution does not go as planned, we quickly know why and can bring corrective measures.

Once again, change is made easier by the fact that sustainability changes are expected and supported by the very top of our organization, and this has enabled the group to make some fundamental changes way ahead of these issues being trendy.

ER: How do you gauge the interest of consumers for environmental and social issues, and are you seeing differences in terms of expectations consumers have from the brands in terms of age, gender, or nationality? Why is sustainability a particularly important topic for the luxury sector versus other industries?

MCD: When buying a luxury product, customers expect it to be perfect from all points of view, whether it is the intrinsic quality of the product, the savoir faire, the design, but of course also the reality that the item was manufactured with a sense of caring for the planet and caring for the people involved in the manufacturing process. For customers purchasing luxury goods, all of this should be a given, and sustainability is an integral part of the perception of quality whatever the age of the consumer or country of origin. This is also the way we see it at Kering: sustainability is inherent to quality. What we do observe, though, is a particular sensitivity of Millennials and Generation Z consumers for product attributes linked to sustainability, such as traceability of the product, greenhouse gas emissions, bio-diversity, and animal welfare. Gen Z especially is asking questions about traceability and raw materials. So, I would say there is a real generational shift rather than big differences by nationality, and the extensive use of social media is also likely to have helped the conversation move forward more rapidly.

Beyond customers, it is also important to understand that employees are also driven by these topics, and the change in culture with a new generation of managers joining luxury groups also means that sustainability issues can play a role in how some gifted students may want to choose the company they will eventually join. If you want to attract and retain the best talent, it is key to understand that employees will likely take pride in working for a company with an environmental conscience and a proven track record. It's great to be an employee in the luxury industry, but beyond that, we all remain citizens of the world first and foremost. As a result, I have been very active with several universities and fashion schools in France, the U.K., the U.S., and China as sustainability issues gradually permeate the education field as well.

ER: Early on, Kering has developed an EP&L account. How does that work, and how is staff at Kering concretely incentivized to implement measures to limit the group's footprint?

MCD: We have been using the EP&L in order to measure, then reduce, our impact on the planet, and it is very much linked to our 2025 action plan. The initial goal of reducing 40% of our footprint by 2025 was looked at brand by brand, with a focus on what products or processes could evolve, and obviously, there are big differences between fashion and jewelry brands within our portfolio. All the brands are involved and need to do the work, and we ask brand CEOs, alongside their regular P&Ls, what their EP&Ls could look like, when assessing new projects. Concretely, from the learnings we've had with our EP&L, we are implementing the right programs, focusing mainly on raw materials sourcing and processing. As such, and to name a few, we implemented a sustainable cashmere program in Mongolia and developed a metal-free leather tanning process— thereby addressing issues with two materials that are important yet harmful to the planet.

ER: In 2017, you laid out a very ambitious 2025 action plan. What are the top priorities for the five years ahead, and what do you see as key challenges?

MCD: The most difficult part is really the environmental aspects. If we look at best practices today, we can cut 20% of our carbon foot-print out of a target of cutting 40%. To ensure the 20-point delta is addressed, we have to find disruptive innovations, and we are in the process of identifying start-ups who are developing new mate-rials and new processes enabling us to go a lot further. The other challenge is for everyone to systematically think about the environ-ment whatever the project. Sustainability should be second nature to managers; our habits need to change, and with that, our suppliers' habits as well.

ER: Ahead of the G7 summit in the summer of 2019, the Kering group was selected by French President Emmanuel Macron to deliver an environmental fashion pact which 32 groups (representing 150 brands) signed. How difficult was this to manage, and what are the gist of the pact and the next steps?

MCD: Our group was given a mandate in late April 2019 to build a coalition by the end of August 2019 that would include a broad rep-resentation of the apparel industry, and while the timing was very tight, it was refreshing to see how willing and reactive the brands we reached out to ended up being. We have been overwhelmed by the contribution and the open-mindedness of most groups we approached, whether from some of the luxury mainstays (e.g., Chanel and Hermès), some of the Italian names (e.g., Moncler, Zegna, Ferragamo), but also more broadly from sporting goods leaders such as Nike, adidas, and PUMA as well as the high-street brands. This is a historic coalition as we have managed to convince 56 groups (representing in all 250 brands) to work together despite the reality of very different sizes, corporate cultures, nationalities, and supply chains. We also managed to gather retailers and suppliers. After the G7 summit, more brands have expressed the willingness to join. The pact really focuses on three key areas: climate change, biodiversity, and ocean protection. The end goal is for all of us to reach carbon neutrality by 2050, aligned with the broader goal of remaining below the 1.5 degrees Celsius maximum increase in global temperatures. The project goes beyond elements of competition and egos; all groups have an interest in participating. The coalition will be accountable and report progress at least once a year. There are initiatives outside of the fashion world which are also helpful. For instance, the CEO of Danone, Emmanuel Faber, has launched a coalition for the food industry, with 19 companies signing on initially in September 2019 to work on sustainability and biodiversity in farming and notably, regenerative agriculture, which is a topic about which we can all learn. In the luxury world, we are fortunate that customers want stronger changes, trust key opinion leaders (KOLs), and purchase our goods. We should also note the same customers, rightly so, will start to trust and follow what scientists are projecting as well, not just KOLs, and as that happens, we should all be better off!

INTERVIEW: On the potential to invest in a more sustainable fashion world

Miroslava Duma is the founder and CEO of Future Tech Lab, a venture capital fund that works with start-ups to develop and promote more sustainable practices in the fashion industry.[12]

ERWAN RAMBOURG: After a successful career as a fashion influencer and digital entrepreneur, you founded Future Tech Lab (FTL) in 2017. What were the key insights that led you to create this company?

MIROSLAVA DUMA: The idea of FTL came to me more than three years ago. I was pregnant with my third child, and I started to think differently, to develop new perspectives. I tend to get bored pretty quickly and constantly work to bring purpose to what I do, and when I like something, I really become obsessed with it, a bit like when you like a piece of music or a specific food; I just can't stop. It was the same with the fashion industry. For ten years, I would start my day at 7 a.m. with a media breakfast, attend shows all day, go to cocktail parties and events. I then suddenly realized I had seen fashion executives more than my family. It was sort of like Groundhog Day, where every day seemed to be built on the same script, and I got fed up with it. It was also a time when it became clear that many practices in the fashion industry were unethical. The Rana Plaza scandal happened in 2013, and I thought: "How can I contribute? I have been a little part of a giant fashion propaganda machine. I need a new role in this world."

At the same time, a friend of mine founded a company called VitroLabs in San Francisco in 2016, a bioengineering company that develops lab-grown leather and pelts for fashion and other sectors, and I started to speak to scientists and thought about what my contribution could be. As I became a social media impactor, my following grew quickly, and while I could have used that following to sell more handbags, I thought that really sounded miserable and I could really leverage that following for a good purpose. I had a eureka moment when my young son asked me: "Are you an actress? How come so many people know you? Surely, you must be doing something important." That really grounded me to think through the philosophical question of why I am here on this earth and what I can bring. I wake up every morning feeling privileged, having had the luxury of education, a caring family, not having to wonder how to put food on my plate.

What I have done so far with FTL is source, scout, dig for alternative technology to help the fashion industry move away from being one of the greatest polluters. I have met more than three hundred companies around the world, from spider silk to seaweed fiber, looking at research and development and helping small, smart concepts scale up.

ER: FTL is split between three activities: investment, an advisory role, and an experimental lab. Can you walk us through the purpose of all three, and how you see them developing in the future? Is there anything else you need within the company?

MD: Future Tech Lab is a company that bridges fashion and technology to lead the transition towards a more sustainable future. We work with the most promising start-ups that have the potential to pioneer and champion the positive impact of innovation in science and technology.

We help engineers and scientists all over the world develop their ideas in fields like material science, bio- and nanotechnology, smart fabrics, and wearable tech. By combining two worlds that are far removed from each other right now—science/technology and fashion/design—we promote the inception and production of unique products. Our team is based all over the world and spends much of their time sourcing and scouting for the next breakthrough across the globe—from China and the U.S. to France and Israel.

ER: How do you explain that sustainability is a topic that consumers and the media are keen to talk about, but many companies in luxury and fashion seem to have been on the back foot, not early adopters of best practices? Do you see that discrepancy evaporating soon?

MD: Some groups, like Patagonia, The North Face, Nike, and adidas, are heavily invested in R&D and are ambassadors of sustainability in their fields. As trend forecaster Li Edelkoort has said time and again: "Fashion is old fashioned." The industry is oftentimes disconnected from the latest technology trends, and while they understand sustainability is a big trend, not a passing fad, many are investing for marketing purposes. Only a minority of brands understand that we have entered world 2.0, and they are fueling the hope. As highlighted in *The Innovator's Dilemma* (Clayton Christensen, 1997), the bigger you are as a company, the greater the risk you face of being disrupted. Kodak was a good example of this, owning 85% of the photo-printing industry, employing 130,000 employees at one stage, and having innovation wipe them out. There remains a sense of arrogance in the fashion industry, and the best piece of advice is the one given by Steve Jobs, founder of Apple: "Stay hungry, stay foolish."

ER: Within your investment portfolio, are there concepts you are particularly excited about? Any gaps you want to fill and if so, in which type of industry or technology?

MD: FTL has been working with some of the most inspiring and innovative companies, who all share the same vision to create global change. Our portfolio company Diamond Foundry creates unique, one-of-a-kind, pure diamonds in a laboratory in San Francisco, which are anatomically identical to mined diamonds, but morally pure as well! There is Bolt Threads, who make spider silk, which is stronger than steel and lighter than a cloud (among many of their other performance-based fibers). I already mentioned VitroLabs, who are producing cruelty-free leather and fur. We really believe that these pioneering companies are among many others that will lead the charge to transition the industry towards a more responsible future.

ER: Within luxury, some groups, like Kering, or some creative minds, like Stella McCartney, have been quite vocal about their sustainability efforts. Do you have partnerships or collaborations with certain brands or groups, or is the goal to supply, and to a certain extent educate, the entire industry?

MD: We really function as an investment company and act as strategic investors. If you go back to the example of VitroLabs, I introduced the company at the Google lab in Paris. We share our deal flows with all the groups, co-invest in some companies, and really present ourselves as a bridge between the fashion and tech worlds. We also partner with Fashion for Good, a platform in sustainable fashion innovation, and I have co-hosted events with Stella McCartney.

The way I see things is if you are a brand, the tsunami is happening with or without you. You have a choice to either hop on and ride the wave or be washed away by it.

ER: Do you perceive some differences in terms of adoption of new technologies or products depending on gender, age, or nationality? Are there some particular barriers consumers have in adopting new materials (for example, can so-called vegan leather ever replace cowhide)?

MD: The adoption rate is slow, and it is happening on a different scale depending on the markets. The U.S. has been at the forefront of change, with the advent of brands like Everlane (long-lasting online clothing with transparent pricing) and Allbirds (environmentally friendly footwear). Today, much is about authenticity. Victoria's Secret is suffering from the association with the dream of an impossible body, while Gucci had a very interesting campaign with real people and highlighting real beauty.

The U.S., Australia, Scandinavian countries, and other parts of Europe started to focus on eating healthy; now, other countries are moving there as well, and there are more topics at play. In fashion, we took a stake in Reformation, a sustainable women's clothing and accessories brand. Other companies are getting there, though it never is quick enough. Chanel announced it was banning exotic skins in late 2018; Prada recently announced it would be using Econyl regenerated nylon from discarded materials in its recent iconic Re-Nylon collection. All of these initiatives are going in the right direction.

ER: What makes you the most optimistic about your adventure being a resounding success? What are the main hurdles you face?

MD: I am a natural optimist, but I believe we have already gone too far and there are likely only fifteen to thirty years left for the planet as we currently know it. It does not mean we should stand still. We are living in the Anthropocene, the so-called human epoch, during which mankind has been shaping the present. If mankind can shape the present, surely mankind can shape the future. I am looking at investments and collaborations that will have the potential to do exactly that.

Summary

Ethical transparency, production traceability, and environmental sustainability are not mere buzzwords for the young generation. Whether due to lab-grown diamonds, faux fur, or secondhand apparel, the next decade will be very disruptive for a sector that has arguably become complacent while enjoying a decade of strong growth rates. Existing luxury companies need to have alternatives in mind and possibly invest in them as a hedge for when their own current businesses might be affected by these emerging categories.

Recognizing the existence of a circular economy, environmental, sustainability, and governance issues will not be merely a fashionable conversation or an opportunity to greenwash. A genuine transformation of processes is needed as the next consumer will not be gullible and they will be asking questions. A substantial amount of growth potential remains to be harvested.

The question is whether the industry will be brave enough to self-disrupt. Sometimes change only comes when managers don't have a choice. During 2020, an ongoing joke was: "Who took care of your digital transformation? Your CTO? Your CEO? No, COVID-19!" External shocks can hold a silver lining: as long as brands remember who they are selling to, events like the pandemic can be catalysts for change that has long been needed to avoid becoming irrelevant.

CONCLUSION
THE NEW LUXURY

The secret of man's being is not only to live
but to have something to live for.
FYODOR DOSTOYEVSKY, *The Brothers Karamazov*

I
S THERE ANY such thing as luxury consumption with a purpose? Perhaps Aldous Huxley's *Brave New World* can provide a
response. Nearly a hundred years since its publication, *Brave New World* still resonates as a contemporary story, and a scary one. In Huxley's dystopian fiction, citizens live in a world of prede-termined classes (or castes) and leaders of the World State city of London have engineered ways to make citizens peaceful to avoid any type of rebellion against the powers in place. Beyond having access to a drug (soma) that generates feelings of soothing and hap-piness, citizens are also encouraged to consume as much as possible, ostensibly to help sustain the world's economy, but also as a means to prevent their asking questions.

Citizens of the Brave New World are subject to advertising slo-gans for groupthink and intense consumerism. These are four striking examples:

• "You can't consume much if you sit still and read books" (i.e., don't think, just buy). By the way, I'm happy you managed to read this book up to here!

- "If one's different, one's bound to be lonely" (i.e., conform or you will be rejected).

- "Ending is better than mending" (i.e., just throw away your stuff and buy more stuff).

- "The more stitches, the less riches" (i.e., only wear new clothes, don't bother repairing what is worn).

Talk about unreasoned consumerism! In Huxley's world, intense consumerism, the encouragement to purchase more and more goods, is presented as a way for the state to ensure economic stability and maintain control of its citizens. Though it was published decades before, it's an exaggerated version of American consumerism during the post-war growth years in the 1950s and 1960s and can also evoke the 1980s, when hippie ideas died and consumerism flourished. The big difference with today's world, though, is that in Aldous Huxley's book, consumers have heavily restricted access to knowledge, whereas in the real world, especially today, information is everywhere and questions will be asked.

Though one can argue that the recent frenzy around fast fashion brands is an example of "ending rather than mending," I believe the future luxury consumer will embody the exact opposite of the mentality imposed on citizens of the Brave New World. I believe a fashion revolution is ahead, in which consumers will want to know where their clothes are made, how they are produced, and what will ensure they can keep them forever, fix them, recycle them, or give them to others rather than throw them away. A circular consumption of luxury products could be seen as the default rather than a notable exception.

That will really be the Brave New World for premium goods, a world with purpose. One proponent of that world is Patagonia, described by the media as a company with a conscience.

The Patagonia paradox

Patagonia, a California-based outdoor clothing brand founded in 1973 by colorful entrepreneur Yvon Chouinard (who started off as a rock climber and turned into one of the most vocal environmentalists in the business world), is a poster child for buying less, protecting the planet, and giving back. (For an example of one of their ads, see page 227.) Chouinard starts his book *Let My People Go Surfing: The Education of a Reluctant Businessman* by writing: "I've been a businessman for almost sixty years. It's as difficult for me to say those words as it is for someone to admit being an alcoholic or a lawyer. I've never respected the profession."[1] In a similarly provocative quote, he writes: "We believe the accepted model of capitalism that necessitates endless growth and deserves the blame for the destruction of nature must be displaced."[2] Starting in 1985, Patagonia has been giving 1% of its annual sales to projects related to protecting the planet. In late 2018, the company's mission itself was changed to say that Patagonia is "in the business to save our home planet"–nothing less. Making consumers comfortable when they go out? Protecting them from the elements? Sure, but that's a given. The company has a purpose at a much higher level.

In November 2011, Patagonia ran an ad in the *New York Times* that still serves as a case study in branding. The ad, showing a Patagonia jacket, simply read: "Don't buy this jacket. The environmental cost of everything we make is astonishing." It ran on Black Friday, a day during which consumers in the U.S. hunt down deals, spend beyond reason, and likely waste a lot. The ad also encouraged Patagonia customers to take a pledge, the Common Threads Initiative, essentially a deal between the brand and the public to consume goods more responsibly. It includes the five following commitments:

REDUCE

WE make useful gear that lasts a long time
YOU don't buy what you don't need
[That in itself is anti-"fast fashion."]

REPAIR

WE help you repair your Patagonia gear
YOU pledge to fix what's broken
[That in itself is common sense or at least anti-waste relative to the
behaviors in *Brave New World*. Eileen Fisher, an American women's
clothing brand, has recently offered a similar program for their
clothing called Renew.]

REUSE

WE help you find a home for Patagonia gear you no longer need
YOU sell or pass it on (eBay is a great place to start)
[That in itself is the definition of circular economy, with the
following pledge.]

RECYCLE

WE will take back your Patagonia gear that is worn out
YOU pledge to keep your stuff out of the landfill and incinerator

REIMAGINE

TOGETHER we reimagine a world where we take only
what nature can replace[3]

Call this naive or suicidal, but the so-called Patagonia pardox,
the theoretical contradiction between profits and purpose, can
be resolved if consumers share the company's values. Patagonia
has increased its bond with its consumers and, yes, counterintuitively, increased its sales: many consumers would rather go to a
brand that has convictions and values than one which is just about
making money. Chouinard is critical of entrepreneurs who grow a

company, make money, and only give some back after they retire. In his view, you have the responsibility to give back all along. He also accuses many companies of "greenwashing," or pretending to be environmentally friendly to placate consumers when in reality the companies are simply obsessed with pursuing growth.

The luxury of genuine purpose

I am not saying luxury brands should embrace the Patagonia way, but embracing the idea of "buying less but better" and having a genuine purpose, something that is not gimmicky or made up, will go a long way.

Stella McCartney, a successful advocate for sustainability in the fashion world, looks at that industry with some cold common sense. The fashion industry is likely to generate up to 25% of global emissions if nothing is done. McCartney believes consumers will force the fashion industry to change because consumers are aware of the issues. In the meantime, she announced the launch of a UN charter for sustainable fashion in late 2018. In an interview following that announcement, she told *Business of Fashion* that for her, luxury is living in a world with fresh air and clean water.[4]

She has a point. Luxury does not have to be about flashy colors or logos. The New Luxury could be about knowledge, respect, and values. With time, knowledge, and money, consumers will go higher within the pyramid of Maslow (hierarchy of needs) and the pyramid of mass-luxe. More importantly, they should move from a "look at me, I've arrived" mentality to one where purchases are more for themselves and align to their values. In the old luxury paradigm, consumers used to flock to brands first and buy products from brands which may have had values or not. The future will start with values, then products, and finally brands.

ACKNOWLEDGEMENTS

W RITING A FIRST book is not as difficult as many seem to think it is, but writing a second one, I felt, was a lot tougher! It was a great help for me to witness my children's enthusiasm when I told them I might be thinking about publishing another book six years after my first. My wife, Dorothée, once again proved to be particularly patient in this second adventure, with the type of constructive criticism you can only hope to get from your best friend. Thank you!

To all the contacts—from the assistants to the CEOs—within the consumer groups, brands, suppliers, retailers, and media, thank you for sharing your insights. The luxury sector has enabled me to travel to some of the most fascinating cities in Europe, Asia, and North America. With a passion for the products and the places they are sold in, you soon start to develop a passion for the people in this industry because their enthusiasm is viral, so I am thankful to many luxury folks for having brought me here. Luxury executives are ever optimists and passionate about their industry. Thank you so much for sharing that passion!

For David May, Jon Marsh, Andrew Inglis-Taylor, Chris Brown-Humes, James Pomeroy, Lucy Dwyer, Antoine Belge, Anne-Laure Bismuth, David Harrington, Nicholas Smithie, John Gerzema, and all who have supported me throughout the years and particularly for this project, thank you. Special thanks to Alexis Cooper and Tessie Petion for your contributions; your time has been precious. To Tom Doctoroff and Farid Mokart, your insights and friendship are an inspiration and a gift.

For Chris Labonté and Michael Leyne at Figure 1 Publishing, thanks for being so straightforward and easygoing and showing me that publishing doesn't need to be an antiquated business.

For all the students and next-generation luxury managers, thanks for the inspiration, and best of luck in your future endeavors.

TWENTY-ONE
PREDICTIONS FOR
'21 AND BEYOND

1. Because luxury sales are essentially driven by female purchases, the limited number of top female executives in the sector is fast becoming an embarrassment—or if it is not, it should be. Luxury has long been driven by a macho culture, but there is no scarcity of female talent in the industry. In the next ten years, I predict that the majority of board members and at least 25% of brand CEOs will be female.

2. While credibility and sales of Chinese brands should increase dramatically in subsegments such as consumer staples or electronics, I project that in ten years' time, Western brands will still dominate in the traditional luxury segments such as high-end leather goods, watches, and jewelry, as well as in sporting goods and cosmetics.

3. One impact of COVID-19 in 2020 will be to accelerate the shift of consumption of Chinese consumers back to mainland China. The year 2020 should prove to be a bit of an exceptional year for luxury, with Chinese being wary about traveling. Still, in ten years, I believe that more than 75% of luxury sales to Chinese citizens will occur in their homeland.

4. The Indian consumer, while still a marginal contributor to luxury sales overall, will become a key contributor to the sector's growth, giving some hope as Chinese growth gradually slows between now and the late 2020s.

5. Founders of Kering and LVMH have given some of their children management responsibilities. Because the average consumer of luxury is young, so should the managers be. Not all young managers have the bandwidth to become a CEO of a luxury brand, like Alexandre Arnault, heir of LVMH's Bernard Arnault, born in 1992 and running RIMOWA since age twenty-five in 2017—but a new generation is coming. At the end of the 2020s, it should not be surprising for brand CEOs to be in their thirties or forties rather than fifty and older, as they are today.

6. Bernard Arnault, chairman and CEO of LVMH, will consistently top the list of the richest individuals in the world, ahead of Amazon's Bezos, as was already the case briefly in late 2019. His group will hold ninety to one hundred brands, up from seventy-seven at the time of writing.

7. Very few luxury brands will remain independent, with the possible exceptions of Hermès, Chanel, and Rolex. Most of them will merge, go out of business, buy others, or be bought. Watch retailers will merge as volumes of watches sold remain under pressure and sales shift more to stores or websites operated directly by the brands.

8. Nike will generate more than 50% of its sales online, mostly via directly operated apps and its own websites. The rest of its business will occur mostly via its own full-price stores and outlets. Brick-and-mortar wholesale partners will contribute less than 25% of group sales.

9. When walking into your favorite store, you will be able to choose whether you want to use the iris scanner at the door. The scanner will call your favorite sales associate and download on their smartphone all the details of your previous transactions, favorite colors, key dates, and other information and tell the associate what products they should be showing you today. Already, at Sephora, you can choose between a red basket if you need help ("I would like to be assisted") or a black one if you want to be let alone ("I would like to shop on my own"). This is just a slightly more contemporary version of that. Welcome to the future of luxury!

10. Luxury will be one of the few sectors to prioritize brick and mortar and physical interaction over online sales. For most luxury brands, a maximum of 20% of sales (versus Nike's more than 50%) will be generated online over the next decade. Most luxury brands will distance themselves from online wholesale, after having broadly eliminated their exposure to brick-and-mortar wholesale. And while luxury brands' own websites will give access to their products online, they should be used essentially for storytelling rather than selling purposes.

11. Given the complexity of managing a low-growth business in affordable luxury handbags, I expect ownership of Michael Kors, Coach, Tory Burch, and/or Furla will have changed in ten years.

12. Leaving aside Swarovski and Pandora, no other affordable jewelry brand has been successful on a global basis. This is clearly a gap, in my view, and I expect new entrants will revolutionize the branded market for affordable jewelry over the next decade.

13. With some of the best management teams in the consumer space, great storytelling, emotional relationships with consumers, and

some of the most inspiring brand ambassadors out there, Nike, adidas, and PUMA will be three of the fastest-growing consumer goods companies over the next decade in terms of sales.

14. Apple will be known as a health-monitoring, visual entertainment (notably, movies and gaming), and banking corporation (and more), with iPhone sales accounting for less than a third of its business, down from more than 60% in 2018.

15. In the next decade, travel, hospitality, cannabis, fine food, e-sports, and e-learning will be the fastest-growing luxury segments.

16. Louis Vuitton, still one of the largest and most influential brands in luxury, will diversify into travel in a big way, not just selling luggage and city guides, like it does today, but also selling VR packages for consumers to discover the world in style without leaving their living room.

17. Wealthy consumers will favor boutique hotels over hotel chains. The latter, while having the incentive of loyalty programs, will suffer from a feeling of "copy and paste" and lack of authenticity.

18. The combination of eco-friendly attitudes and COVID-19 impacts will mean that cruises and commercial flights will be transformed; flygskam, or flight shaming, might become more than just an obscure Swedish concept; and fast rail and self-driving electric vehicles will become preferred means of transportation.

19. The majority of suitcases and athletic shoes from top brands will be made out of recycled and/or recyclable material. Meanwhile, most handbags will still be made from real leather, but fur will be banned in many countries as substitutes take over (despite not being earth friendly, because they are made with plastic derivatives).

20. Cartier, Tiffany, and Bulgari will be using mostly lab-grown diamonds for their watches and jewelry, though center stones on the higher-end jewelry pieces will still be from mined diamonds.

21. With Louis Vuitton now producing in the U.S. for the U.S., with sites in California and in Texas, being a locavore will extend into wanting to buy other products that are manufactured closer to home. Supply chains in luxury will shift a lot closer to their end markets: "made in Italy" or "made in France" will gradually shift to "made in a production site near you." For watches, "made in Switzerland" will persist, but fewer clients will buy those watches.

A GUIDE TO LUXURY GOODS COMPANIES

THIS IS A snapshot of the various major companies involved in the luxury goods trade. It is not a comprehensive list.

Multi-brand groups

Some families have created veritable luxury empires through a collection of brands purchased over time. While many more exist, here are the main multi-brand groups in the sector.

Kering (formerly known as PPR)

Kering is mostly driven by soft luxury goods, having in its midst one of the biggest brands in the space: Gucci. Alongside this brand—generating close to EUR10bn (USD11bn) in sales—the group runs many smaller brands such as Bottega Veneta (recently repositioned), Balenciaga (up-and-coming star), and Saint Laurent (formerly known as Yves Saint Laurent). Before it was renamed Kering, the group was invested in many retail assets and sporting goods brand PUMA, and these have since been disposed of.

The group has been run for the past fifteen years by François-Henri Pinault, the husband of actress Salma Hayek and the son of François Pinault, the group's founder. The author of the foreword to this book, F-H P, as he is nicknamed internally at Kering, took over the reins of the company, which was then known as PPR, as in Pinault-Printemps-Redoute, a name which soon disappeared along with the assets associated: the Printemps, one of Paris's foremost department stores, and La Redoute, a struggling mail-order business. F-H P took over what was a very diversified conglomerate to transform it into a pure luxury player, renaming it Kering in 2013. The group's sales halved between 2008 and 2017 while profits quadrupled!

The Pinault father, François, is now known for being one of the most prominent contemporary art collectors and led the battle to purchase Gucci against another self-made French billionaire, Bernard Arnault, who runs the LVMH group (see below). At the time of writing, the Pinault family holds close to 41% of Kering shares via its holding structure called Artémis.

LVMH—*Moët Hennessy Louis Vuitton*

The self-described "world leader in high-quality products" is by far the largest diversified group in luxury. LVMH was born in 1987 from the merger of Louis Vuitton, the largest luxury brand to date with close to EUR13bn (USD14bn) in annual sales, with Moët Hennessy, itself a 1971 merger between cognac leader Hennessy and champagne powerhouses Moët & Chandon. The group generates annual sales of close to EUR55bn (USD61bn) and employs more than 160,000 people.[1] It now runs seventy-seven brands in five different divisions as follows:

1. Fashion and leather goods: this is dominated by Louis Vuitton and includes Christian Dior, Marc Jacobs, Givenchy, Fendi, Celine, Loewe, and Berluti.

2. Wines and spirits: LVMH is by far the dominant group in champagne with leaders Moët (and its high-end vintage champagne, Dom Pérignon) and Veuve Clicquot; and in cognac with Hennessy. It also holds a few wineries and Glenmorangie scotch.

3. Perfumes and cosmetics: this includes one of the fine fragrance leaders (Parfums Christian Dior), as well as Guerlain, Givenchy, and smaller cosmetics and makeup brands.

4. Watches and jewelry: the bigger brands here are Roman jeweler Bulgari, recently acquired New York icon Tiffany, and watchmaker Tag Heuer.

5. Selective retailing: this includes duty-free giant DFS and fragrance and cosmetics specialty retailer Sephora.

Outside of the five core activities, LVMH also holds eleven "houses" that are linked to culture and "art de vivre," including investments in the French press, yachts, Italian coffee shop Cova, and some assets in hospitality (e.g., Cheval Blanc and the recently acquired Belmond chain of forty-six properties).

LVMH, while being a professionally run, diversified group, is also a family affair, with Bernard Arnault at the helm. Children Delphine and Antoine from his first marriage are involved with the group. Delphine was the first female member of the group's board in 2003 and since 2013, has been director and executive vice president at Louis Vuitton, the key brand within the group, accounting for close to half of the group's profits. Antoine started his career at Louis Vuitton, overseeing memorable advertising campaigns for the brand (including the core values campaign with Mikhail Gorbachev, Muhammad Ali, Sean Connery, and Keith Richards) and serves as the CEO of Berluti and the chairman of Loro Piana, two high-end fashion and accessories brands. Younger children from a second

marriage are also going up the ranks and seen as potential succes-
sors: Alexandre, who has been the CEO of high-end luggage brand
RIMOWA since age twenty-five and is instrumental in shaping the
group's digital strategy, and Frédéric, an outstanding pianist and a
graduate from his father's alma mater, the prestigious École Poly-
technique, and who started to work for the group's largest watch
brand, Tag Heuer, in late 2018. At the time of writing, the Arnault
family holds more than 47% of shares in LVMH.

Richemont

Formerly a diversified group including tobacco and pay TV, Richemont is now mostly focused on hard luxury with leading diversified
brand Cartier, jeweler Van Cleef & Arpels, and many brands in the
watch industry, such as IWC, Panerai, Jaeger-LeCoultre, and Montblanc. In early 2018, the Richemont group bid for the 50% it didn't
already own of YNAP, a leading luxury e-commerce group.

Richemont was set up in 1988 by Johann Rupert, a South African
financier and visionary sometimes known as "Rupert the Bear" for
his dire predictions before the global financial crisis of 2008. The
group was created when Rupert spun off the international assets of
the Rembrandt Group, which his father, Anton, had founded in the
1940s. Via a system of multiple voting rights, he owns 9.1% of the
equity in the company but 50% of the voting rights. Johann Rupert
has a son, Anton Rupert Jr., who has been serving on the board
since 2017 and is also a director of Watchfinder & Co., a secondhand
watch business the group bought in 2018. Unlike Arnault's children
at LVMH, Rupert's children are unlikely, in my opinion, to be participants to succession planning for the Richemont group.

The Prada Group

Some might think of Prada as a mono-brand company as the Miu
Miu brand is a sort of exuberant, female-only version of sister brand
Prada, which is much bigger and more institutional. The bulk of sales

for both brands are in leather goods and accessories. While shares of the group are listed on the Hong Kong stock market after an IPO in June 2011, CEO Patrizio Bertelli, his wife and creative director (Miuccia Prada), and other family members hold close to 80% of group shares.

The Swatch Group

The leading Swiss watch manufacturer (note that now more Apple watches than Swiss watches are sold every year) holds many brands. While indeed the Swatch brand itself is part of the portfolio, the bigger ones are Omega, Tissot, Longines, Rado, and Mido. The Swatch Group is seen as having saved the Swiss-made watch industry from the threat of Casio-type watches, by focusing on mechanical movements and investing in the early 1980s for the entire industry. Similar to the other multi-brand groups, the Swatch Group is run by a family. Nick Hayek Jr. took over from his father, the founder of the group, in 2010. Sister Nayla is the chair of the board of directors and the CEO of the Harry Winston jewelry brand, which the group bought in early 2013. Nayla's son, Marc Hayek, is in charge of some of the higher-end brands within the portfolio (Blancpain, Breguet, Jaquet Droz) as well as of Latin America. At the time of writing, the Hayek family holds 53% of registered shares in the Swatch Group.

Capri

Capri Holdings has been the new name of Michael Kors Holdings since early 2019. Michael Kors, an American designer, launched his brand in 1981. As the brand was forced into bankruptcy in 1993, he worked for other labels and notably, became the ready-to-wear designer for French brand Celine. The business was then relaunched in 1997, and in 2003, the designer left Celine to focus on his own brand, which became a fierce competitor to affordable luxury brand Coach (part of the Tapestry group) with a positioning targeting the modern jet-setter. A bit like Coach within Tapestry, Michael Kors within Capri is by far the largest brand in terms of revenues. The group acquired Jimmy Choo (footwear) in 2017 and the iconic Italian fashion brand Versace a year later. Like Tapestry, Capri is a publicly listed company in the U.S. with no majority shareholding or major family involvement, leaving aside the presence of Donatella Versace, the sister of founder Gianni Versace, as artistic director of the eponymous brand.

Tapestry

The inventor of democratic or affordable luxury, this American leather goods and accessories group started with the Coach brand, born in 1941 and known for durable leather products. The brand was spun off of Sara Lee in 2000 and IPO-ed that year. In 2015, the company bought Stuart Weitzman, a footwear company, and in 2017, Kate Spade, another affordable handbags and accessories brand known for its positioning around optimistic femininity. That year, Coach Inc. rebranded itself Tapestry Inc. As the integration of Kate Spade proved a lot tougher than expected, the group made a series of senior management changes in late 2019.

The Tod's Group

Though this is technically a group with four brands—Tod's, Hogan, Fay, and Roger Vivier—the core Tod's brand, an Italian leather shoe icon, remains the key business. Founder and chairman Diego Della Valle has had investments in soccer in Italy, owns the fashion brand Schiaparelli, and has had a seat on boards such as those of Ferrari, Maserati, and LVMH. Separately, he has participated financially in the restoration of the Coliseum in Rome. At the time of writing, the Della Valle family owns close to three-quarters of the group's capital.

Mono-brand companies

Other companies are characterized by a focus on a single brand. Strategically, this approach can be more efficient than running a multi-brand venture, but it also is theoretically much riskier if for some reason that given brand goes out of favor, an idea I develop in chapter 4 of the book. Here are a few examples.

Burberry

Known for outerwear initially and its iconic trench coat, this British brand has successfully managed to diversify into a broader set of subsegments, notably leather, accessories, and fragrances. The brand, founded in 1856, has gone through a lot of change recently, with the latest repositioning starting in 2018 intended to elevate the brand towards becoming a high-end fashion luxury brand, with a new CEO and a new designer both coming from the LVMH group. This is the only truly global British brand of significance in the luxury industry.

Chanel

Probably the most respected luxury brand in the minds of consumers, competitors, and distributors alike, the company started by Gabrielle "Coco" Chanel in 1909 is big in fashion, fragrance, and cosmetics. It has more recently developed its third division: watches and jewelry, known notably for the J12 watch range, launched in 1999. The Chanel brand has been disclosing accounts since management decided to relocate headquarters from New York to London in 2018, and the brand generated USD11bn in sales that year, making it a very large brand, alongside Louis Vuitton and Gucci. The company is privately owned by the Wertheimer brothers, Gérard and Alain, the latter acting as CEO since early 2016. Their younger half-brother, Charles Heilbronn, runs Mousse Partners in New York, an investment firm running the family's funds.

Hermès

Known for its silk-based products and its handbags (Kelly, Birkin, Bolide, and more), for which there are waiting lists, this family-controlled brand founded in 1837 is synonymous with absolute luxury. It is a rare brand where the perception of scarcity is not incompatible with growth. While the company is listed on the stock market, at the time of writing the family holds around two-thirds of shares and has resisted assaults from potential predators, such as LVMH, to remain independent. Since 2014, once again a member of the founding family, Axel Dumas, has been running the company.

Moncler

This luxury outerwear company known for premium down jackets has a motto which is self-explanatory: "Born in the mountains, living in the city." The company's headquarters are indeed in a city: Milan, Italy's fashion capital. The chairman and CEO, Remo Ruffini, owned indirectly a bit more than 22% of listed shares. Moncler is dominating its niche by not competing directly with some of the more functional outerwear brands such as Canada Goose, The North Face, and Patagonia.

Rolex

The leading watch brand globally is private and technically speaking, a foundation for the arts in terms of its legal status. While many watch brands have sold different shapes and styles, Rolex is well known for keeping to round watches.

NOTE THAT THERE are many companies in the luxury space. In soft luxury goods, these include Armani, Hugo Boss, Brunello Cucinelli, D&G, ESCADA, Ferragamo, Missoni, Ralph Lauren, and SMCP. In hard luxury goods, examples include Audemars Piguet, Asprey, Chopard, Graff, and Patek Philippe.

NOTES

INTRODUCTION: A BIG AND BRIGHT FUTURE FOR LUXURY

1 Claudia D'Arpizio et al., "The Future of Luxury: A Look into Tomorrow to Understand Today," Bain & Company, January 10, 2019, https://www.bain.com/insights/luxury-goods-worldwide-market-study-fall-winter-2018/.

2 Lauren Landry, "Tory Burch to Babson Graduates: 'If It Doesn't Scare You, You're Not Dreaming Big Enough,'" BostInno, May 18, 2014, https://www.americaninno.com/boston/transcript-of-tory-burchs-2014-commencement-speech-at-babson/.

1: THE FUTURE IS FEMALE

1 Katie Mettler, "Hillary Clinton Just Said It, but 'The Future Is Female' Began as a 1970s Lesbian Separatist Slogan," *Washington Post*, February 8, 2017, https://www.washingtonpost.com/news/morning-mix/wp/2017/02/08/hillary-clinton-just-said-it-but-the-future-is-female-began-as-a-1970s-lesbian-separatist-slogan/.

2 See, for instance, "When It Comes to Spending Decisions, Women Are in Control," *Insights*, June 22, 2011, https://www.nielsen.com/us/en/insights/article/2011/when-it-comes-to-spending-decisions-women-are-in-control/; Michelle King, "Want a Piece of the 18 Trillion Dollar Female Economy? Start with Gender Bias," *Forbes*, May 24, 2017, https://www.forbes.com/sites/michelleking/2017/05/24/want-a-piece-of-the-18-trillion-dollar-female-economy-start-with-gender-bias/; Vivian Ni, "Consumption Trends and Targeting China's Female Consumers," *China Briefing*, March 8, 2012, https://www.china-briefing.com/news/consumption-trends-and-targeting-chinas-female-consumer/; Corinne Abrams, "Indian Women Seize Spending Power: 'I Just Tell My Husband I Am Buying This Stuff,'" *Wall Street Journal*, April 1, 2018, https://www.wsj.com/articles/indias-women-gain-consumer-clout-1522580408.

3 Ryan Gorman, "Women Now Control More Than Half of US Personal Wealth, Which 'Will Only Increase in Years to Come,'" *Business Insider*, April 7, 2015, https://www.businessinsider.com/women-now-control-more-than-half-of-us-personal-wealth-2015-4.

4 "Women's Wealth Is Rising," *Economist*, March 8, 2018, https://www.economist.com/graphic-detail/2018/03/08/womens-wealth-is-rising.

5 Daichi Mishima, "Japan Sees Record Number of Women Working, but Challenges Remain," *Nikkei Asian Review*, July 30, 2019, https://asia.nikkei.com/Economy/Japan-sees-record-number-of-women-working-but-challenges-remain.

6 Jessica Semega et al., "Income and Poverty in the United States: 2018," U.S. Department of Commerce, U.S. Census Bureau, September 2019, https://www.census.gov/content/dam/Census/library/publications/2019/demo/p60-266.pdf.

7 "World Marriage Data 2017," United Nations, Department of Economic and Social Affairs, Population Division, 2017, https://www.un.org/en/development/desa/population/theme/marriage-unions/WMD2017.asp.

8 "Historical Marital Status Tables," United States Census Bureau, November 2019, https://www.census.gov/data/tables/time-series/demo/families/marital.html.

9 Quoctrung Bui and Claire Cain Miller, "The Age That Women Have Babies: How a Gap Divides America," *New York Times*, August 4, 2018, https://www.nytimes.com/interactive/2018/08/04/upshot/up-birth-age-gap.html.

10 Jonathan Woetzel, "The Power of Parity: How Advancing Women's Equality Can Add $12 Trillion to Global Growth," McKinsey & Company, September 2015, https://www.mckinsey.com/featured-insights/employment-and-growth/how-advancing-womens-equality-can-add-12-trillion-to-global-growth.

11 Cae Luzio, "A Missing Factor in Women's Leadership: Leave the Mean Girl Behind," *Forbes*, July 24, 2019, https://www.forbes.com/sites/cateluzio/2019/07/24/a-missing-factor-in-womens-leader-leave-the-mean-girl-behind/.

12 Emma Hinchliffe, "Funding for Female Founders Stalled at 2.2% of VC Dollars in 2018," *Fortune*, January 28, 2019, https://fortune.com/2019/01/28/funding-female-founders-2018/; "Imposons la mixité dans l'économie numérique," *Les Echos*, December 3, 2018, https://www.lesechos.fr/idees-debats/cercle/imposons-la-mixite-dans-leconomie-numerique-202503.

13 Avivah Wittenberg-Cox, "What Do Countries with the Best Coronavirus Responses Have in Common? Women Leaders," *Forbes*, April 13, 2020, https://www.forbes.com/sites/avivahwittenbergcox/2020/04/13/what-do-countries-with-the-best-coronavirus-reponses-have-in-common-women-leaders/.

14 Linda Landers, "Top Strategies for Marketing to Millennial Women," Business 2 Community, April 23, 2018, https://www.business2community.com/marketing/top-strategies-for-marketing-to-millennial-women-02048109; "Women in 2020: Understanding the New Female Consumer," Insights in Marketing, n.d., https://www.insightsinmarketing.com/media/1170/women2020_millennial_051415_2_.pdf.

15 Brecken Branstrator, "Study: 51 Percent of Millennial Women Buy Jewelry for Themselves," National Jeweler, August 10, 2018, https://www.nationaljeweler.com/independents/retail-surveys/6885-study-51-percent-of-millennial-women-buy-jewelry-for-themselves.

16 Suzy Menkes, "Woman-to-Woman Jewellery," *Vogue*, February 11, 2019, https://www.vogue.co.uk/article/woman-to-woman-jewellery.

17 Nicola Nice, email message to the author, October 22, 2019.

2: ALL POINTS EAST

1 Homi Kharas, "The Unprecedented Expansion of the Global Middle Class: An Update," Brookings, Global Economy and Development Working Paper 100, February 2017, https://www.brookings.edu/wp-content/uploads/2017/02/global_20170228_global-middle-class.pdf.

2   Tania Branigan, "Xi Jinping Vows to Fight 'Tigers' and 'Flies' in Anti-Corruption
    Drive," *Guardian*, January 22, 2013, https://www.theguardian.com/world/2013/jan/22/
    xi-jinping-tigers-flies-corruption.
3   Yuval Atsmon and Max Magni, "Meet the Chinese Consumer of 2020," *McKinsey
    Quarterly*, March 2012, https://www.mckinsey.com/featured-insights/asia-pacific/
    meet-the-chinese-consumer-of-2020.
4   Lambert Bu et al., "Chinese Luxury Consumers: More Global, More Demanding,
    Still Spending," McKinsey & Company, August 2017, https://www.mckinsey.com/
    business-functions/marketing-and-sales/our-insights/chinese-luxury-
    consumers-more-global-more-demanding-still-spending.
5   Bruno Lannes, "What's Powering China's Market for Luxury Goods?" Bain & Company,
    March 18, 2019, https://www.bain.com/insights/whats-powering-chinas-
    market-for-luxury-goods/.
6   Marcus Fairs, "Coronavirus Offers 'a Blank Page for a New Beginning' Says
    Li Edelkoort," *Dezeen*, March 9, 2020, https://www.dezeen.com/2020/03/09/
    li-edelkoort-coronavirus-reset/.
7   "The Results Are In—Womenomics Is Working," *Foreign Policy*, n.d.,
    https://foreignpolicy.com/sponsored/japanus/896258-2/.
8   Cyrille Vigneron, in discussion with the author, July 9, 2019.

3: THE POWER OF YOUTH, INCLUSION, AND DIVERSITY
1   Based on World Bank and UN Population Division data, which defines "digital native"
    as anybody who turns eleven years old when the country has a 50+% Internet adoption
    rate. It is linearly scaled for the preceding ten years.
2   Katherine Schaeffer, "The Most Common Age among Whites in U.S. Is 58—More
    Than Double That of Racial and Ethnic Minorities," Pew Research Center,
    Fact Tank, July 30, 2019, https://www.pewresearch.org/fact-tank/2019/07/30/
    most-common-age-among-us-racial-ethnic-groups/.
3   Anthony Cilluffo and D'Vera Cohn, "6 Demographic Trends Shaping the U.S. and
    the World in 2019," Pew Research Center, Fact Tank, April 11, 2019,
    https://www.pewresearch.org/fact-tank/2019/04/11/6-demographic-trends-
    shaping-the-u-s-and-the-world-in-2019/.
4   Matt Weeks, "Minority Markets See Economic Growth," UGA Today, March 21, 2019,
    https://news.uga.edu/multicultural-economy/.
5   Rachel Tashjian, "How Jennifer Lopez's Versace Dress Created Google Images," *GQ*,
    September 20, 2019, https://www.gq.com/story/jennifer-lopez-versace-google-images.
6   Claude Lévi-Strauss, *A World on the Wane,* originally published 1955, Trans. John
    Russell (Whitefish: Literary Licensing, LLC, 2013).
7   Imran Amed et al., "What Radical Transparency Could Mean for the Fashion Industry,"
    McKinsey & Company, February 2019, https://www.mckinsey.com/industries/retail/
    our-insights/what-radical-transparency-could-mean-for-the-fashion-industry.
8   Imogen Calderwood, "88% of People Who Saw 'Blue Planet II' Have Now Changed
    Their Lifestyle," Global Citizen, November 1, 2018, https://www.globalcitizen.org/en/
    content/88-blue-planet-2-changed-david-attenborough/.
9   Robin Givhan, "'I Was the Person Who Made the Mistake': How Gucci Is Trying to
    Recover from Its Blackface Sweater Controversy," *Washington Post*, May 7, 2019,
    https://www.washingtonpost.com/lifestyle/style/i-was-the-person-who-made-
    the-mistake-how-gucci-is-trying-to-recover-from-its-blackface-sweater-
    controversy/2019/05/06/04eccbb6-6f7d-11e9-8be0-ca575670e91c_story.html.

10 Rob Picheta, "'Suicide Isn't Fashion': Burberry Apologizes for Hoodie with Noose around the Neck," CNN, February 19, 2019, https://www.cnn.com/style/article/burberry-noose-hoodie-scli-gbr-intl/index.html.

11 Remo Ruffini, email message to the author, September 10, 2019.

4: SIZE MATTERS

1 The phrase appears frequently in company press releases and letters to shareholders, most recently in LVMH, "LVMH 2017 Record Results," press release, January 25, 2018, https://www.lvmh.com/news-documents/press-releases/2017-record-results/.

2 George Anders, "Jeff Bezos's Top 10 Leadership Lessons," *Forbes*, April 4, 2012, https://www.forbes.com/sites/georgeanders/2012/04/04/bezos-tips/.

3 Anaïs Lerévérend, "As SMCP Looks to New Horizons, an Acquisition Could Be on the Cards," FashionNetwork.com, February 1, 2019, https://us.fashionnetwork.com/news/As-smcp-looks-to-new-horizons-an-acquisition-could-be-on-the-cards,1063299.html.

5: BRICK AND MORTAR IS IMMORTAL

1 Jordan Valinsky, "Macy's Is Closing 28 Stores and a Bloomingdale's Store," CNN Business, January 8, 2020, https://amp.cnn.com/cnn/2020/01/08/business/macys-store-closures/index.html.

2 Clement Kwan, in discussion with the author, December 3, 2019.

3 Steve Dennis, "Omnichannel Is Dead. The Future Is Harmonized Retail," *Forbes*, June 3, 2019, https://www.forbes.com/sites/stevendennis/2019/06/03/omnichannel-is-dead-the-future-is-harmonized-retail/.

4 Farfetch, "Farfetch and JD.com Expand Strategic Partnership to Build the Premier Luxury Gateway to China," press release, February 28, 2019, https://www.farfetchinvestors.com/financial-news/news-details/2019/Farfetch-and-JDcom-Expand-Strategic-Partnership-to-Build-the-Premier-Luxury-Gateway-to-China/default.aspx.

5 Carol Ryan, "Luxury Brands Follow the Money to Airports," *Wall Street Journal*, March 27, 2019, https://www.wsj.com/articles/luxury-brands-follow-the-money-to-airports-11553681663.

6 Lan Luan, Aimee Kim, and Daniel Zipser, "How Young Chinese Consumers Are Reshaping Global Luxury," McKinsey & Company, April 2019, https://www.mckinsey.com/featured-insights/china/how-young-chinese-consumers-are-reshaping-global-luxury.

7 Jason Holland, "Louis Vuitton Duplex Store Plans at Hong Kong Airport on Track Despite Downtown Closure Reports," The Moodie Davitt Report, January 6, 2020, https://www.moodiedavittreport.com/louis-vuitton-duplex-store-plans-at-hong-kong-airport-on-track-despite-downtown-closure-reports/.

8 Caitlin Jascewsky, "What I Learned about Customer Experience from The Retail Prophet," Storis, n.d., https://www.storis.com/retail-prophet/.

9 Doug Stephens, "The Store Is Media and Media Is the Store," The Retail Prophet, April 2013, https://www.retailprophet.com/the-store-is-media-and-media-is-the-store/.

10 Doug Stephens, "The Most Important Metric in Retail," *Business of Fashion*, July 9, 2019, https://www.businessoffashion.com/articles/opinion/measuring-the-store-of-the-future.

11 Katie Harris Storer, email message to the author, November 15, 2019.

6: DEMOCRATIC LUXURY

1 Rakesh Kochhar, "Through an American Lens, Western Europe's Middle Classes Appear Smaller," Pew Research Center, Fact Tank, June 5, 2017, https://www.pewresearch.org/fact-tank/2017/06/05/through-an-american-lens-western-europes-middle-classes-appear-smaller/.

2 "The Chinese Consumer in 2030," *The Economist*, Intelligence Unit, November 2, 2016, http://country.eiu.com/article.aspx?articleid=1584774142.

3 Homi Kharas, "The Unprecedented Expansion of the Global Middle Class: An Update," Brookings, February 28, 2017, https://www.brookings.edu/research/the-unprecedented-expansion-of-the-global-middle-class-2/.

4 "Beer Still Number One on Drinks List in Great Britain and United States, but the Challenge Is Engaging Younger Drinkers," CGA, August 1, 2019, https://www.cga.co.uk/2019/08/01/beer-still-number-one-on-drinks-list-in-great-britain-and-united-states-but-the-challenge-is-engaging-younger-drinkers/.

5 Daniel Lalonde, email message to the author, September 8, 2019.

7: THE LUXURY OF HEALTH

1 Nicola Davison, "Rivers of Blood: The Dead Pigs Rotting in China's Water Supply," *Guardian*, March 29, 2013, https://www.theguardian.com/world/2013/mar/29/dead-pigs-china-water-supply.

2 Gary Fuller, "Pollutionwatch: China Shows How Political Will Can Take on Air Pollution," *Guardian*, March 14, 2019, https://www.theguardian.com/environment/2019/mar/14/pollutionwatch-china-shows-how-political-will-can-take-on-air-pollution.

3 United Nations Environment Programme, "Half the World to Face Severe Water Stress by 2030 Unless Water Use Is 'Decoupled' from Economic Growth, Says International Resource Panel," press release, March 21, 2016, https://www.unenvironment.org/news-and-stories/press-release/half-world-face-severe-water-stress-2030-unless-water-use-decoupled.

4 Lisa Friedman and Claire O'Neill, "Who Controls Trump's Environmental Policy?" *New York Times*, January 14, 2020, https://www.nytimes.com/interactive/2020/01/14/climate/fossil-fuel-industry-environmental-policy.html; Nadja Popovich, Livia Albeck-Ripka, and Kendra Pierre-Louis, "95 Environmental Rules Being Rolled Back under Trump," *New York Times*, December 21, 2019, https://www.nytimes.com/interactive/2019/climate/trump-environment-rollbacks.html.

5 "Nielsen, Worldwide Consumers Choose Food Health Consciousness," ItalianFOOD.net, September 12, 2016, https://news.italianfood.net/2016/09/12/nielsen-worldwide-consumers-choose-food-health-consciousness/.

6 Xinhua, "China's 'Marathon Fever' Continues with Running Industry Up by 7 Percent in 2018," en.people.cn, March 12, 2019, http://en.people.cn/n3/2019/0312/c90000-9555304.html.

7 Ella Alexander, "Life Lessons from Dolly Parton: What Would Dolly Do?" *Harper's Bazaar*, January 19, 2018, https://www.harpersbazaar.com/uk/people-parties/people-and-parties/news/a26180/dolly-parton-quotes/.

8 Jo Best, "Apple's Research App: What Does It Want Your Health Data For?" ZDNet, November 18, 2019, https://www.zdnet.com/article/apples-research-app-what-does-it-want-your-health-data-for/.

9 Bjørn Gulden, in discussion with the author, October 8, 2019.

8: THE "PREMIUMIZATION" OF EVERYTHING

1 Nick Jones, quoted in Jeremy Wakeham, "With Us Magazine: The Growth Story of Soho House," withersworldwide, October 4, 2016, https://www.withersworldwide.com/en-gb/insight/with-us-magazine-the-growth-story-of-soho-house.
2 John Gapper, "How Millennials Became the World's Most Powerful Consumers," *Financial Times*, June 6, 2018, https://www.ft.com/content/194cd1c8-6583-11e8-a39d-4df188287fff.
3 Andrew Daniller, "Two-Thirds of Americans Support Marijuana Legalization," Pew Research Center, Think Tank, November 14, 2019, https://www.pewresearch.org/fact-tank/2019/11/14/americans-support-marijuana-legalization/.
4 Uday Sampath Kumar and Nichola Saminather, "Corona Owner Invests Another $4 Billion in Cannabis Producer Canopy," Reuters, August 15, 2016, https://in.reuters.com/article/us-canopy-growth-stake-constellation/corona-owner-invests-another-4-billion-in-cannabis-producer-canopy-idINKBN1L0155.
5 Francis Belin, in discussion with the author, November 26, 2019.

9: TRAVEL—AND ARRIVE

1 IATA, "IATA Forecast Predicts 8.2 Billion Air Travelers in 2037," press release no. 62, October 24, 2018, https://www.iata.org/en/pressroom/pr/2018-10-24-02/.
2 Richard Lung, "Travel Wanderlust: Age Is Not a Constraint, but Income Might Be," Visa Travel Insights, February 22, 2017, https://usa.visa.com/partner-with-us/visa-consulting-analytics/senior-travel-wanderlust.html.
3 Dion Rabouin, "For Estée Lauder, Airports Are the New Malls," Axios, June 18, 2019, https://www.axios.com/estee-lauder-airport-retail-duty-free-650bf866-a32f-4abb-9e3b-e74d8a8be783.html.
4 "China Focus: 70 Years on, Chinese Travel Abroad More Easily in Much Larger Number," Xinhuanet, September 28, 2019, http://www.xinhuanet.com/english/2019-09/28/c_138430646.htm; "Reports and Statistics," U.S. Department of State, n.d., https://travel.state.gov/content/travel/en/about-us/reports-and-statistics.html.
5 Chelsea Ritschel, "Millennials When Booking Holidays Think of Instagram Photos above All Other Factors," *Independent*, December 28, 2017, https://www.independent.co.uk/life-style/millennials-holiday-decision-instagram-photos-factors-think-first-social-media-a8131731.html.
6 Paul Peeters et al., "Overtourism: Impact and Possible Policy Responses," ResearchGate, 2018, https://www.researchgate.net/publication/330502264_Overtourism_Impact_and_possible_policy_responses.
7 Hiroko Tabuchi, "'Worse Than Anyone Expected': Air Travel Emissions Vastly Outpace Predictions," *New York Times*, September 19, 2019, https://www.nytimes.com/2019/09/19/climate/air-travel-emissions.html.
8 Kyle Gendreau, email message to the author, October 11, 2019.

10: DISRUPTING LUXURY: THE DECADE AHEAD

1 Hannah Ritchie, "Food Production Is Responsible for One-Quarter of the World's Greenhouse Gas Emissions," Our World in Data, November 6, 2019, https://ourworldindata.org/food-ghg-emissions.
2 "Cattle Ranching in the Amazon Region," Yale School of Forestry & Environmental Studies, Global Forest Atlas, n.d., https://globalforestatlas.yale.edu/amazon/land-use/cattle-ranching; Lorraine Chow, "WWF: 60% of Global Biodiversity Loss Due to Land Cleared for Meat-Based Diets," EcoWatch, October 5, 2017, https://www.ecowatch.com/biodiversity-meat-wwf-2493305671.html.

3   "Flexitarianism: Flexible or Part-Time Vegetarianism," United Nations, Sustainable Development Goals, May 4, 2012, https://sustainabledevelopment.un.org/partnership/?p=2252.

4   Caroline Bushnell, "Newly Released Market Data Shows Soaring Demand for Plant-Based Food," Good Food Institute, September 12, 2018, https://www.gfi.org/newly-released-market-data-shows-soaring.

5   Dee-Ann Durbin, "Beyond Meat's Shares More Than Double with a Monumental IPO," *Inc.,* May 3, 2019, https://www.inc.com/associated-press/beyond-meat-ipo-shares-more-than-double.html.

6   Tatiana Schlossberg, "How Fast Fashion Is Destroying the Planet," review of *Fashionopolis: The Price of Fast Fashion and the Future of Clothes,* by Dana Thomas, *New York Times,* September 3, 2019, https://www.nytimes.com/2019/09/03/books/review/how-fast-fashion-is-destroying-the-planet.html.

7   Nathalie Remy, Eveline Speelman, and Steven Swartz, "Style That's Sustainable: A New Fast-Fashion Formula," McKinsey & Company, October 2016, https://www.mckinsey.com/business-functions/sustainability/our-insights/style-thats-sustainable-a-new-fast-fashion-formula.

8   Paul Zimnisky, email message to the author, March 9, 2020.

9   "MVI's Latest Lab-Grown Diamond Consumer Research," MVI Marketing, July 30, 2019, https://www.mvimarketing.com/reports.php.

10 Jean Pigozzi, quoted in Osman Ahmed, "Can Lab-Grown Diamonds Become a Girl's Best Friend?" *Vogue,* November 29, 2018, https://www.vogue.in/content/how-diamonds-grown-in-a-lab-are-shaking-up-the-world-of-fine-jewellery.

11 Marie-Claire Daveu, email message to the author, November 10, 2019.

12 Miroslava Duma, in discussion with the author, September 12, 2019; email message to the author, October 23, 2019.

CONCLUSION: THE NEW LUXURY

1   Yvon Chouinard, *Let My People Go Surfing: The Education of a Reluctant Businessman* (New York: Penguin, 2006), 3.

2   Chouinard, *Let My People Go Surfing,* 4.

3   "Don't Buy This Jacket, Black Friday and the New York Times," Patagonia, n.d., https://www.patagonia.com/stories/dont-buy-this-jacket-black-friday-and-the-new-york-times/story-18615.html.

4   Tamison O'Connor, "Stella McCartney Announces UN Charter for Sustainable Fashion," *Business of Fashion,* November 29, 2018, https://www.businessoffashion.com/articles/news-analysis/stella-mccartney-announces-un-charter-for-sustainable-fashion.

A GUIDE TO LUXURY GOODS COMPANIES

1   LVMH, "LVMH: Management Report of the Board of Directors," December 31, 2019, https://r.lvmh-static.com/uploads/2020/03/rapport-de-gestion_lvmh_va.pdf.

INDEX